JUDAIC APPROACHES TO THE GOSPELS

University of South Florida
INTERNATIONAL STUDIES IN FORMATIVE
CHRISTIANITY AND JUDAISM

EDITORIAL BOARD

VOLUME 2
JUDAIC APPROACHES TO THE GOSPELS
by
Bruce Chilton

JUDAIC APPROACHES TO THE GOSPELS

Bruce Chilton

Scholars Press
Atlanta, Georgia

Judaic Approaches to the Gospels

by
Bruce Chilton

Published by Scholars Press
for the University of South Florida

Library of Congress Cataloging in Publication Data
Chilton, Bruce.
    Judaic approaches to the Gospels / Bruce Chilton.
        p.   cm. — (University of South Florida international studies
    in formative Christianity and Judaism ; v. 2)
        Includes index.
        ISBN 0-7885-0001-5
        1. Bible. N.T. Gospels—Criticism, interpretation, etc.
    2. Christianity and other religions—Judaism. 3. Judaism—History—
    Talmudic period, 10-425. 4. Judaism—Relations—Christianity.
    5. Rabbinical literature–Relation to the New Testament.
    6. Christianity—Origin. 7. Church history—Primitive and early
    church, ca. 30-600. I. Title. II. Series.
    BS2555.2.C492   1994
    226'.06—dc20   94-22119
                                                                CIP

Printed in the United States of America
on acid-free paper

For Henry, a spring of hope

CONTENTS AND ACKNOWLEDGEMENTS

---

[1]Forthcoming in *Forum.*

[2]In proof in *The Pseudepigrapha and the New Testament: Comparative Studies* (eds J. H. Charlesworth and C. A. Evans; Sheffield: Sheffield Academic Press).

[3]Appeared in *The Four Gospels: 1992. Festschrift Frans Neirynck* (eds F. van Segbroeck, C. M. Tuckett, G. van Belle, J. Verheyden; BETL 100: Leuven, 1992) 203-218, and in *Approaches to Ancient Judaism. Religious and Theological Studies*: South Florida Studies in the History of Judaism 81 (ed. J. Neusner; Atlanta: Scholars, 1993) 97-114.

---

[4]First published in *Forum* 7 (1991) 45-50.

[5]Scheduled to appear in *Forum*.

[6]A study in honor of my doctoral supervisor, first published in *Templum Amicitiae. Essays on the Second Temple presented to Ernst Bammel*: Journal for the Study of the New Testament Suppement Series 48 (ed. W. Horbury; Sheffield: Sheffield Academic Press, 1991) 330-344.

[7]First published in *Targum Studies* 1 (1992) 89-100.

[8]First published in Ex Auditu 4 (1988) 27-37.

---

[9]First published in *The Jewish Quarterly Review* 79 (1989)
93-100.

[10]Forthcoming in a volume edited by Robert Berchman in the
series "Studia Philonica."

[11]First published in *From Ancient Israel to Modern Judaism:
Intellect in Quest of Understanding. Essays in Honor of
Marvin Fox:* Brown Judaic Studies 173 (edited by Jacob
Neusner, Ernest S. Frerichs, Nahum S. Sarna; Atlanta:
Scholars Press, 1989) 119-137.

PREFACE

The twelve studies presented here are either published here for the first time or were published recently. They broaden the perspective of an earlier collection, *Targumic Approaches to the Gospels.*[1] Targumim continue to be at issue from time to time in the present volume, but within a wider consultation of Judaic literature. And my focus includes John and Paul here.

The first eight essays are addressed to the canon of the New Testament; the last four deal with issues in the interpretation of Judaic materials. Readers of *The Temple of Jesus*[2] and *A Feast of Meanings*[3] will discover in these essays some of the roots of my theory of Jesus as a teacher of purity. Others may find the essays interesting in their own right.

---

[1]*Essays in the Mutual Definition of Judaism and Christianity*: Studies in Judaism (Lanham and London: University Press of America, 1986).

[2]*His Sacrificial Program Within a Cultural History of Sacrifice* (University Park: The Pennsylvania State University Press, 1992).

[3]*Eucharistic Theologies from Jesus through Johannine Circles*: Supplements to Novum Testamentum (Leiden: Brill, 1994).

Professor Jacob Neusner encouraged the production of this book; I would like to register my continuing gratitude to him, my most stimulating colleague. Three students at Bard College -- Clinton Adams and Michelle Dunn (on various computers and an obscure software) and Annette Reed (with pencil, paper, and an eye for indexing) -- were closely involved with the production.

B. D. C.

Annandale-on-Hudson

JOHN THE PURIFIER

Robert Webb's recent book, *John the Baptizer and Prophet*, may be thought of as a reasonable statement of a long-established consensus regarding John. He is portrayed as a "popular prophet," by which it is meant that John set out to behave as did the leaders whom Josephus styles "false prophets:" convinced he was leading Israel into the final, messianic judgement, John called the people to "repentance baptism," that is, to a "conversionary repentance" of which his own ministry was the symbol.[1] Webb's John is the lineal descendant of Wink's characterization of him as "the frontier character of the Christian proclamation,"[2] and more generally of the prophetic representations of John which have dominated the secondary literature.[3]

---

[1]Webb, 214, 215. For details of publication, see the bibliography.

[2]Walter Wink, *John the Baptist in the Gospel Tradition*, 113. As Wink's title suggests, he appropriately focuses on what the tradition makes of John, rather than upon John in himself. But his concern to correct the impression that the tradition is governed by an anti-baptist polemic leads him to make assertions of John, as if in respect of an historical figure.

[3]Cf. Jean Steinmann, *John the Baptist and the Desert Tradition*; Charles H. H. Scobie, *John the Baptist*. For general reference to the literature, cf. Webb, Wink, and

The irony of the allegedly critical consensus which has emerged is that it so neatly confirms the evaluation of John in the Gospels' presentation. Scholars who by training and habit dispute whether Jesus really compared John to the messenger of Malachi (that is, to Elijah), which is the identification ascribed to Jesus in the sayings' source (Matthew 11:7-19/Luke 7:24-35), are, apparently, more willing to accept that John actually was such a figure. The same romanticism which makes John a more vivid figure than Jesus in Rembrandt, Kazantzakis, and "Godspell," makes him a more historical figure than Jesus in much contemporary scholarship, despite the complete lack of evidence deriving directly from John's own movement.[4] Ed Sanders, for example, takes it as the

---

Ernst Bammel, "The Baptist in Early Christian Tradition."

[4]Wink, p. 100 n. 2 amply documents the demise of the speculation that John was connected with the rise of the sources of Mandaeanism. The present statement obtains, even if one asserts that the materials related to John within the first two chapters of Luke ultimately derive from a Baptist source. That contention is itself suppositious; cf. Stephen Ferris, *The Hymns of Luke's Infancy Narratives*. On pp. 86-98, Ferris discusses the problematic features of the supposition of a baptist source behind the first two chapters of Luke. Fitzmyer is more open to the possibility in *The Gospel According to Luke (I-IX)*, 303-330. But even if such a source did exist, it would not be *directly* represented in Luke. The fundamental difficulties of historiography are identified in Bammel's article. In particular, cf. his telling

first among "[t]he almost indisputable facts" regarding Jesus that he "was baptized by John the Baptist,"[5] and then accepts at face value the attribution in the Gospels to John of a preaching of eschatological repentance.[6] Sanders even maintains that he is sufficiently informed regarding John's position that he can characterize Jesus as relatively deemphasizing the importance of repentance as compared to John.[7]

Before scholars who think of themselves as critical accept the historical reliability of the Gospels' portraits of a prophetic John, certain cautions are in order. In the first place, whether or not Jesus compared John to Elijah, it is evident that the christology of "Q" has an interest in the comparison. Within "Q," Malachi is cited after the presentation of John's question from prison, whether Jesus is ὁ ἐρχόμενος (Matthew 11:2–6/Luke 7:18-23). As followed by Jesus' citation of Malachi (Matthew 11:7-19/Luke 7:24-35), ὁ ἐρχόμενος appears to be

---

criticism of the resuscitation of the "old genre of a *Leben Jesu*...in the form of a *Leben Johannis*," p. 96.

[5]*Jesus and Judaism*, 11.

[6]Pp. 108f., 227; he acknowledges his debt to Ernst Bammel in his formulation (p. 117).

[7]Cf. p. 227. For criticism of Sanders's position in respect of a preaching of repentance, cf. Chilton, "Jesus and the Repentance of E. P. Sanders."

a messianic title, but it is of far less precise meaning, taken on its own terms or within the context of John's question from prison (even assuming the term itself reflects John's interest).[8] Moreover, the "citation" from Malachi has been distorted in a messianic direction;[9] the messenger is sent "before you," rather than "before me." It cannot be argued that the identification of John with the messenger from Malachi is anything but tendentious, and applied in the service of an exaltation of Jesus' status within "Q," whatever the origin of that identification.

The identification of John as Elijah by means of Malachi 3 (suitably distorted) is also represented within Markan tradition, specifically (1:2), where an "overlapping"

---

[8]So, with greater confidence than I would claim to have, John S. Kloppenborg, *The Formation of Q*, 104, 105, 107, 108.

[9]Cf. Fitzmyer, p. 672. As he points out, the very notion that the Elijah redivivus of Malachi 3:1, 23 precedes the *messiah* is innovative. Jesus, of course, may have compared John to Elijah without thereby claiming he was the (or a) messiah. For the alteration of the persons of pronouns in dominical "citations," cf. Chilton, *God in Strength* 157–177 and "Announcement in *Nazara*: redaction and tradition in Luke 4:16–21." Both Fitzmyer and I use the term "messiah" with a non-technical meaning at this point, and it should be acknowledged that Exodus 23:20 may have been at least as important as Malachi 3 at the originating level of Jesus' allusion.

with "Q" is to be explained. Streeter makes the telling comment that "the overlapping of Mark and Q is more certain than the existence of Q."[10] The problem so vexed Streeter that he changed his mind on the subject over the years. Earlier, he had come quite firmly to the conclusion that Mark knew the source in writing,[11] and even that Mark "wrote to *supplement* Q."[12] By 1924, however, when Streeter came to write his classic contribution to the study of the Synoptics, he considered that Mark was "taken down from rapid dictation by word of mouth,"[13] so that he viewed the relationship between Mark and "Q" as more attenuated than he had earlier argued. Now he is not certain "Q" was a written document,[14] and disowns attempts to specify its contents.[15] What intervened between 1911 and 1924 to alter Streeter's approach was his work with A. J. Appansamy (published in 1921) on the the Indian mystic, Sadhu Sundar Singh. That

---

[10]Burnett Hillman Streeter, *The Four Gospels*, 186.

[11]Cf. Sanday, *Studies in the Synoptic Problem*, 165, 166, 176, 177.

[12]*Studies*, 219.

[13]*The Four Gospels*, 163.

[14]*The Four Gospels*, 184, 187, 237.

[15]*The Four Gospels*, 185, 239–242. Indeed, by the time he came to formulate his position in its classic shape, Streeter held that Q had been combined with "Proto-Luke" prior to the writing of Luke (pp. 199–222), and even that there was an overlap between Q and "M" (pp. 251, 252).

research brought Streeter face to face with the overlapping of written and oral sources within cycles of tradition, and he consciously attempted to account for such phenomena within his work on the Synoptics.[16]

The problem of "overlapping" only remains for Streeter, and for his followers, because two features of "Q" which he postulated within the argument of 1911 are imported into the very different analysis of 1924. If one follows Streeter's later formulation, there is no reason to assume that "Q" is an early, written product of a Galilean phase of the movement.[17] Indeed, its production in Syria is betrayed by its assumption of a missionary setting within which Judaism is marginal and there is an established community of eschatologically fervent Christians.[18] That setting, in turn, assumes that an apostolic gospel has already been preached and heard, a gospel which commenced with the preaching of John (cf. Acts 10:34-43, and the reference to the spirit in vv. 44-48) as typologically related to that of Jesus. In

---

[16]*The Four Gospels*, 192-195. In a recent work, I have attempted to craft the insights of the late Streeter with those of the early Westcott into a solution which takes account of the nature of early rabbinic transmission, cf. *Profiles of a Rabbi.*

[17]*Pace* J. S. Kloppenborg, M. W. Meyer, S. J. Patterson, M. G. Steinhauser, *Q-Thomas Reader*, 5, 6.

[18]Cf. Siegfried Schulz, *Q. Die Spruchquelle.*

short, there is no reason, on the formulation of the later Streeter, to assume that the source was a primitive, written "Q," or that knowledge of that "document" must be attributed to "Mark" (as if the text were a person). A Syrian setting of the material in "Q" (whether or not a document, whatever we might mean by "document') would also account for the use of the material in Antioch (within Luke) and Damascus (within Matthew) especially, and for its evenual mutation into an aphoristic form in Edessa (within Thomas). The relative non-appearance of "Q" in Mark is also more easily understood on the supposition of a Syrian provenience, and "overlapping" is a natural feature, if Mark is a later representation of the sort of apostolic gospel which the mishnaic source we call "Q" supplements.

Whatever is made of the "overlapping" with "Q," Mark proceeds to cohere with the triple tradition as a whole in offering a citation of Isaiah 40 and a portrayal of John as a prophet in the wilderness (Matthew 3:1-6/Mark 1:4-6 cf. Luke 3:4-6). The point of John's preaching is the one who is stronger than he, whose baptism of judgement is to follow John's baptism with water (Matthew 3:11/Mark 1:7, 8/Luke 3:16). When the scene in which Jesus is baptized follows (Matthew 3:13-17/Mark 1:9-11/Luke 3:21, 22), there can be no doubt but that he

fulfills John's reference to a figure greater than he.[19]
But it is equally plain that the pointing of John's
preaching and activity towards Jesus is achieved by a
shaping of its contextual presentation *at the very least*,
and the probability is high that the conviction that John
was a messianic messenger in the manner of Malachi 3 and
Isaiah 40 distorted whatever meaning he and his followers
originally attached to what he did and said. John 1:21
may just preserve an awareness of such distortion, by
presenting the baptist as denying he is Elijah or "the
prophet."

John the baptist's role in the Synoptic Gospels, then, is
both catechetical and christological. He points the way
forward to believers' baptism after the manner of Jesus,
who is greater than John. That is the case both in the
apostolic catechesis of the triple tradition which

---

[19]The Lukan interpolation of John's arrest in 3:19, 20 is
designed to loosen any notion of Jesus' dependence upon
John, since it might be taken to suggest that John did
not personally baptize Jesus (Cf. Fitzmyer, p. 477). See
the *Gospel of the Nazaraeans* 2, where Jesus refuses to be
baptized by John. In a similar vein, Luke 3:15f., like
John 1:19-23, has John reject the notion that his own
ministry has a messianic significance, and John's Gospel
focuses so uniquely on John's witness to Jesus' identity
(1:29-34 cf. 1:6-8), there is no mention of the baptism.
On the other hand, the oblique reference to Jesus' own
baptismal ministry in John 3:22; 4:1-3 may be an actual
index of his relationship to the baptist.

conveys the scene of Jesus' own baptism in association with John's movement, and in the assertion in the sayings' source that the least in the kingdom is greater than John the baptist (Matthew 11:11b/Luke 7:28b). John's preaching of repentance in the mishnaic source conventionally known as "Q" is replete with warnings and encouragements for potential converts: Jewish opponents are a brood of vipers (Matthew 3:7/Luke 3:7); what matters is producing fruits worthy of repentance rather than genetic kinship with Abraham (Matthew 3:8, 9/Luke 3:8), and the urgency of the imperative to repent is as keen as an ax laid at the root of a tree (Matthew 3:10/Luke 3:9). Whatever may or may not be reflected of John's preaching here, it is evidently cast within the needs of Christian catechesis[20] and addressed to sympathetic hearers who are assumed to be at the margins of Judaism. Likewise, the advice to relatively prosperous converts in Luke 3:10-14 -- presumably from the Lukan version of "Q"[21] -- is redolent of a social setting more reminiscent of Lukan Antioch than of the baptist's

---

[20]The similarity to sayings ascribed to Jesus is striking, although infrequently considered; cf. *God in Strength*, p. 188, citing Matthew 3:10 with 7:19; 3:12 with 13:30; 3:7 with 12:34, and E. Klostermann, *Das Mattäusevangelium*, 29.

[21]Bammel, pp. 105, 106, attributes the material to "Luke's own pen," although he associates it closely with "Q."

Peraea: charitable giving by revenue contractors[22] and Roman soldiers is not likely to have been the burden of the historical John's message.

That John should be taken as a prophet within the Gospels, then, is entirely natural. It permits him to be seen as a prototype of Christian teachers who were also seen as prophets.[23] But the more natural it is within evangelical preaching to portray John as a prophet, the less reasonable it is to claim that is what he was within his own estimate or that of his sympathizers. Webb nonetheless considers the category of prophet alone as suitable for understanding John: his only indecision is whether John was a "clerical prophet," a "sapiential prophet," a "solitary popular prophet," or a "leadership popular prophet."[24]

---

[22]Cf. Fritz Herrenbrück, *Jesus und die Zöllner*. He challenges the understanding that τελῶναι in the Gospels are to be equated with *portitores*, collectors in the service of *publicani* within Roman society. Herrenbrück's preferred models, intimated in a discussion of matters of translation in chapter 2, are the τελῶναι of the hellenistic world (not Rome itself), local contractors (*Kleinpächter*) charged with the collection of various revenues for Rome. They are *Abgabenpächter*, revenue contractors, rather than tax or toll collectors (p. 37, cf. p. 225, where the suggested English rendering confuses the issue somewhat).

[23]Cf. David Aune, *Prophecy in Early Christianity*, 189–231.

[24]Webb, pp. 307–348. The wording is largely Aune's,

Such subdivisions are alleged to derive from Josephus, but that derivation is only possible by means of tendentious exegesis. What is a "sapiential prophet" but a sage? Josephus indeed describes Essenes who foretell the future, and whose wisdom derives from study and purification (*Jewish War* II @ 159).[25] John may have been comparable to them in some ways, but that does not make him or them prophetic by pretension. It is to be borne in mind that Pharisaic or early rabbinic teachers were disinclined to accept designation as prophets, and their attitude is embodied in classic stories concerning Hanina ben Dosa and Hillel.[26] Similarly, Josephus refers to those who can predict the future; we naturally refer to such people as prophets, but Josephus calls them oracles (cf. μάντις in *Antiquities* XIII @ 313), and John is reputed in neither Josephus nor the New Testament for predictions of the future. Only the "popular prophet" among Webb's categories can claim a verbal affinity with Josephus, in that those who led groups into symbolic actions which the

---

although the solecism involved in the third category is Webb's own.

[25] Cf. Webb, pp. 322–326, and *War* I @ 78–80; II @ 113; *Antiquities* XII @ 310–313..

[26] Cf. Berakhoth 34b for Hanina, discussed in *A Galilean Rabbi and His Bible*, 31f. The vignette concerning Hillel is found in Tosephta Sotah 13:3 and Sanhedrin 11a, and is discussed in *Profiles of a Rabbi*, pp. 77–89.

Romans interpreted as seditious are styled "false prophets."

Josephus' relative reserve in using prophetic designations is not unusual, when viewed in the context of rabbinic views[27] and of the usage within 1 Maccabees 4:46; 9:27; 14:41; and Psalm 74:9. Nonetheless, it is evident that Josephus, as we have seen, understood that prophetic functions continued to be exercised; the old generalization that "according to Josephus as well as the rabbis, prophecy ceased"[28] is simply inadequate. By contrast, Aune goes out of his way to insist that "Israelite prophecy did not disappear" in early Judaism.[29] But in choosing to reverse Moore's judgement, instead of nuancing it, Aune creates a problem for himself: he finds cause to regret the "paltry evidence" for actual reference to prophets in early Judaism.[30] The problem lies more in Aune's conception than in the inadequacy of the "evidence." The notion that prophecy simply ceased with

---

[27]In addition to the passages cited above, cf. Aboth 1:1 and Megillah 3a, 14a.

[28]So George Foot Moore, *Judaism*, 240. For a treatment of Josephus' self-portrait in priestly and prophetic terms, cf. *The Temple of Jesus*, chapter 5, "Joseph bar Matthias's Vision of the Temple," pp. 69–87.

[29]Aune, 103.

[30]Aune, 189.

Ezra is indeed simplistic, but the idea that canonization did not influence the practice of claiming directly prophetic authorization is unrealistic.

Webb follows in the wake of Aune's loose usage of the category of prophet, and argues that John was a Josephan "popular prophet," in that he baptized people in the Jordan:

> People would leave their homes in Jerusalem/Judea, where they experienced a sense of oppression and deprivation, perhaps reminscent of what their ancestors experienced in Egypt. They would travel through the wilderness to the Jordan river following the call of the prophet John, again reminiscent of the people of Israel travelling through the wilderness under the leadership of a great prophetic figure, Moses. They would come to the Jordan river and enter it (possibly crossing to the other side), reminding them of the other "crossings": the Red Sea and the Jordan river in the Exodus and Conquest. Here they were baptized by John with a repentance-baptism which functioned to initiate them into the group of prepared people, the true Israel. As such, they expected imminently the restoring ministry of God's agent who would make them a holy

group and remove the wicked from their midst...[31]
Webb must admit, however, that John's ministry was not
limited to the river itself[32] and that, unlike the false
prophets, John did not engage in a single, dramatic
symbol of liberation.[33] But his admission does scant
justice to the clear indications that the reference to
the Jordan in Matthew 3:6/Mark 1:5 is not to be taken as
a limitation: the specific word "river" is omitted in
significant witnesses, and the Lukan analogue (3:3, καὶ
ἦλθεν εἰς πᾶσαν περίχωρον τοῦ Ἰορδάνου) is a purely
regional reference. Moreover, the baptist is explicitly
portrayed as baptizing at other sites in John (Bethany in
1:28, Aenon in 3:23); and although his setting is
Judaean, the Jordan river is not mentioned as a place
where people are baptized.[34] Within the fourth Gospel, the
Jordan is more a point of reference (1:28; 3:26, cf.
10:40) than a place where action unfolds.

In any case, the symbolism of bathing is not

---

[31]Webb, 364.

[32]He does so with only passing reference to the works of
other scholars, p. 363 n. 27. See especially Scobie, pp.
41–48.

[33]Webb, 265.

[34]Jesus' baptismal activity is portrayed in Judaea (John
3:22, 26) and even in Galilee (John 4:3). Webb backs away
from John's explicit association with the river on p.
365, but without a discussion of the relevant material.

transparently revolutionary. It can scarcely be compared with what Josephus said the false prophets did: one scaled Mount Gerezim to find the vessels deposited by Moses (*Antiquities* XVIII @ 85-87), Theudas waited at the Jordan for the waters to part (*Antiquities* XX @ 97, 98), the Egyptian marched from the Mount of Olives so that he might conquer Jerusalem (*War* II @ 261-63).[35] If there is an act in the Gospels which approximates to such fanaticism, it is Jesus' entry into Jerusalem and his occupation of the Temple, an enactment of the eschatological prophecy of Zechariah.[36] When Jesus is called a prophet in that context,[37] it is arguable that there is some affinity with the sort of usage which Josephus presupposes (but personally rejects). There is, no doubt, a certain theological convenience in making John the symbolic rebel and Jesus the pacifist, but that typology is counter-factual.

---

[35]In *Antiquities* XX @ 169-72, he expected the walls of the city to fall at his command.

[36]Cf. *The Temple of Jesus*, chapter 6, "Jesus' Occupation of the Temple," pp. 91-111, and chapter 7, "The Sacrificial Program of Jesus," pp. 113-136.

[37]Cf. Matthew 21:11, 46. By contrast, John's repute as a prophet may be no more than a retroversion of his significance within Christianity, cf. Matthew 14:5; Matthew 21:26/Mark 11:32/Luke 20:6. In the last complex cited, it is notable that what is a narrative comment in Mark is retrofitted to the Judaic authorities in Matthew and Luke.

If, as seems only reasonable, we remove the prophetic mantle from John, in that his garb appears more apologetic than historical, in what category are we to clothe him? Webb rightly insists that Josephus' testimony should be accorded privilege, but -- as we have seen -- his actual method (derived from David Hill's) is to press Josephus into the service of the apologetic tendency of the Gospels.[38] For Josephus, John is not a false prophet, and he does not predict the future. Rather, he practices ablutions and preaches righteousness in the wilderness (*Antiquities* XVIII @ 116-119). Josephus does not provide John with a category, and in that regard his treatment invites comparison with the presentation of Bannus, the ascetic sage with whom Josephus claims to have lived and studied for three years (*Life* 10-12). Bannus is both wise and pure, and his frequent ablutions in cold water are a part of the pattern of his wisdom. That purity may also be associated with the purity of the Essenes whom Josephus describes as able to tell the future (see above).

---

[38]Cf. Hill, *New Testament Prophecy*, 43-47, where the historical John is simply treated as Jesus' forerunner. Hill supervised Webb's research (cf. Webb, p. 11); his less than reflective appropriation of the Gospels' paradigm of John appears to have been contagious.

But there are three related features which distinguish John from Bannus within Josephus' presentation. First, a large following is attributed to John, while Bannus is a studiously solitary figure.[39] Second, there is a self-consciously public dimension involved in John's preaching, which leads to his execution at the hands of Antipas.[40] And third, John does not simply make ablution a personal practice, but urges the activity upon those who come to him. In a word, John makes baptism a public program, which both earns him his sobriquet and distinguishes him from Bannus.

The practice of frequent ablutions at Qumran has led to a comparison of John with the Essenes. That comparison has been somewhat complicated by the issue of whether or not the covenanters of Qumran and the Essenes are identifiable. A collation of Josephus, Philo, Pliny and the scrolls nonetheless results in a reasonably coherent picture, which has been masterfully represented by Todd

---

[39]Webb's characterization of Bannus as a "solitary popular prophet" conceals an important difference from John within an oxymoron.

[40]The attribution of Antipas' rage to John's criticism of marriage to a brother's wife is arguably implied in Josephus (*Antiquities* XVIII @ 109–115), and explicit in the Synoptics (Matthew 14:3, 4/Mark 6:17, 18/Luke 3:19). In any case, it is difficult to conceive how the story can have served a specifically Christian apologetic. Cf. Harold W. Hoehner, *Herod Antipas*, 110–171.

S. Beall.[41] Robert H. Eisenman, on the other hand, stresses that Pliny was writing in the period after the revolt in *Natural History* 5.15 @ 70-73 when he described Essenes as living on the western shore of the Dead Sea with Engedi below them.[42] His contention is that the community of the scrolls centered on James as the righteous teacher. But his reading of Pliny hypothesis must also confront an anachronism: Qumran was destroyed by the Romans in A. D. 68.[43] Whoever Pliny described was living in conditions ill suited for habitation, or at some site other than Qumran, or in fact dwelled there at an earlier period. In that Pliny appears to be referring to a site which had not been destroyed and Qumran suits the location as described, the most plausible explanation is that he is describing an earlier setting on the basis of his authorities (a list of which he provides in book one). And the earlier setting, of course, would not allow time for a sect to have emerged which venerated the dead James. In addition, Eisenman's theory must impute to James views which there is no record that he held, and

---

[41]See *Josephus' description of the Essenes*, a citation and comprehensive discussion of both the texts and the issues.

[42]The passage is miscited as 5.17 by Eisenman; cf. *James the Just in the Habakkuk* <u>Pesher</u>, 83, 84.

[43]For a discussion of the archaeology of Qumran, cf. Roland de Vaux, *Archaeology and the Dead Sea Scrolls*, 1-45.

posit a hermetic separation between his movement and early Christianity which the continued memory of James within the Church makes improbable. Finally, he must also suppose that the deposit of the scrolls in the caves nearby had nothing whatever to do with the history of earlier habitation at Qumran. It is not at all clear that the theory explains anything sufficiently important to compensate for the obscurity it generates.[44]

The Essene movement appears to have its origins in opposition to the Hasmoneans. The Essenes pursued their own system of purity, ethics, and initiation, followed their own calendar, and withdrew into their own communities, either within cities or in isolated sites such as Qumran.[45] There they awaited a coming, apocalyptic war, when they, as "the sons of light," would triumph over "the sons of darkness:" not only the Gentiles, but anyone not of their vision (see *The Manual of Discipline* and *The War of the Sons of Light and the Sons of Darkness*). The culmination of those efforts was to involve complete control of Jerusalem and the Temple,

---

[44]Cf. the theories that the righteous teacher was Jesus (J. L. Teicher, "Puzzling Passages in the Damascus Fragments") and John the Baptist (B. E. Thiering, *The Gospels and Qumran*). *Mutatis mutandis*, the same objections apply to them.

[45]Cf. David Flusser, "The Social Message from Qumran," *Judaism and the Origins of Christianity*, 193–201.

where worship would be offered according to their
revelation, the correct understanding of the law of Moses
(cf. *Zadokite Document* 5:17–6:11). Their insistence upon
a doctrine of two messiahs, one of Israel and one of
Aaron, would suggest that it was particularly the
Hasmoneans' arrogation of priestly and royal powers which
alienated the Essenes, and such a usurpation of what the
Essenes considered divine prerogatives also characterized
Herodian settlements with Rome.

On a routine level, the Essenes appear to have focused on
the issue of purity, thus maintaining a tense
relationship with the cultic establishment which
comported well with their apocalyptic expectation that
control of the Temple would one day be theirs. Some of
them lived in cities, where they performed ablutions,
maintained distinctive dietary regulations, observed
stricter controls on marital relations than was common,
and regulated the offerings they brought to the Temple
according to their own constructions of purity. A more
extreme form of the movement lived apart from cities in
communities such as Qumran: in them celibacy and a break
with ordinary, sacrificial worship was the rule. The aim
throughout, however, was the eventual governance of the
Temple by Essene priests, the first phase of the war of
the sons of light against the sons of darkness.

The practice of regular ablutions at Qumran shows that Bannus, John the baptist, and the Pharisees were in no sense unique, or even unusual, in their insistence upon such practices. But the entire direction of Essene practice, the interest in the actual control of worship in the Temple, appears unlike John's. The notion that John somehow opposed the cult in the Temple is weakly based. The argument is sometimes mounted that, because John preached a baptism of repentance for the forgiveness of sins, he challenged the efficacy of sacrificial forgiveness.[46] Such assertions invoke a supposed dualism between moral and cultic atonement which simply has no place in the critical discussion of early Judaism,[47] and they in no way suffice to establish that John opposed worship in the Temple. The motif of his preaching "a

---

[46]Cf. Webb, pp. 192, 193. Webb's claims are ultimately based upon Joseph Thomas, *Le mouvement baptiste*. But the thesis of a widespread movement of "nonconformity" in which there was a substitution of "baptizing rites for the observation of Temple sacrifice," was long ago discredited by Matthew Black, "Patristic Accounts of Jewish Sects," 54.

[47]Even within the sacrificial systems of the Hebrew Bible, the link between purity and righteousness is implicit, and the book of Psalms brings to open expression the systemic association of righteousness and purity (cf. 18:21 [v. 20 in English versions]; 24:3-6; 26:4-7; 51:4, 8, 9, 12 [English vv. 2, 6, 7, 10]; 119:9). Cf. *The Temple of Jesus*, chapter 4, "Sacrifice in 'Classic' Israel," pp. 45-67 and chapter 7, "The Sacrificial Program of Jesus," pp. 113-136.

baptism of repentance for the forgiveness of sins" may in any case represent the anachronistic assignment to John of an element of the language of catechesis within early Christianity. The phrase appears in Mark 1:4; Luke 3:3 (cf. 1:77) in relation to John, but εἰς ἄφεσιν ἁμαρτιῶν appears in obviously Christian contexts at Matthew 26:28; Luke 24:47. Webb can see the problem posed for his thesis by such passages as Acts 2:38, and his only defense is a methodological bias against any "skeptical conclusion."[48] Josephus more accurately observed that John's baptism was not understood to seek pardon for sins, but was intended to purify the body (*Antiquities* XVIII @ 117).

The motif of John's priesthood is similarly beside the point of any alleged antagonism to worship in the Temple.[49] The fact of being born a priest did not necessarily involve anyone in the Temple on a regular basis, although it might conceivably have prompted the increased concern with purity which evidently characterized John. Even so, the fact that Josephus was a priest did not imbue the author we know with a marked sensitivity to the issue. He had no scruples regarding where Jews in Syria were to buy their oil (cf. *The Jewish War* II @ 590-594), and expressed none in regard to

---

[48]Cf. Webb, 171.

[49]Cf. Webb, 193.

fighting on the sabbath or dealing with the uncleanness occasioned by corpses.[50] He mentions Herod's construction of the golden eagle in the Temple only when certain (apparently Pharisaic) rabbis object to it, and ventures no vigorous opinion of his own (I @ 648-650). The only time he refers to the impurity of food, an issue which must have plagued many military campaigns during the period, it is in order to assail the impiety of John of Gischala at the end of the war (VII @ 264).[51]

Some priests, especially among the privileged families in Jerusalem, were notoriously pro-Roman. The story of sons of the high priest having the surgery called epispasm, in order to restore the appearance of a foreskin (for gymnastic purposes) is well known (cf. 1 Maccabees 1:14, 15; *Antiquities* XII @ 240, 241). There is little doubt but that such families, the most prominent of which were the Sadducees and Boethusians, were not highly regarded by most Jews (cf. *b. Pesaḥim* 57a). They are typically

---

[50]Cf. his attention to the lapse at a later period, in *Antiquities* III @ 262.

[51]Reference might be made in this regard to Josephus' fascination with menstrual blood for such diverse purposes as removing asphalt (IV @ 480) and neutralizing the supposed movements of the Baaras root (VII @ 181), which he expresses without compunction, although he knows quite well that menstruants are to be excluded from the Temple (V @ 227).

portrayed in a negative light, as not teaching the resurrection of the dead (cf. *War* II @ 165; Matthew 22:23; Mark 12:18; Luke 20:27; Acts 23:8), but the issue may have been one of emphasis: the Torah had stressed that correct worship in the Temple would bring with it material prosperity, and the elite priests attempted to realize that promise. The arrangement gave them such consistent control that they became known as "high priests," although there was in fact only one high priest. But Josephus indulges in the usage, as well as the Gospels, so that it should not be taken as an inaccuracy: the plural is a cultic mistake, but a sociological fact.

Members of most priestly families were not "high priests," and did not in any sense exercise control over the Temple, or even participate ordinarily in the conduct of worship there. The well known courses of 1 Chronicles 23; 24; Ezra 2:36-39; 10:18-22; Nehemiah 10:3-9; 12:1-7, 12-21; *Antiquities* VII @ 365, 366; *Life* 2; *Against Apion* 2 @ 108 provided for only occasional service (cf. Luke 1:8, 9).[52] Within the Gospels, priests appear locally, in adjudications of purity (Matthew 8:1-4; Mark 1:40-45; Luke 5:12-16 cf. Luke 10:31; 17:14, and the exceptional

---

[52]For a brief discussion of the passagaes, cf. Fitzmyer, p. 322; the standard remains Joachim Jeremias, *Jerusalem in the Time of Jesus*, 98-207.

role of Zechariah in 1:5-23), while high priests are essentially limited to Jerusalem, or use Jerusalem as a base of power (cf. Matthew 2:4; 16:21; 20:18; 21:15, 23, 45; 26:1-28:11; Mark 8:31; 10:33; 11:18, 27; 14:1-15:31; Luke 3:2; 9:22: 19:47; 20:1-24:20; John 1:19; 7:32, 45; 11:47, 49, 51, 57; 12:10; 18:3-19:21). Several priests were also prominent in the revolt against Rome, however, and it should not be thought that such priestly nationalists, among whom were Joseph bar Matthias, better known as Flavius Josephus, emerged only at the end of the sixties (*War* II @ 562-568). The precedent of the Hasmoneans was there for any priestly family to see as a possible alternative to Roman rule, direct or indirect. Indeed, some priests were not only nationalists, but revolutionaries, who joined with the Essenes, or with rebellious Pharisees, although any alliance with a prophetic pretender is, perhaps, not a likely supposition. In any case, John well may not have been a priest: the claim that he was is weakly attested (Luke 1:5), and made within the same complex of material which asserts that Jesus was related to him (cf. Luke 1:36), although of Davidic ancestry (cf. 1:27 *and* 1:69). The line which divides historical reminiscence from theological typology is particularly difficult to draw here.

Once it is appreciated that John is not known to have

shared the cultic program of the Essenes, the argument that he is to be associated with the covenanters of Qumran loses its foundation. W. H. Brownlee gave currency to the view that the usage of Isaiah 40 in *The Manual of Discipline* viii.14; ix.19 shows that "John must have been familiar with Essene thoughts regarding the coming of the Messianic age."[53] More accurately, one might say that the analogy suggests that Isaiah 40 was known both to the covenanters and to the Christians who revered John's memory as their master's forerunner. To build upon such analogies and Luke 1:80 the speculation that John was orphaned and raised by the Essenes is an exercise in hagiography.

Essene practice, together with Pharisaic, Sadducean, and Bannus' practice, does suggest by analogy a likely feature of John's baptism which contemporary discussion has obscured. It is routinely claimed that John preached a "conversionary repentance" by baptism, an act once for all which was not repeatable nor to be repeated.[54] That is a fine description of how baptism as portrayed in the Epistle to the Hebrews 6:1-8, and such a theology came to

---

[53]"John the Baptist in the New Light of Ancient Scrolls," 73; cf. Steinmann, p. 59.

[54]Cf. Webb, 197-202. Brownlee, p. 76, realized at an early stage that Essene ablutions could not be regarded as an initiation.

predominate within catholic Christianity. But ablutions in Judaism were characteristically repeatable, and even Hebrews must argue against the proposition that one might be baptized afresh. Only the attribution to John of a later, catholic theology of baptism can justify the characterization of his baptism as symbol of a definitive "conversion."

If John's baptism was not in the interests of "conversion," or permanent purification, or opposition to atonement by means of cultic sacrifice, what was its purpose? Josephus in *Antiquities* XVIII @ 117 asserts that John's baptism was to serve as a ritual of purity following a return to righteousness. Righteousness and bathing together made one pure. Josephus makes a nearly or actually dualistic distinction between the righteousness which effects purification of the soul and the baptism which symbolizes the consequent purification of the body, and that is consistent with his portrayal of others with whom he expresses sympathy, the Essenes, the Pharisees, and Bannus.[55]

Webb argues that John attempted to found a sect after the

---

[55]Cf. Webb, p. 192, and *The Temple of Jesus,* chapter 5, "Joseph bar Matthias's Vision of the Temple," pp. 69–87.

manner of the Essenes.[56] The thesis founders on several considerations. There is no evidence whatever that baptism for John constituted an initiation, comparable to the ceremony for novices at Qumran.[57] It is not even to be assumed -- as we have seen -- that baptism for John was not to be repeated. Moreover, no discipline but "righteousness" was required by John, as far as the available evidence would suggest. His execution was not occasioned by placing an unusual requirement upon Antipas, but for insisting Antipas keep the Torah of purity as any person might understand it (cf. Leviticus 20:21).

The purpose of John's baptism must be sought, not in an unfounded hypothesis of sectarian motivations, but in the nature of his activity as compared to ordinary practices of purification. It is just here that contemporary students of John have been most misled by the supposition that he was a prophet with a recoverable message which explains his activity. Historically, his activity is itself as much of his program as we are ever likely to

---

[56]Cf. Webb, pp. 197-202. His stance is that of Steinmann, p. 5, and opposed to that of Wink. p. 107. He discusses neither.

[57]Indeed, David Flusser contrasts John's stance with the Essenes on the precise issue of initiation, cf. "The Social Message from Qumran," p. 109.

grasp.

John practiced his baptism in natural sources of water. It is sometimes taken that his purpose was to use living water,[58] but that it not specified in any source, and the waters of the Jordan or a pool in Peraea or an oasis in the valley of the Jordan would not necessarily be flowing.[59] Indeed, Sanders has plausibly suggested that water from a spring was equated with the category of naturally collected water by the first century.[60] Moreover, even if John did use living water by preference, the especial corruption of what was thereby purified was not thereby marked, as is sometimes supposed:[61] corpse contamination, after all, was dealt with by means of the still water of the ashes of the red heifer, not living water (cf. Numbers 19).[62] John's baptism made no statement as to the nature of what was to be purified: his activity took that as being as self-evident as Antipas' lapse. John's baptism was, however, an implicit claim that there was no advantage in

---

[58]Cf. Webb, p. 195.

[59]Cf. Herbert G. May, *Oxford Bible Atlas*, 50.

[60]*Jewish Law*, 215.

[61]Cf. Webb, 193.

[62]For an indication of how the ashes and the water were regarded by Pharisees and rabbis, cf. Parah 5:1–8:11.

the pools of Qumran, the double vatted *miqvaoth* of the
Pharisees, or the private baths of aristocratic groups
such as the Sadducees.[63] He enacted what amounted to
generic purification, in contrast to the deliberate
artifice involved in several other movements, sectarian
and non-sectarian. In that sense, his purpose was
deliberately anti-sectarian.

Inferentially, it might be maintained that John's baptism
was driven by an eschatological expectation, not
necessarily of a messiah, but of divine judgement.[64] Of
all the statements attributed to John, the claim that
after him a baptism of spirit was to come stands out as
possibly authentic.[65] Whether or not it is, the
anticipation of imminent judgment would both supply a
suitable motivation for John's activity and help to
account for his appropriation within early Christianity.

---

[63]Cf. E. P. Sanders, *Jewish Law*, 214–227, for a
preliminary discussion. The later development of the
immersion of proselytes (cf. Yebamoth 47a, b) accords
with the understanding that such bathing is an ordinary
act of integration within Israel.

[64]Cf. Flusser, "The Magnificat, the Benedictus and the War
Scroll," *Judaism*, 126–149, 148.

[65]Cf. Webb, 262–278. His citation of *Jubilees* 1:23 on p.
224 is especially apposite. The phrase καὶ πυρί in the
version of Mark 1:8 reflected in Matthew 3:11/Luke 3:16
is, however, probably an apologetic addition inspired by
Malachi 3:2.

But whatever his own motivation, and those of subsequent interpreters, that he acted as a purifier on the basis of ritual bathing is the most certain -- as well as the most obvious -- feature of his public activity.

Works Consulted

David Aune, *Prophecy in Early Christianity and the Ancient Mediterranean World* (Grand Rapids: Eerdmans, 1983)

Ernst Bammel, "The Baptist in Early Christian Tradition," *New Testament Studies* 18 (1971-1972) 95-128.

Todd S. Beall, *Josephus' description of the Essenes illustrated by the Dead Sea Scrolls*: Society of New Testament Studies Monograph Series 58 (Cambridge: Cambridge University Press, 1988)

Matthew Black, "Patristic Accounts of Jewish Sects," *The Scrolls and Christian Origins* (London: Nelson, 1961) 48-74

W. H. Brownlee, "John the Baptist in the New Light of Ancient Scrolls," *Interpretation* 9 (1955) 71-90

B. D. Chilton, "Announcement in *Nazara*: redaction and tradition in Luke 4:16-21," *Gospel Perspectives* 2 (1981) 147-172

-------------- *A Galilean Rabbi and His Bible: Jesus' Use*

of the Interpreted Scripture of His Time (Wilmington: Glazier, 1984)

--------------- *God in Strength. Jesus' Announcement of the Kingdom*: Studien zum Neuen Testament und seiner Umwelt 1 (Freistadt: Plöchl, 1979; reprinted in "The Biblical Seminar" of Sheffield: JSOT, 1987)

--------------- "Jesus and the Repentance of E. P. Sanders," *Tyndale Bulletin* 39 (1988) 1-18.

--------------- *Profiles of a Rabbi. Synoptic Opportunities in Reading about Jesus:* Brown Judaic Studies 177 (Atlanta: Scholars Press, 1989)

--------------- *The Temple of Jesus. His Sacrificial Program within a Cultural History of Sacrifice* (University Park: Pennsylvania State University Press, 1992)

Roland de Vaux, *Archaeology and the Dead Sea Scrolls* (London: Oxford University Press, 1973)

Robert H. Eisenman, *James the Just in the Habakkuk* Pesher: Studia Post-Biblica (Leiden: Brill, 1986)

Stephen Ferris, *The Hymns of Luke's Infancy Narratives.*

Their Origin, Meaning and Significance: Journal for the Study of the New Testament Supplements Series 9 (Sheffield: JSOT, 1985)

Joseph A. Fitzmyer, *The Gospel According to Luke (I-IX)*: The Anchor Bible (Garden City: Doubleday, 1981)

David Flusser, *Judaism and the Origins of Christianity* (Jerusalem: Magnes, 1988)

Fritz Herrenbrück, *Jesus und die Zöllner: Historische und neutestamentlich-exegetische Untersuchungen*: WUNT 2/41 (Tübingen: Mohr-Siebeck, 1990)

D. Hill, *New Testament Prophecy* (London: Marshall, Morgan & Scott, 1979)

Harold W. Hoehner, *Herod Antipas* (Grand Rapids: Zondervan, 1980)

Joachim Jeremias (trans. F. H. and C. H. Cave), *Jerusalem in the Time of Jesus* (London: SCM, 1969)

John S. Kloppenborg, *The Formation of Q. Trajectories in Ancient Wisdom Collections* (Philadelphia: Fortress, 1987)

------------------------, M. W. Meyer, S. J. Patterson, M. G.

Steinhauser, *Q-Thomas Reader* (Sonoma: Polebridge, 1990)

E. Klostermann, *Das Mattäusevangelium* (Tübingen: Mohr, 1927)

Herbert G. May (with G. N. S. Hunt, R. W. Hamilton, J. Day), *Oxford Bible Atlas* (New York: Oxford University Press, 1984), 50.

George Foot Moore, *Judaism in the First Centuries of the Christian Era* I (Cambridge: Harvard University Press, 1927)

William Sanday (ed.), *Studies in the Synoptic Problem* (Oxford: 1911)

E. P. Sanders, *Jesus and Judaism* (Philadelphia: Fortress, 1985)

-------------- *Jewish Law from Jesus to the Mishnah* (Philadelphia: Trinity Press International, 1990)

Siegfried Schulz, *Q. Die Spruchquelle der Evangelisten* (Zürich: Theologischer Verlag, 1972).

Charles H. H. Scobie, *John the Baptist* (Fortress: Philadelphia, 1964).

Jean Steinmann (tr. M. Boyes), *John the Baptist and the Desert Tradition* (Harper: New York, 1958)

Burnett Hillman Streeter, *The Four Gospels. A Study of Origins* (London: Macmillan, 1924)

----------------------- and A. J. Appansamy, *The Sadhu: A Study in Mysticism and Practical Religion* (London: Macmillan, 1921).

J. L. Teicher, "Puzzling Passages in the Damascus Fragments," *Journal of Jewish Studies* 5 (1954) 139–143

B. E. Thiering, *The Gospels and Qumran. A New Hypothesis*: Australian and New Zealand Studies in Theology and Religion (Sydney: Theological Explorations, 1981)

Joseph Thomas, *Le mouvement baptiste en Palestine et Syrie* (150 *av. J. C. --* 300 *ap. J. C.)* (Gembloux: Duculot, 1935)

Robert Webb, *John the Baptizer and Prophet. A Socio-Historical Study*: Journal for the Study of the New Testament Supplement Series 65 (Sheffield: Sheffield Academic Press, 1991)

Walter Wink, *John the Baptist in the Gospel Tradition*:
Society of New Testament Studies Monograph Series 7
(Cambridge: Cambridge University Press, 1968)

GOD AS "FATHER" IN THE TARGUMIM,
IN NON-CANONICAL LITERATURES
OF EARLY JUDAISM AND PRIMITIVE CHRISTIANITY,
AND IN MATTHEW

Interest in what has come to be called "midrash" in contemporary scholarship has corresponded and contributed to a program to locate Christianity within early Judaism. That program is not simply a matter of treating Judaism as a "background," as if it were a static frame within which the dynamics of Christian faith emerged. Rather, our period has seen the possibility emerge of treating Christianity and Judaism together, both sympathetically and critically, as mutually explicating, if definitively distinctive, variants of biblical religion. Indeed, some of us would insist that their relationship is so close as to require that both be understood, if either is to be comprehended.

Because scripture is a vital force within both religious perspectives, and because the contents of what they call the book or "Bible" are largely shared, a natural point of departure is the simple question, "how is the Bible read within each of the systems of belief?" Although that question is simple, to answer it is not, and there is the further complication that modern scholars have chosen to refer to the issue under the ancient category, "Midrash." The common approach is to point out that the noun מדרש

refers to anything which one "searches out," and therefore to what one might call the inquisitive use of scripture. That definition is a hybrid of ancient etymology and modern hermeneutics, but it has nonetheless won a place for itself in current parlance. Within early Judaism, "midrash" refers to the deliberate exposition of scripture. If such exegesis is not at issue, the term in its ancient sense cannot appropriately be applied. But some of my contemporaries also use the noun to refer to the process of thought which stands behind midrash (which I should call interpretation), and to the subsequent use made of what an exposition states (which I should call a history of thought).

The desire to characterize the use and influence of scripture in broad terms is understandable, because the fact is that scripture is deeply implicated in the visions of God which Judaism and Christianity convey. But it is as well to be clear that, when a statement is made about God by means of a biblical text, what is said may reflect the speaker's theological conviction more than his comprehension of the text or his adherence to exegetical norms. For that reason, a comparison of religious systems must not be limited to an evaluation of their "midrash" because the danger emerges that we will mistake properly theological differences for happenstances of exegetical policy.[1]

Reference to God as "father" in primitive Christianity and early Judaism is a likely point of comparison, and one which will shortly take us to the heart of a properly comparative study of distinct, religious systems. But before the material can do that for us, we need to clear away some undergrowth, left us by recent discussion.

Joachim Jeremias is still widely cited, in the literature and in the classrooms, for his analysis of the place of God's fatherhood in Jesus' teaching. Jeremias held that, among the rabbis, "Johanan b. Zakkai, a contemporary of the apostles, who taught *c.* AD 50–80, seems to be the first to use the designation 'heavenly Father' ('our heavenly Father,' or 'Israel's heavenly Father') for God,"[2] and that Jesus' direct address of God as "Abba"

---

[1]Cf. Chilton, "Commenting on the Old Testament (with particular reference to the pesharim, Philo, and the Mekilta)," *It is Written: Scripture Citing Scripture. Essays in Honour of Barnabas Lindars, SSF* (ed. D. A. Carson and H. G. M. Williamson; Cambridge: Cambridge University Press, 1988) 122–140; "Varieties and Tendencies of Midrash: Rabbinic Interpretations of Isaiah 24:23," *Gospel Perspectives* 3 (1983) 9–32.

[2](Tr. J. Bowden and C. Burchard), *The Prayers of Jesus*: Studies in Biblical Theology 6 (London: SCM, 1967) 16. Jeremias immediately explains, however, that he has in mind only that Yohanan popularized the usage. After all, the conception itself is rooted in the Hebrew Bible, cf.

was unique.[3] He pointed out that, within Rabbinic literature, the reference could not be found in a passage datable prior to Yoḥanan.[4] The obvious problem in Jeremias's analysis is that passages in Rabbinica are *generally* difficult to date prior to Jesus, owing to the chronology of the documents themselves. When one considers the number of references to God's fatherhood in Rabbinica, and takes into account the improbability that Jesus' usage somehow stands behind them, it is far more likely, as Gottlob Schrenk concluded, that the reference was conventional within the first century. Schrenk's analysis is supported by his citation of passages in *Jubilees, the Sibylline Oracles, 3 Maccabees*, Tobit, *the Apocalypse of Moses*, and the *Testament of Judah*; his point is that Rabbinica and the Pseudepigrapha together (along with Philo) attest a usage which was widespread within early Judaism.[5] Schrenk is concerned also to

---

Jeremias, pp. 12–15, and Deuteronomy 32:6; 2 Samuel 7:14; Psalm 68:5; 89:26; Isaiah 63:16; 64:18; Jeremiah 3:4, 19; 31:9; Malachi 1:6; 2:10.

[3] Pp. 53–65, and above all, p. 57, for its famous reference to "*ipsissima vox Jesu.*"

[4] Pp. 16, 17.

[5] Schrenk, "Der Vaterbegriff im Spätjudentum," *Theologisches Wörterbuch zum Neuen Testament* 5 (G. Friedrich; Stuttgart: Kohlhammer, 1954) 974–981. The English version appears as "The Father Concept in Later Judaism," (G. Friedrich, tr. G. W. Bromiley), *Theological Dictionary of the New Testament* 5 (Grand Rapids:

forestall any attempt to suggest that Jesus was unique in imputing a particular sense or emphasis to the locution.[6] The first volume of the *Wörterbuch*, in an article on ἀββᾶ, takes a similar line, and it is telling that neither editor, Kittel or Friedrich, invited Jeremias to contribute an article relevant to "Abba," a topic upon which his reputation in Anglo-Saxon circles is largely built, although Jeremias did, of course, make other contributions to the *Wörterbuch*.

The published findings of the *Wörterbuch* make it unmistakably clear that Jeremias's perspective was not shared by the editors, who in fact saw to it that it was refuted. That point is worth recognizing, because in his work on the subject of "Abba," Geza Vermes has claimed that Jeremias' position has been dominant in the study of the New Testament,[7] and that the *Wörterbuch* is to be

---

Eerdmans, 1967) 974–982.

[6]"Die individuelle Fassung der Beziehung zum himmlischen Vater tritt also keineswegs erst bei Jesus auf...," p. 980. The English rendering of the statement appears more reserved by comparison, "Certainly the individual version of relationship to the heavenly Father does not appear for the first time in Jesus..."

[7]*Jesus and the World of Judaism* (Philadelphia: Fortress, 1984) 41, 42. It should be observed that, at one, crucial point, Vermes misrepresents Jeremias's position. He claims that Jeremias regarded ἀββᾶ as "the 'chatter of a small child'" (p. 42), and then adduces examples where

associated with the ideology of the Third Reich.[8] The first contention has already been shown to be false. The second is more difficult to refute, because it relies on the old technique of imputing guilt by association: because Kittel was sympathetic with National Socialism, anti-Semitism is attributed to contributors to the *Wörterbuch*. Vermes is interested in claiming that his own perspective is original, according to which "Abba" was particularly used as an address to God amongst people he calls charismatic Hasids.[9] Two specific figures are in Vermes's mind, Honi, known as the circle-drawer, and Hanina ben Dosa. A story is told according to which a grandson of Honi, named Abba Hilkiah, was approached by children during a drought, saying, "Abba, Abba, give us

---

the term is used among adults. But what Jeremias wrote was (p. 62, and cf. p. 16 n. 9):
One often reads (and I myself believed it at one time) that when Jesus spoke to his heavenly Father he took up the chatter of a small child. To assume this would be a piece of inadmissible naivety.
Jeremias elsewhere (cf. pp. 58–62) gives a much fuller linguistic discussion of the usage among adults than Vermes does, and to see some of the same evidenced marshaled *against* Jeremias by Vermes is what might be called an exercise in creative midrash.

[8]Pp. 64–66. On p. 65, Vermes remarks that scholars of the New Testament treat the *Wörterbuch* "as a gospel truth above all criticism."

[9]Cf. *Jesus the Jew. A historian's reading of the Gospels* (London: Collins, 1973) 69–82.

rain!" He then prayed to the "Lord of the universe," to help those who did not know the difference between the Abba who gives rain and the Abba who does not.[10]

Vermes' solution is troubled by many of the same problems that afflict Jeremias's. The focus, first of all, is too narrowly restricted to Rabbinica, and even then, the instances within Rabbinica are misconstrued. The examples of Honi and Hanina do not, as Vermes maintains, establish a type of charismatic Hasid. The fact is that both of them are referred to within Rabbinica as among rabbis, and, as George Foot Moore pointed out, Aqiba also (and effectively) prayed for rain, so that the ability is scarcely a unique charism.[11] That Aqiba was associated with powers to pray for divine aid in the course of nature did not in any way reduce his status as a teacher,

---

[10] *Jesus the Jew*, p. 211; *Jesus and the World*, p. 42, on both occasions citing Ta'anith 23b. In neither book does Vermes mention that Jeremias cites the passage in full and discusses it (pp. 61, 62), and also gives credit for the reference to J. Leipoldt in *Jesu Verhältniss zu Juden und Griechen* (Leipzig: 1941) 136f.

[11] *Judaism in the First Centuries of the Christian Era* 2 (Cambridge: Harvard University Press, 1927) 235. Moore's presentation of stories about Honi and Hanina (pp. 222, 235f.) -- which Vermes does not cite -- makes it plain that efficacious prayer did not constitute the line of demarcation of a special group among or apart from the rabbis, although it did mark out certain teachers as especially favored.

or demand another category for him. Even if the existence
of such a category be granted, for the sake of argument,
Hilkiah's paternity would by no means demonstrate he
belongs within it. Further, as we will shortly see, God
could be appealed to as "father" by those outside the
circle of rabbinic teachers. In any case, Jeremias
observed that Abba Hilkiah does not address God as
"father", even though he knows he is as a father. He
calls him "Lord,"[12] a change from "father" which is also
made in Targum Jeremiah.[13] Although Vermes's purpose is
comprehensively to refute Jeremias's position, he in fact
only aggravates the methodological weaknesses of the
latter's approach, by limiting his survey of the evidence
of Judaism to late Rabbinic sources, and by attempting to
justify a christological reading of Jesus. Vermes's
charismatic Hasid is certainly less orthodox than
Jeremias's unique Jesus, peculiarly conscious of a filial
relationship with God, but both represent the sort of
effort at christology which is appropriate only after
evidence has been adduced, not at the foundational stage
of inquiry.

The Pentateuchal Targumim called Neophyti, the Fragments

---

[12]Jeremias, pp. 61, 62.

[13]Cf. 3:4, 19, cf. 31:9 (with the Masoretic Text, in each
case), and Robert Hayward, *The Targum of Jeremiah*: The
Aramaic Bible 12 (Wilmington: Glazier, 1987).

Targum, and Pseudo-Jonathan, with their expansive, often innovative readings, provide clear evidence of an understanding of God as father within Judaism. For the present purpose, only Pentateuchal Targums may be considered,[14] and Onqelos, the most literal of the Targumim, is excluded from consideration here precisely because, as the most accurate translation of the Hebrew text, it is the least obviously reflective of the Rabbinic ethos. Commonly, and even in recent, critical introductions, the expansive Targumim to the Pentateuch are held to reflect a definite "Palestinian Targum," datable within the first century.[15] The fact of the matter

---

[14]The development of a more circumspect approach to God's fatherhood is evident in the Targumim to Isaiah (63:16; 64:8), Jeremiah (3:4, 19; 31:9), and Malachi (1:6; 2:10). Cf. Chilton, *The Isaiah Targum*: The Aramaic Bible 11 (Wilmington: Glazier, 1987); Hayward, *op. cit.*; Kevin J. Cathcart, Robert P. Gordon, *The Targum of the Minor Prophets*: The Aramaic Bible 14 (Wilmington: Glazier, 1989). In aggregate, what the readings demonstrate is that a more reverential approach to God was probably current, at least linguistically, among the Rabbis as compared to some circles of Judaism during the first century. Both Jeremias and Vermes attempt to employ a nuance of usage in order to posit a categorical distinction of Jesus, when a model involving gradations of usage would be more productive.

[15]Cf. Roger Le Déaut, "The Targumim," *The Cambridge History of Judaism. Volume two. The Hellenistic Age* (Cambridge: Cambridge University Press, 1989) 563-590, cf. p. 578 and p. 581 in particular. Unfortunately, the article as a whole simply fails to take account of recent

is that the freer, more paraphrastic Targumim are called "Palestinian" because they are more expansive than and exegetically distinct from Onqelos, which was accepted in Babylon, and their dialect of Aramaic is different. We may not conclude that they all derive from a common, written source, nor that such a source is to be located in Palestine, much less in the first century. As the texts stand, they reflect the perspectives of later periods: Neophyti derives from the third century, Pseudo-Jonathan from the seventh, and the Fragments Targum from no earlier than the Middle Ages. We will consider the question of their relevance for the study of the New Testament after their vision of the divine fatherhood has been considered.

Neophyti constitutes the most convenient point of departure, because its references (inclusive of the margins) are the most typical. Each reference provides a distinctive point of view. At the close of Genesis 21, it is said in the margin of Neophyti that Abraham, having given hospitality to strangers, and being offered something in return, insisted:

Pray before your father in heaven, from whose hands

---

research, and criticism of the stance Le Déaut has championed for some thirty years.

you have eaten and from whose hands you have drunk.[16] Abraham proceeds in the passage to proselytize the grateful foreigners, teaching them to worship. The recognition of God as father, in the sense of the one who provides sustenance, is therefore taken to be the incipient point of correct faith, and potentially the beginning of a fruitful, prayerful relationship with God.

Quite a different situation is presumed in Exodus 1:19. There, the Egyptian midwives describe to Pharaoh why they fail to kill the male children of Israel at birth. As in the Masoretic Text, the problem is that they actually bring forth before the midwives arrive, but the reason for their vitality is given:

> They pray before their father in heaven, and he answers them and they deliver.[17]

In the present case, the conception of fatherhood is narrower than in Genesis 21:33 of Neophyti, in that the pregnant Israelites pray to *their* father, and he responds to their particular need by giving them the force to bring forth.

---

[16]Cf. Alejandro Díez Macho, *Neophyti 1. Targum Palestinense Ms de la Biblioteca Vaticana. Tomo 1* (Madrid: Consejo Superior de Investigationes Científicas, 1968).

[17]Díez Macho, *op. cit. Tomo 2* (1970).

The particularity with which divine fatherhood might be
depicted is especially plain in Neophyti at Numbers
20:21. Edom refuses Israel the freedom to pass through
its territory, but Israel does not attack:

> they were ordered by their father in heaven not to
> form up against them in the formations of war.[18]

The underlying notion at this point is that some definite
revelation attends Israel's relationship to God as
father. The particularity of that relationship is
emphasized in a clever rendering at Deuteronomy 32:6:

> Is he not your father, who acquired you and who
> created you and perfected you?

It will readily be seen that the Hebrew text of
Deuteronomy already has God as the father who "created
you, made you, and established you." The first verb,
translated "created," is קָנָה, and קָנָא is what appears in
Neophyti. But in Aramaic, the term means "acquire" more
than "create," so that the redundancy of expression in
the Masoretic Text is avoided, and a much more directly
particularistic impression is conveyed.[19]

At Deuternomy 33.24 Neophyti would appear to offer a
conception of that link which is foundational for

Cf. Díez Macho, *op. cit. Tomo 4* (1974).

[19]Cf. the fine note in Bernard Grossfeld, *The Targum
Onqelos to Deuteronomy*: The Aramaic Bible 12 (Wilmington:
Glazier, 1988) 91.

Israel's   existence,   and   which   requires   Asher's
intercession, when it falls into disrepair:

> Blessed above sons. In the tribes he shall interpose
> his   pasture (מרעיה) between his brothers and their
> father who is in   heaven, and his land shall be
> washed by the waters, and he shall bathe his feet in
> oil.

The manuscript of Fragments Targum in the Vatican has
Asher providing pasture to his brothers during sabbatical
years. That   is   probably   the   sense   here,   as   well,[20]
although it is notable that in Midrash Rabbah, Asher is
credited with an ancillary role in the Temple (or in the
camp in the wilderness): he provides light from the oil
of his land (Numbers 2.10), or oil of anointing (Genesis
97), or daughters for anointed priests (Genesis 71.10,
cf. 98.16).[21]

---

[20]Díez Macho, however, renders the passage differently;
cf. *Neophyti 1. Tomo 5* (1978). For the edition of the
Fragments Targum, see n. 23 below.

[21]Cf. Judah J. Slotki, *Numbers: Midrash Rabbah* (London:
Soncino, 1983); H. Freedman, *Genesis: Midrash Rabbah*
(London: Soncino, 1983). A comparison might be made with
the teaching ascribed to Yohanan ben Zakkai, that the
stones of the altar, upon which no iron tool was to be
lifted, establish peace between Israel and "their father
in heaven." By using the argument *kal vahomer*, he reasons
that a person who establishes peace is to be protected.
Cf. Mekhilta Bahodesh 11.80-92 in Jacob Z. Lauterbach,
Mekilta   de-Rabbi   Ishmael (Philadelphia: Jewish
Publication Society of America, 1933).

Neophyti offers, then, a coherent conception of God's fatherhood: it is mediated to the Gentiles, as a fact of creation, by Abraham, but is the central feature of Israel's particular appeal to God, to God's answer to Israel, and in fact to the essential link between Israel and his God. But before we proceed further, it is crucial to recognize, and to appreciate, that the coherence of the Targumim in the matter of God's fatherhood is deceptive. Within Neophyti itself, we have already observed that the reading at Genesis 21:33 appears in a marginal gloss, not within the main text of the ms, and such glosses appear to have been quite consciously added, as alternatives, perhaps when the document was copied during the sixteenth century.[22] Moreover, at Exodus 1:19, "the LORD" replaces "their father" in an interlinear gloss within the ms itself, a location which may suggest greater antiquity as a reading of Neophyti than a marginal gloss. Although it seems best, on the whole, to accept the reading of "father" at Exodus 1:19, and to reject it at Genesis 21:33 (that is, as the text of Neophyti), the crucial point (from the present

---

[22]Cf. Shirley Lund and Julia Foster, *Variant Versions of Targumic Traditions within Codex Neofiti 1*: Society of Biblical Literature Aramaic Studies 2 (Missoula: Scholars Press, 1977). Lund and Foster argue for the affinity between the Fragments Targum and at least one of the versions reflected in the marginalia.

perspective) remains that there is textual instability in the attestation, and that "father" was a designation subject to correction during the course of the transmission of Neophyti.

The likely source of Neophyti's reading at Genesis 21:33 is the Fragments Targum, a collection of variants to Targumic readings which was compiled during the eleventh to the thirteenth centuries.[23] Taking the ms of the Bibliothèque Nationale of Paris (a document of the fifteenth century) as our basis, we find an interpretation cognate with that of the margin of Neophyti, also at Genesis 21:33. The case is similar at Exodus 1:19; Numbers 20:21; Deuteronomy 32:6. In addition, the Fragments Targum includes additional references to God as father, which fill out the usage we have already typified on the basis of Neophyti, without altering its essentials. At Exodus 17:11, it is said that Israel was victorious in battle when Moses prayed with arms outstretched to his father in heaven; presumably, such a positive understanding of God's military support is the background of the usage in Numbers 20:21, where it

---

[23]Cf. Michael L. Klein, *The Fragment-Targums of the Pentateuch According to their Extant Sources*: Analecta Biblica 76 (Biblical Institute Press: Rome, 1980) 25; Moses Ginsburger, *Das Fragmententhargum* (Berlin: Calvary, 1899).

is assumed that God can also give an order not to attack. When, in the Fragments Targum, turning towards the bronze serpent is coordinated with Israel's prayer for healing to God as father (Numbers 21:9) that fills out the sort of usage one can see at Exodus 1:19, both in Neophyti and the Fragments Targum, and the promise of "good reward" (אגר טב) to the righteous at Numbers 23:23 may also be held to be consistent with the usage. But a highly imaginative rendering at Exodus 15:12 pictures the very earth as afraid to receive the Egyptian dead of the Exodus, for fear the acceptance of them would tell against it in the world to come at the judgment by its father in heaven.[24]

The last usage is a vivid reminder that the Fragments Targum may on occasion provide, not just the background of a usage in Neophyti (as, perhaps, at Exodus 17:11), or further examples of the same usage (as at Numbers 21:9; 23:23), but conceptions of a different order altogether, which probably reflect its later date. After all, the Fragments Targum was consciously composed as a collection

---

[24]Cf. also the mss from the Cairo Geniza presented in Michael L. Klein, *Genizah Manuscripts of Palestinian Targum to the Pentateuch* 1 (Cincinatti: Hebrew Union College Press, 1986) 240, 241, 244, 245. Although the substance of the haggadah is given in both fragments, so that its existence c. A. D. 1000 is established, neither refers to God as father.

of variants, by rabbis whose primary language (and whose community's primary language) had ceased -- essentially since the Arabic conquests -- to be Aramaic. It would be odd not to find later (sometimes esoteric) conceptions developed within it. On the other hand, we also may not assume that the Fragments Targum simply inflates prior developments such as are reflected in Neophyti, since the reference of Deuteronomy 33:24 does not appear there, although the haggadah does (in the Vatican ms). In the same connection, it should be pointed out that the Targum called Pseudo-Jonathan, from the seventh century, does not preserve most of the references cited above, although it does present analogous renderings at Exodus 1:19; Deuteronomy 32:6, and an *innovative* usage at Deuteronomy 28:32, 33, where it is a question of praying to God with good works (עובדים טבים) in one's hands for release in judgment.[25] Clearly, as we come to later sources, there is

---

[25] The analogy to the reading at Exodus 15:12 in the Fragments Targum is evident, and further suggests that the forensic reference to God as father is relatively late within the Targumim. For editions of Pseudo-Jonathan, cf. Brian Walton, *Triplex Targum: Biblia Sacra Polyglotta* 4 (Roycroft: London, 1657); Moses Ginsburger, *Pseudo-Jonathan* (Hildeshein: Olms, 1971); David Rieder, *Pseudo-Jonathan* (Jerusalem: Salmon, 1974); Ernest G. Clarke, *Targum Pseudo-Jonathan of the Pentateuch* (Hoboken: Ktav, 1984). Until the Targum is published in "The Aramaic Bible," we have recourse for a translation only to J. W. Etheridge, *The Targums of Onkelos and Jonathan ben Uzziel on the Pentateuch* (New

a tendency both to embellish and to qualify the notion of
God as father.

Given that the Targumim reflect a rich conceptual
development of God as father, and do so in a way which
makes it impossible immediately to characterize what the
usage of the first century might have been, the
"Pseudepigrapha" -- non-canonical literatures of Judaism
and Christianity -- are potentially of great usefulness.
Although their chronology as a collection is no more
unequivocally pre-Christian than that of the Targumim,
they do hold out the prospect of enabling us to determine
elements of commonality with the Targumim which may be
held to evidence a datable consensus concerning God's
fatherhood within Judaism and Christianity. Any analysis
is, however, complicated further by the fact that
geographically and theologically, the provenience of the
"Pseudepigrapha" is almost always quite other than that
of Rabbinic literature. For that reason, even documents
of approximately the same period may reflect quite a
different concept of the divine fatherhood. Indeed, it
must be stated at the outset that the "Pseudepigrapha"
generally -- especially the non-canonical documents of
Judaism -- are far more parsimonious in their usage of
the *theologoumenon* than either the New Testament or the

York: Ktav, 1968), reprinted from the last century.

Targumim.

The Testament of Job nonetheless stands out as an instance of a document of early Judaism in which the designation of God as father occupies an importance place. In his fine introduction to the translation of the document, R. P. Spittler places the *Testament* within the first century B. C. or A. D., and ascribes it to the Therapeutae, the Egyptian wing of the Essenes.[26] But the evocative date of the *Testament* is only part of its appeal from the present point of view: it also presents an unusually high number of references to God as father among the non-canonical documents of Judaism.

The references in question, however, are quite different, at first acquaintance, from what the Pentateuchal Targumim have accustomed us to. At 33:3, Job says in response to the lament of Eliphas:

> My throne is in the upper world (ὑπερκοσμίῳ), and its glory and dignity come from the right hand of the father.[27]

"Father" is the reading only in the ms of the

---

[26] Cf. R. P. Spittler, "Testament of Job," *The Old Testament Pseudepigrapha* 1 (ed. J. H. Charlesworth; Garden City: Doubleday, 1983) 829–838.

[27] Cf. S. P. Brock, *Testamentum Iobi*: Pseudepigrapha Veteris Testamenti Graece (Leiden: Brill, 1967).

Bibliothèque Nationale,[28] which suggests that a similar tentativeness accompanied the designation among the scribes of Hellenistic Judaism as is evidenced among the meturgemanin and scribes of the Targumim. But the most striking feature of the reference is its originality, as compared to the usage of the Targumim. In the *Testament*, the initial usage describes the provenience of the glory and dignity which attend Job's heavenly throne. Similarly, Job claims in 33:9 that his kingdom is possessed of a glory and dignity installed in "the chariots of the father" (ἐν τοῖς ἅρμασιν τοῦ πατρὸς), phrase obviously inspired from Ezekiel 1, and an early example of speculation concerning the divine chariot as the cosmological locus of God. In 40:2, the usage and its cosmological, or visionary, meaning, achieves a climax, when Job replies to his wife's disconsolation for her dead children by acknowledging God as father (καὶ τότε σταθεὶς ἐξωμολογησάμην πρὸς τὸν πατέρα), and then conveying a vision of his children crowned with divine splendor (40:3).

Just here, however, when the usage might seem to be quite distant from that of the Targumim, it becomes unmistakably plain that the cosmological and visionary reference of the divine fatherhood is rooted in the

---

[28]Cf. Spittler, p. 855 n. "g."

understanding that God as father is first and foremost the object of prayer. Job first acknowledges God as father, and then conveys his vision; moreover, he is said to speak of his vision (40:3) *after* he has acknowledged God as father (40:2), *and his acknowledgement is called a prayer* (καὶ μετὰ τὴν εὐχήν, 40:3). Quite evidently, although *the Testament of Job* does not directly refer to God's fatherhood as a locution of prayer, as in the Targumim, it does presuppose that such a reference is conventional. The particular references of the Targumim which refer to God as "father" in the context of prayer are, of course, not shown to be pre-Christian for that reason, but the usage in itself is presupposed by the reading of *the Testament of Job*.

The two further instances in the *Testament of Job* represent further developments, quite unlike what we read in the Targumim, of the association of divine fatherhood and efficacious prayer. In 47:11, Job provides his daughters with what he calls a "phylactery of the father" (φυλακτήριόν ἐστιν τοῦ πατρός), in order that they might see the heavenly beings who come to take Job's soul.[29] The

---

[29]My interpretation here differs from Spittler's, who takes the "father" to be Job himself (although he capitalizes the initial letter in his translation). As he himself observes, however (865, n. j), the mss at Messina and Rome read "the Lord," much as they do at 40:2, so that his exegesis would appear unnatural.

association of phylacteries with prayer is normative within the period, and the usage of "father" is entirely natural within the context of the *Testament*. Nonetheless, the magical effect imputed to the phylactery (which is actually rendered "amulet" by Spittler), is a reminder that prayer is understood within a particular context in the *Testament*. The resulting vision of one of the daughters is referred to as of "the paternal glory" (τῆς πατρικῆς δόξης) in 50:3: clearly, there is a coherent conception with *the Testament of Job*, according to which prayer to God as father -- sometimes assisted with mediatory objects -- leads to a vision of his throne and what is associated with it. A later, one might say vulgarized, development of that conception is represented by "The Prayer of Jacob," from Egypt in the fourth century, in which God is actually invoked as the cosmological father, with the aim that the petitioner might become angelic in his wisdom (18, 19).[30]

---

[30]Cf. Karl Preisendanz, *Papyri Graecae Magicae* II: Sammlung Wissenschaftliche Commentare (Stuttgart: Teubner, 1974) 148, 149 and James H. Charlesworth, "Prayer of Jacob," *The Old Testament Pseudepigrapha* 2 (ed. J. H. Charlesworth; Garden City: Doubleday, 1985) 715-723. Charlesworth contention that the prayer is neither "peculiarly gnostic" nor "a charm" (p. 718) is well taken; on the other hand, his attempt to back the dating up to as early as the first century is tendentious. It is partially based on an alleged similarity to the "Prayer of Joseph," which must be earlier than the third century, when it was quoted by

The Testament of Abraham presents but pale reflections of an understanding of God as father. Abraham tells Sarah she is blessed by God, even the father, for her recognition of an angelic visitor (6:6), and the angels are described in 20.12 as bringing Abraham to heaven, for the worship of God, the father (ἐις προσκύνησιν τοῦ θεοῦ καὶ πατρός).[31] In both cases, the divine fatherhood appears to be linked to God's cosmological grandeur. Sanders's opinion, which places *the Testament of Abraham* in Egypt around A. D. 100, would appear to be confirmed by the usage in respect of God as father: it simply picks up, without developing, the thronal imagery of *the Testament of Job*. Indeed, the relationship between the two documents might be taken to support the contention of Matthias Delcor, that *the Testament of Abraham*

Origen, but the range of parallels to the angelology of its few lines certainly do not support Smith's confident ascription of it to the first century (cf. J. Z. Smith, "Prayer of Joseph," *APOT* 2, 699–714). Charlesworth himself acknowledges "parallels" with documents of the second century, and he nowhere addresses the central point of Preisendanz's chronology: in form and function, the "Prayer of Jacob" comports well with other incantations of the fourth century, which also were designed to summon deities.

[31]Cf. Montague Rhodes James, *The Testament of Abraham*: Texts and Studies 11.2 (Cambridge: Cambridge University Press, 1892); E. P. Sanders, "Testament of Abraham," *APOT* 1, 871–902.

intentionally transfers to its hero the virtues depicted in *the Testament of Job*, and that therefore a date within the second century is preferable.[32]

The picture which has so far emerged is one in which the Targumim, from a period later than the New Testament, presents a coherent usage of the divine fatherhood, one which is partially confirmed as a Judaic usage of the first century by non-canonical Jewish documents. On the other hand, those documents, while earlier in aggregate, are also to some extent representative of a visionary, sometimes magical, version of Judaism, which is unlike the ethos of the Targumim (and, perhaps, of the New Testament). The question remains whether it is possible to discern a type of usage which may reasonably be held to have been a part of the milieu in which the Gospels emerged.

Around A. D. 100,[33] or somewhat later during the second

---

[32]Cf. Matthias Delcor, *Le Testament d'Abraham*: Studia in Veteris Testamenti Pseudepigrapha (Leiden: Brill, 1973) 49; Chilton, "'Amen': an Approach through Syriac Gospels," *Zeitschrift für die nestestamentliche Wissenschaft* 69 (1978) 203-211 and *Targumic Approaches to the Gospels* (Lanham: University Press of America, 1986) 15-23.

[33]So James H. Charlesworth, "The Odes of Solomon," APOT 2 (Garden City: Doubleday, 1985, 725-771, 727.

century,[34] *the Odes of Solomon* were composed in Edessa[35] (or perhaps Antioch[36]); they utilize the address of God as father more frequently, and with far greater density, than any of the documents adduced above. That feature of the usage of the *Odes* is easily explained on the basis of their Christian provenience, and some of the usages in fact join the evidence which indicates that is their provenience. After the unambiguously Christian statement, "you are saved in him who was saved" (8:21c), the *Odes* go on to speak of being found incorrupt "on account of the name of your father" (לשמה דאבוכון, 8:22).[37] The Christian idiom, "God the father," on the way towards becoming trinitarian, is also evidenced (cf. 9:5; 14:1, cf. v. 8), as when Christ calls God "my father" (cf. 10:4). But that doctrinal development becomes most explicit at 19:1, 2:

A cup of milk was offered to me,

---

[34]Cf. Rendel Harris and Alphonse Mingana, *The Odes and Psalms of Solomon* 2 (Manchester University Press, 1920) 64.

[35]Cf. Harris and Mingana, 64, 36–40, 42–47, 68, 69.

[36]So Charlesworth, 727, although Ignatius' knowledge of *the Odes* can scarcely be used as evidence of their *origin*; it only shows they were widely disseminated. Given the tradition of wisdom at Edessa (evidenced in the Thomaean corpus), and the tradition of hymnody there, above all in the case of Bardaisan, an Edessene origin is more probable.

[37]Cf. the Syriac text in the first volume of Harris and Mingana (1916).

and I drank it in the sweetness of the Lord's
kindness.

The Son is the cup,

the Father is he who was milked;

and the Holy Spirit is she who milked him.[38]

The incipient trinitarianism as well as the vivid imagery
of the passage, which goes on to speak of the virginal
conception of Jesus (vv. 6f.), marks it out as
characteristic of the devotional purpose of the *Odes*.

From the point of view of the sources discussed earlier,
the *Odes* are distinct in provenience, geographically, to
some extent chronologically, and above all theologically.
Their correspondence with types of usage current within
early Judaism is therefore all the more striking. In
7:11, God is described as "the perfection of the worlds
(שולמנא דעלמא) and their father," because he provides for
the benefits of sacrifice (cf. 7:10). The link by means
of the term "father" between the notions of God's
cosmological power and of the acceptable worship of God
is reminiscent of *the Testament of Job*. Of course, the
reminiscence we can observe is a matter of a pattern of
usage, not dependence (literary or otherwise), but it
does tend to confirm that God's fatherhood was connected
with his cosmological grandeur and his availability

---

[38]The translation and the capitalizations are Charlesworth's.

through worship within the first century. The same chapter of the *Odes* also presents an innovative usage, in comparison to what we have seen so far, in which God's fatherhood is related specifically to his wisdom (7:7):

The father of knowledge is the word of knowledge.

By itself, that aphorism need not refer to God. In isolation, it could mean, "The principle of knowledge is the expression of knowledge." But in fact, the passage goes on to speak of the creation of the speaker by God (7:9), so that the reference to the divine fatherhood in context is unmistakable. It would appear that, just as in Egypt the cosmological usage was developed in the idiom of vision, above all in *the Testament of Abraham*, in Syria the key was that of wisdom.

The last usages in the *Odes* refer to the father's vindication of Christ.[39] Christ is in view (cf. v. 1) when it is said that his face was justified by the father (31:5); that justification corresponds to power over darkness and error (vv. 1, 2); as well as to graceful speech (v. 3) and the offering back to God of "those who had become sons through him" (v. 4). The identity of the speaker as Christ is even more obvious at 41:9, where he says:

---

[39]The identity of the speaker with Christ in each of the examples to be cited is also asserted by Charlesworth.

The father of truth remembered me, he who acquired
me from the beginning.

Given the Christian stance of the *Odes*, that statement is
not surprising in the mouth of one who says that God
begat him with his riches and his thought (v. 10). But it
is startling that Christ says that God "acquired me from
the beginning" (הו דקנני מן ברישיה), when that is what
Neophyti says emphatically of Israel in its clever
rendering of Deuteronomy 32:6. It is apparent that the
tradition that the father would answer the prayers of the
people he acquired when they are in distress has been
applied particularly to Christ in the *Odes* in respect of
his cosmic triumph, a triumph whose cosmic aspect also
corresponded to another association in the designation of
God as father within the first century.

The usages of the Pseudepigrapha and the Targumim in
aggregate suggest that, within early Judaism, God was
known as father especially (1) for the purposes of
prayer, particularly prayer in straits, (2) in reference
to the vision or revelation which such a prayer might
involve, (3) because he responds to prayer, (4) in view
of his power over the entire creation, and (5) in respect
of the peculiar relationship between God and his people.
For the most part, it will be readily seen that the usage

of Jesus, as attributed to him in the Synoptic Gospels,[40] is quite conventional. Matthew is the best text to illustrate the usage, since Matthew attributes it more to Jesus than any other Synoptic Gospel, and the most crucial usages in Matthew are paralleled in other Gospels.

The prayer attributed to Jesus addresses God in the usual way, although the direct connection with the kingdom is innovative (Matthew 6:9, 10),[41] and many Matthean passages which refer to God as father in the context of prayer belong to the first category identified above. Several of them refer explicitly to the manner in which prayer as instructed by Jesus should be offered (6:6,[42] 8), but there is also an insistence upon the place of forgiving others within prayer (6:14, 15; 18:35). The latter aspect

---

[40]Considerations of space preclude a consideration of John here.

[40.]The qualification must be registered, however, that the address of God as "our father, our king" became conventional in Rabbinic prayer (cf. Jeremias, pp. 24-26). Moreover, in Tobit 13:1, praise is directed to God and his kingdom, and he is called "father" in v. 4.

[42]The present usage also refers to the reward of prayer, and might therefore be included in the third category. For the purpose of the present investigation, only the most obvious category for each usage will be observed, in order to avoid inflating the apparent number of instances.

is without question unusual, but the point at issue is by
no means the address of God as father, but the nature of
prayer as taught by Jesus. Towards the close of the
Gospel, Jesus is portrayed as addressing God fervently
and intimately in his time of greatest need (26:39, 42,
53), as we should expect on the basis of early Judaic
usage.

Similarly, Jesus' statements of the father's revelation
in Matthew are consistent with the second category of
usages we have considered, and it is notable that in
11:25-27, a pivotal passage within the development of
christology, Jesus "acknowledges" (ἐξομολοῦμαι) the
father's grandeur, just the verb used in the Testament of
Job 40:2 (see also Tobit 13:3). Peter is also said to
benefit from God's revelation (16:17) and "little ones"
are said to have "angels" which see the father (18:10),
in a manner also somewhat reminiscent of the angelology
of the Testament. The father is held to retain certain,
specific knowledge (20:23; 24:36), but the surprise is
more the nature of the knowledge than the designation
"father," much as is the case (mutatis mutandis) within
the first category.

The idea of God's response to prayer (category 3)
is consistent with the focus upon reward in Matthew (6:1,
4, 18), but there is also a more direct appeal to the

imagery of fatherhood in order to express God's merciful response in prayer (7:11). Much more startlingly, Matthew's Jesus claims that God will respond, as father, whenever two petitioners agree (18:19), and that promise is made in the context of one of the imperatives for forgiveness (18:18). It seems clear that a distinctive view of prayer is being promulgated by Matthew's Jesus, but most unclear that any unusual idiom of God as father is the precedent. The appeal to the cosmological father is, on the other hand, quite as direct as we find in the Pseudepigrapha (category 4). The images are sometimes striking (6:26; 10:29), but one of the usages under the fourth category can only be described as banal (18:14). The idea of election, as compared to the Gentiles (6:32), is also unexceptional, but the distinction from those who call people "father" is unusual (23:9). There, too, however, as in the cases of forgiveness in prayer and the father's apocalyptic knowledge, category five is not notable for the usage of "father" in respect of God, but for what is said by means of that Judaic idiom.

Many usages within Matthew do not fall into the categories developed above. In the case of the final instance in the Gospel, where the risen Jesus calls for the disciples to baptize all nations in the name of the father, the son, and the holy spirit (28:19), the Christian provenience of the usage is obvious, and

comports well with *the Odes of Solomon*. The odd reference
to "the kingdom of my father" in 26:29 is another such
instance,[43] and the confidence that the father will
provide the disciples with the holy spirit when they are
under duress (Matthew 10:20) might have come directly
from the *Odes*. The passages are a reminder that the whole
of Matthew represents signal developments of Jesus'
message, although the present investigation is not in the
least concerned to disentangle Jesus from Matthew. The
issue is solely Matthew's Jesus, and how his reference to
God as father might be illuminated in the light of the
Targumim and the Pseudepigrapha.

Two sorts of usage within Matthew remain to be discussed,
however. In the first, the "father" features particularly
in the context of the final judgment, a
characteristically Matthean concern. The scene might be
the angelic assize (10:32, 33), the brilliance of
vindication (13:43), the destruction of what is not God's
(15:13), or the coming of the son of man (16:27). In all
such cases, however, it is clear that the issue is more
than God's response, vindication, or cosmological power:
there is a specifically apocalyptic thrust to his
fatherhood. It might be remembered, in this connection,

---

[43]The parallel in Mark 14:25, and the more distant echo in
Luke 22:18, confirm the suspicion.

that the Targum Pseudo-Jonathan, for all that the document itself is late, does present the father under the particular aspect of judgement (Deuteronomy 28:32, 33, cf. also Numbers 23:23 in the Fragments Targum).

Similarly, although the idea of doing good works so that God might be glorified by others (Matthew 5:16) is not a category of usage established above as current within the first century, it is precisely what Abraham did at Beersheba, and Neophyti at Genesis 21:33 associates his proselytism with God's fatherhood. Tobit's prayer at Tobit 13:4, moreover, directs that God, as father, should be exalted among the Gentiles. But Matthew 5:16 is only one of some half dozen usages in Matthew in which the divine fatherhood is held immediately to make ethical demands of disciples, to become truly his sons (5:45, 48), by doing his will (7:21; 12:50; 21:31; 25:34, 41). Although there is no question of a category of such usage having been established within the first century, the fact is that Pseudo-Jonathan at Leviticus 22:28 presents the innovative command:

> My people, children of Israel, since our father is merciful in heaven, so should you be merciful upon earth.[44]

---

[44]Jeremias, p. 19, also discusses the teaching ascribed to Judah in Qiddushin 36a, that "If you behave like children, you are called children; if you do not behave

Given that the bulk of the usages of Matthew's Jesus fall
within the norms of early Judaism, in the light of the
readings of Pseudo-Jonathan and Neophyti, late though
they undoubtedly are, it is historically dubious to use
the distinctiveness of the Matthean usage to argue that
Jesus was "unique," "radical," or in some other way
"transcended" Judaism, and to argue that his talk of God
as father somehow put him in a special category of
Judaism is simply specious.

The present essay, it must be stressed, is by no means a
full account of references to God as father in the
relevant literatures. There are sporadic references in
the Apocrypha, elsewhere in the Pseudepigrapha, and in a
score of Rabbinic documents (particularly within prayers
and parables). Documents have been considered here which
present clear profiles of usage, for the sake of
comparison. That comparison leads to a simple finding:
Matthew's Jesus does not say anything radically new about
God in calling him "father". He simply prays, enjoys or
speaks of the visions and revelations of prayer,
anticipates God's response, praises him as the father of
all and of his own followers particularly. That he also
stresses the judgment of the father and his demand for
ethical conduct is unusual, but hardly unprecedented. The

---

like children, you are not called children."

persistence and character of the usage in Matthew is distinctive, but no mystery; and the usage of Matthew is a suitable starting point for proceeding to discover the usage of Jesus, which may well emerge as distinctive, but hardly as unique or esoteric.

THE SON OF MAN, HUMAN AND HEAVENLY

An Aramaic idiom, "(the) son of (the) man" (a rendering to be explained) has recently received renewed attention, as providing a possible antecedent of the characteristically dominical expression, "the son of the man" (as a slavish translation of ὁ υἱὸς τοῦ ἀνθρώπου would have it). In Aramaic, the phrase essentially means "human being," and the issue which has emerged in the study of the Gospels centers on whether Jesus used the phrase with that broad, non-messianic reference. Amongst recent contributors, Geza Vermes has perhaps been the most conspicuous exponent of the view that the Aramaic idiom is the only key necessary for understanding Jesus' preaching, at least in this regard.[1] His own particular generalization, that the phrase is a circumlocution for "I," has rightly been attacked:[2] the fact is that "(the) son of (the) man" in Aramaic is generic, in the sense

---

[1] Cf. Vermes, *Jesus the Jew. A Historian's Reading of the Gospels* (London: Collins, 1973) 160-191; "'The Son of Man' Debate," *JSNT* 1 (1978) 19-32.

[2] Cf. J. A. Fitzmyer, "Another View of the 'Son of Man' Debate," *Journal for the Study of the New Testament* 4 (1979) 58-68; "The New Testament Title 'Son of Man' Philologically Considered," *A Wandering Aramean. Collected Aramaic Essays*: SBLMS 25 (Chico: Scholars, 1979) 143-160, 153-155.

that, insofar as it is self-referential, the speaker is included in the class (or a class) of human beings, but the class normally refers to mortal humanity (or a group of people), not to one human being alone.[3]

One of the passages   cited by Vermes, from Yerushalmi (Shebi'ith 9:1), should have made the last point entirely plain to him:

כ"ש בן יוחי עביד טמיר במערתא תלת עשר שנין במערת
חרובין דחרומה עד שהעלה גופו חלודה לסיף תלת עשר
שנין אמר לינה נפיק חמי מה קלא עלמא נפיק ויתיב
ליה על פומא דמערתא חמא חד צייד צייד ציפרין פרס
מצודוי שמע ברת קלא אמרה דימוס ואישתיזב ציפור
אמר ציפור מבל עדי שמי לא יבדא כ"ש בר נשא.[4]

---

[3] Cf. J. W. Bowker, "The Son of Man," *Journal of Theological Studies* 28 (1977) 19-48; B. D. Chilton, *The Isaiah Targum. Introduction, Translation, Apparatus, and Notes:* The Aramaic Bible (Wilmington: Glazier, 1987) lvi-lvii. Barnabas Lindars refers to "the idiomatic use of the generic article, in which the speaker refers to a class of persons, with whom he identifies himself" (*Jesus, Son of Man. A fresh examination of the Son of Man sayings in the Gospels in the Light of Recent Research* [Grand Rapids: Eerdmans, 1983] 24). I would prefer to describe the usage as "generic" with or without the article, in order to refer to people globally or to certain people under some set of circumstances. Cf. P. M. Casey, "General, Generic, and Indefinite: the Use of the Term 'Son of Man' in Aramaic Sources and in the Teaching of Jesus," *JSNT* 29 (1987) 21-56.

[4] A useful translation might be:
Rabbi Simeon ben Yoḥai made a hide-out in a cave thirteen

Quite evidently, the syllogism (such as it is) cannot function unless both "bird" and "(the) son of (the) man" are understood as classes of being, not particular entities. The point is that the divine care for animals demonstrates by analogy that human beings are not left hopeless, and Simeon goes on to leave the cave. The genre of being which is described by "(the) son of (the) man" obviously includes Simeon, since otherwise, he could not reach the conclusion, and undertake the action, which he does. But the genre is no mere circumlocution for Simeon, since otherwise the class could not be compared to that of which the bird in the narrative is an instance, not the entire set.[5]

The generic quality of the phrase might be more apparent if, as Aramaic grammar permits, the determined state of "man" were not held to equate to the usage of the definite article in English. As it happens, בר נש ("son of man") and בר נשא ("the son of the man") are closely

---

years, in a cave of carobs and dates, until his flesh came up scabby. At the end of thirteen years, he said, If I do not go forth to see (sic!) what the voice of the world is.... He went forth and sat at the mouth of the cave. He saw one hunter, hunting birds, spreading his net. He heard a bath qol saying, Release, and the bird was saved. He said, A bird apart from heaven will not perish, how much less (the) son of (the) man!

[5] Cf. Casey (1987) 25.

related in usage, and the line of demarcation between them is subject to dialectical variation;[6] there was an increasing tendency for the determined state to be used with an indefinite sense as the language developed. By the time of Jesus, the form was probably בר אנש(א): the prosthetic א is more securely attested than the usage or the precise meaning of the determined state.[7] That is the reason for the parenthetical qualification of "the" in renderings from Aramaic here. Nonetheless, the generic force in the usage to hand is obvious. If God cares for birds, and his care for humans can be inferred therefrom, Simeon has grounds for assurance; if his resolve to leave the cave is based solely on his observation of a single bird's illustration of his own destiny, his thinking is wishful, not positively forceful.

The function of the bath qol is similar to what may be observed in other stories: the heavenly voice requires earthly explication. As in the case of the bath qol in respect of Hillel,[8] where a message concerning his

---

[6]Cf. Casey (1987) 30, 31.

[7] Cf. Fitzmyer, "Another View," 62; "The New Testament Title," 149-151. For a characterization of the debate between Fitzmyer and Vermes, cf. J. R. Donahue, "Recent Studies in the Origin of 'Son of Man' in the Gospels," *CBQ* 48 (1986) 484-498, 486-490.

[8] Cf. Tosefta Sotah 13:3; Yerushalmi Sotah 9:13; Sotah 48b.

fitness to receive the holy spirit is given, a new language is used, but in the case of Simeon the language is Latin, "Release" (*dimissio*), rather than Aramaic.[9] Given the setting of the story, in the hard period subsequent to the revolt of Bar Kokhba, when the Roman Imperium exerted its power definitively over Palestine, the language of the voice is apposite. A version of the story with slightly more by way of setting occurs in Genesis Rabbah 79:6; in that case, Simeon also sees a bird taken when the voice cries "*Spekula*". Even more clearly than in Yerushalmi, the narrative concerns a genre of being, which is comparable to the class of humanity, not to a particular bird, in that Simeon decides that both he *and his son* should leave the cave. Unfortunately, Vermes does not observe this aspect of the story, which is also found (substantively) in Ecclesiastes Rabbah 10:8. All these versions are presented, neatly laid out, in Hugh Odeberg's *The Aramaic*

---

[9]The choice of language is not beside the point. Simeon goes forth to "see" what he calls "the voice of the *world*," and he hears a bath qol ("the daughter of a voice") in *Latin*.

Portions of Bereshit Rabbah,[10] from which Vermes drew his examples.[11]

The fact is also worth mentioning, since it has been consistently overlooked, that Odeberg called attention as well to the value of the story concerning Simeon for understanding the Gospels.[12] Vermes's assertions of originality have been so exaggerated as to suggest that he for the first time identified the various versions of the haggadah, and for the first time related them to the Gospels.[13] Neither suggestion is appropriate. In addition to providing the fullest citation of the versions available (even today), Odeberg makes specific mention of Matthew 10:29, where Jesus insists that the very sparrows which are bought cheaply do not fall to earth apart from the father's will. By analogy, people ought to take comfort (v. 31). Odeberg observed that "apart from your father" in Matthew 10:29 is substantively equivalent to "apart from heaven" in Genesis Rabbah (and, one might add, Yerushalmi and Ecclesiastes Rabbah). His observation may also be applied to "before God" in the Lukan

---

[10] Lunds Universitets Arsskrift 36.3 (Lund: Gleerup, 1939) 92,   154–157.

[11] Vermes (1973) 257 n. 26.

[12] Odeberg (1939) 154.

[13] Cf. Vermes (1978).

equivalent of the saying (12:6, 7). (Luke 12:6 envisions sparrows being "forgotten" [ἐπιλελησμένον], not falling, and they are cheaper than Matthew's birds; otherwise, the agreement with Matthew 10:29 is striking, albeit not verbatim.) It would appear that essentially the same observation of nature is employed by Jesus and Simeon. In the case of Jesus, the observation seems to urge carelessness upon disciples, in view of providence; in the case of Simeon, the lesson derived from the bird is courage in view of providence, and the observation is explicitly directed to Simeon himself (with his son, as relevant), although the very transmission of the haggadah intimates that there is also a wider application.

Odeberg's comparison of the passages may be pressed further; it becomes evident that his laconic citation of a single verse from Matthew is an invitation to see the power of a theologoumenon as it unfolds in texts of differing periods and circumstances. For just as the haggadah of Simeon is directed to the circumstances of persecution, when the Romans prowled for followers of a failed revolt, so the haggadah of Jesus is couched in the form of advice to those who confront the punishing power of civil rulers (who "kill the body, but are not able to kill the soul," Matthew 10:28, cf. Luke 12:4.) Underlying the sayings of Jesus and Simeon, despite their evident independence from a genetic point of view (be it at the level of literary or of oral influence), is a common, metaphorical transposition. The target of the saying (disciples or Simeon) is compared to birds which may perish (by natural causes or hunting), but then the divine care for such humble creatures is used to assure the target. In just this application of assurance, Simeon's saying is aesthetically superior to Jesus', because the image of the bird ensnared is far more evocative (from the established perspectives of both sayings) than that of the bird as fallen or (worse still) forgotten.

A striking feature of a comparison of Jesus' saying and Simeon's (again, passed over in silence by Odeberg -- consciously or not -- in his laconic citation), is that Jesus does *not* here employ the theologoumenon "(the) son of (the) man" in any form. That is, Jesus' saying performs a meaning comparable to Simeon's, by means of the same, essentially generic contrast between birds and those people who are in circumstances of persecution, but it does so without reference to the phrase which concerns Vermes. In itself, the question of the origins of the dominical usage "the son of the man," in all its complexity, cannot be adequately answered here. That is (still) a suitable subject for monographic treatment. But it might be noted immediately how Vermes' omission to cite Odeberg fully has distorted the course of recent

research. Vermes has been able to argue for an analogy
between Jesus' and rabbinic usage which is so perfect as
to approach identity, but only by ignoring evidence of
obvious disanalogy. Everyone who has ever read Odeberg
knows (1) that the usage is well and truly generic (not
circumlocutional, as Vermes would have it) and (2) that
Matthew 10:29-31 (with Luke 12:6, 7) represents a
tendency *not* to employ the usage when essentially the
same meaning as in Simeon's dictum is at issue. But
because Vermes failed adequately to cite Odeberg, in his
pretension to originality, it has required considerable
discussion (and several contributions from J. A.
Fitzmyer) to establish the first point, and scholars
continue to be misled in respect of the second.

In his recent and otherwise excellent study of "the son
of the man" in the Gospels, Barnabas Lindars[14] cites
Vermes' collection of haggadoth concerning Simeon, and he
also accepts the analogy posited by Vermes with Jesus'
usage. Had sound scholarly technique stood behind Vermes'
treatment, Lindars would have been encouraged to include
Odeberg's analysis, in which it becomes evident that "the
son of the man" is not used generically in a saying of
Jesus (namely, Matthew 10:29-31; Luke 12:6, 7), when the
comparison with the haggadah of the cave might lead us to

---

[14] Lindars (1983) 228-231.

expect just that. In the event, Luke 12:8, 9 has Jesus refer to "the son of the man" immediately *after* his remark concerning sparrows (cf. Matthew 10:32, 33);[15] it emphatically refers, not generically, but particularly, to a specific figure in the heavenly court. That fact is explicit within the Gospel. It has been possible to ignore it within the most recent discussion only because Dr Vermes ignored Prof. Odeberg's insight.

As has already been suggested, no solution can yet be offered definitively to the perplexing question of what the dominical phrase, "the son of the man," refers to. Essentially, the question is only obfuscated by the issue of authenticity (as will be discussed below). Clarity is only possible when we impute the spectrum of meanings to the phrase which is appropriate to the sphere of language in which it was spoken on any given occasion by any speaker. The advantage of a comparative analysis is that it helps texts mutually to define their spheres of discourse. Our initial attention must therefore fall on a feature of the comparison of haggadoth concerning Simeon and Jesus, a feature which is a regular phenomenon of textual comparison. In other studies, I have treated

---

[15]The Matthean reference is to *Jesus* in the heavenly court, implicitly as "the son of the man" (with whom he is emphatically identified, cf. 10:23), as analogous to the "men" before whom one has confessed or denied him.

texts in which a single tradition (be it of Yoḥanan and the problem of the Levites in Numbers 3 or of Jesus and the problem of divorce) occasioned construals of that tradition which were mutually explicable; the synoptic relationship among common construals of single traditions is first of all an invitation to observe meanings unfold, not a puzzle to be deciphered.[16] The same opportunity obtains in the case of a haggadah concerning such a teacher: the transfiguration and the story of Hillel and the bath qol were considered from that point of view.[17] But in the latter case, we also encountered alternative developments within traditions which went beyond what we might ordinarily refer to as "construal." Within Yerushalmi, the additional instances of bath qol which are cited tend to shift the emphasis, from the exaltation of Hillel to the phenomenon of bath qol generally. Even more dramatically, the story of Jesus and the bath qol in John 12 is so distinctive a version of the haggadah as to demand the designation of "transformation," rather than "construal." But now, as we compare the haggadoth

---

[16] Cf. Bekharoth 5a; Yerushalmi Sanhedrin 1:4; Numbers Rabbah 4:9; and Matthew 19:3-12; Mark 10:2-12; Luke 16:18. The treatment concerned here (and cf. the following remark) appears in *Profiles of a Rabbi. Synoptic Opportunities in Reading about Jesus*: Brown Judaic Studies 177 (Atlanta: Scholars, 1989).

[17] Cf. the Rabbinic texts cited in n. 8 and Matthew 17:1-13; Mark 9:1-13; Luke 9:28-36.

concerning Jesus and Simeon, it is perfectly plain that we are dealing with neither construals nor transformations of a common tradition, for the simple reason that no common tradition evidently lies behind them.

The force of these observations is to the effect that Odeberg put his finger on an order of relationship between texts which does not demand the supposition of their genetic dependence upon the same tradition. "Simeon" and "Jesus" (or whichever speakers are represented by Yerushalmi, Genesis Rabbah, and Ecclesiastes Rabbah on the one hand, and by Matthew and Luke on the other hand)[18] simply use a similar topos of the comparative value of the human and ornithological in order to provide assurance of divine care in the midst of real or potential persecution. Notably, their similarity in the conveyance of a cognate meaning by comparable means does not extend to the usage of the theologoumenon, "(the) son of (the) man." Simeon and Jesus are comparable -- and better understood in one another's light -- in respect of the meaning performed within haggadah attributed to them: they urge similar things by a single

---

[18] For the present purpose, issues of "authenticity," which are themselves often invoked in an inexact manner, are not of concern: the focus here is upon describing the relationships of texts and their meanings.

topos developed distinctively. But what they perform --
as far as presently can be seen -- are not the traditions
of others (that would be construal or transformation),
but their own insights within the theological language
available to them. In other words, for all that their
sayings are comparable, Simeon and Jesus have no need of
a tertium quid, a yet more ancient dictum, to explicate
for us why they say what they say.[19] They simply speak,
and traditions are created, which are then subject to
haggadic construal and/or transformation. They are
performers, not tradents. For the purposes of creating
these sayings, they required only a language, eyes, ears,
and a mouth; appeal to some prior tradition (in the
absence of evidence to that effect) only distracts us
from our appreciation of the distinctive performances.

---

[19]During a meeting of the Seminar on the Aramaic
Background of the New Testament, within the *Studiorum
Novi Testamenti Societas* (Dublin; 25 July 1989) the
suggestion was made by Prof. Otto Betz that Amos 3:5
constitutes precisely such a tertium quid. There is no
question but that proverbial reasoning from the fate of
birds and other wildlife to the condition of humanity
before God is a feature of the Hebrew Scriptures, and as
such one of the elements of early Judaism. But the
members of the Seminar were not compelled by the
argument of any particular dependence of the dominical
saying upon Amos. From the point of view of the idiom
under discussion, Ecclesiastes 9:12 in any case presents
a closer analogy.

Indeed, it should be emphasized that our distinctions among performances, transformations, and construals are heuristic, in respect of readers' cognition: they appear sensible given the lay of texts at a given moment. A "performance" is not something actually said (or, for that matter, not said) by Simeon or Jesus at some time; it is a distinctive, autonomous conveyance of meaning within the language of early Judaism. A "transformation" is not a tradent's attempt to alter a performance, any more than a "construal" is a deliberate effort at nuance; they are simply the names we might use to describe greater or lesser degrees of congruence in that promulgation of performance which is known as tradition. "Simeon" and "Jesus" are, in the first instance, nothing more than names given to performances, just as "Yerushalmi," "Genesis Rabbah," "Ecclesiastes Rabbah," "Matthew," and "Luke" are, in the first instance, nothing other than names given to transformations and construals by anonymous tradents (orally and/or in writing) of such performances.

The relative absence of Simeon's theologoumenon, "(the) son of (the) man," from Jesus' saying should by itself alert us to the possibility, already mentioned, that the phrase carries a different significance within the sayings attributed to Jesus. Precisely that possibility comes evidently to expression in a saying in which "the son of the man" is employed, again in the material known as "Q" (Matthew 8:19, 20, cf. Luke 9:57, 58):

καὶ προσελθὼν εἷς γραμματεὺς εἶπεν αὐτῷ διδάσκαλε, ἀκολουθήσω σοι ὅπου ἐὰν ἀπέρχῃ. καὶ λέγει αὐτῷ ὁ Ἰησοῦς αἱ ἀλώπεκες φωλεοὺς ἔχουσιν καὶ τὰ πετεινὰ τοῦ οὐρανοῦ κατασκηνώσεις ὁ δὲ υἱὸς τοῦ ἀνθρώπου οὐκ ἔχει ποῦ τὴν κεφαλὴν κλίνῃ.

The saying explicitly addresses the issue of discipleship in both Gospels. The famous dictum, ἄφες τοὺς νεκροὺς θάψαι τοὺς ἑαυτῶν νεκρούς, follows in each case (Matthew 8:21, 22; Luke 9:59, 60). Moreover, the same issue is developed within the construals of each Gospel.

In Matthew, a scribe is the interlocutor, and such figures in the first Gospel might be "trained for the kingdom" (13:52); that is evidently the understanding here, because the next interlocutor is described as "another of his disciples" (8:21). The story of the stilling of the storm follows (vv. 23-27), a paradigmatic instance of discipleship.

The Lukan construal attains a cognate presentation of the saying, by its own means, as can be traced by observing the usage of the verb, "to travel" (πορεύεσθαι), within this complex of material. Jesus is said programmatically to "set his face to travel to

Jerusalem" in 9:51, and he sends messengers before him (v. 52a). They proceed to "travel" (v. 52b), but do not manage to prepare a welcome for him in a village of Samaritans "because his face was traveling to Jerusalem" (v. 53). Jesus rebukes the manifestly odd suggestions that fire be called down from heaven (vv. 54, 55); rather, "they traveled to another village" (v. 56). It is, then, "While they were traveling on the way" that an unnamed interlocutor appears and says what is attributed to a scribe in Matthew (v. 57). But there is an addition to the Lukan complex. Just as Jesus' disciples had suggested they call down fire from heaven, in the manner of Elijah (cf. 2 Kings 1:10, 12), so the Lukan Jesus closes this group of sayings with the observation that no one who exercises domestic responsibility, by putting his hand to the plough in the manner of Elisha (1 Kings 19:20), is worthy of the kingdom (vv. 61, 62). The following material concerns the commissioning of seventy disciples, who promulgate precisely that kingdom (10:1–12, vv. 9, 11).

There is an evident adjustment of meaning involved as the reader moves from the Matthean to the Lukan construal of Jesus' saying in respect of foxes, birds, and "the son of the man." What is in the former case a paradigm of scribal discipleship is in the latter case a paradigm of peripatetic discipleship. Nonetheless, Matthew and Luke share the understanding that "the son of the man" is christologically redolent, and that the issue of the saying is discipleship in respect of precisely that "son of man." Nothing intrinsic to the saying, within the language of early Judaism, requires such a presentation of it. "Son of man" need mean no more than "person," and generally should not be pressed for more meaning without warrant. Within that sense of the phrase, it is hardly natural to understand the saying in reference to discipleship. The exigencies of human life are, perhaps, more plausibly at issue:

Foxes[20] have dens and birds their nests: only man has nowhere to lay his head.[21]

If such a gnomic (if cynical) sense is held to have been the performed meaning of the saying,[22] then what we see in Matthew and Luke are two construals of a single and fundamental transformation of that meaning, into the new keys of christology and discipleship.

---

[20] P. M. Casey, "The Jackals and the Son of Man (Matt. 8.20//Luke 9.58," *JSNT* 23 (1985) 3-22, 8 suggests an alternative reading, but M. H. Smith, "No Place for a Son of Man," *Forum* 4.4 (1988) 83-107, 89 replies that "foxes regularly dwell in burrows, while jackals seek such shelter only to bear young."

[21] Cf. the observation of R. Simeon b. Eleazar in Qiddushim 82b, that he had never seen a fox keeping a shop; discussion in Casey (1985) 9.

[22] Cf. Smith (1988) 98-100.

The question naturally arises, whether the performed meaning posited in the last paragraph should be ascribed to Jesus. At just this point, a note of caution needs to be sounded. "The historical Jesus," who was bequeathed to us by the liberal theology of the last century, was an empirically knowable figure, who transcended the doctrines of Christianity. His epitaph was written by Albert Schweitzer and William Wrede. Schweitzer, for all his evident inadequacies,[23] did demonstrate that whatever Jesus said, thought, and did, was -- historically speaking -- conditioned by doctrinal constraints and religious perspectives no less compelling than those which influence Christians (and other religious people) generally. What has chiefly alienated many readers of Schweitzer is his perfectly sensible observation that the constraints and perspectives in the case of Jesus were not Christian in any definable sense, but Jewish and eschatological. Rather more profoundly, Wrede[24]

---

[23] Cf. Chilton, *The Kingdom of God in the Teaching of Jesus:* Issues in Religion and Theology 5 (Philadelphia: Fortress, 1984) 8, 9; A. Schweitzer (tr. W. Montgomery), *The Quest of the Historical Jesus. A Critical Study of its Progress from Reimarus to Wrede* (London: Black, 1954).

[24] Cf. W. Wrede, *Das Messiasgeheimnis in den Evangelien. Zugleich ein Beitrag zum Verständnis des Markusevangelium* (Göttingen: Vandenhoeck und Ruprecht, 1901), translated under the title *The Messianic Secret* by J. C. G. Greig

demonstrated that to search for data concerning Jesus (as distinct from christological interpretations of him) in the Gospels is as sensible as looking for objectivity in an apologetic discourse. Attempts to revive the sort of historical Jesus liberal theology required, an archaeological datum which might refute modern dogmatism, are fashionable only among those who have remained unmoved by developments during this century. Among Christians, certain conservatively inclined Evangelicals[25] continue to treat the Gospels as if they were concocted as puzzles which contain all the necessary facts of history, provided they are re-arranged cleverly. Among certain Jewish interpreters of Jesus, an equally astonishing naïveté is apparent. Harvey Falk[26] has recently represented the attitude that the Gospels are to be taken as relaying Jesus' ipsissima verba, and Vermes apparently believes such data can be gleaned, provided the texts are shorn of their hellenistic accretions.[27]

(Greenwood: Attic, 1971).

[25]Cf. J. W. Wenham, *Do the Resurrection stories contradict one another?* (Exeter: Paternoster, 1984); Michael Green, *The Empty Cross of Jesus:* The Jesus Library (London: Hodder and Stoughton, 1984).

[26] Cf. *Jesus the Pharisee. A New Look at the Jewishness of Jesus* (New York: Paulist, 1985).

[27]Cf. *Jesus and the World of Judaism* (London: SCM, 1983) 85.

Aside from "the historical Jesus" of liberal Protestantism (and his ghost among badly informed contributors), no other contenders have clearly emerged as viable. "The new quest of the historical Jesus" has been hailed from time to time in the period since the war, but its claims have never been realized. It was an attempt to discover the dialectic between Bultmann's "eternal Logos, the Word,"[28] who required a decision for or against himself in the texts as they stand, and Bultmann's messianic prophet, the Judaic teacher who could be investigated by historical means.[29] In order to be successful, "the new quest" required grounding in the sources of Judaism, but its practitioners were even less skilled in that regard than Bultmann himself was. Instead, "new questers" of the 'fifties and 'sixties have turned to "the new hermeneutic" (cf. Fuchs),[30] Gnosticism (cf. Robinson),[31] doctrinal interests (cf. Keck),[32] or some

---

[28] *Jesus Christ and Mythology* (New York: Scribner, 1958) 80.

[29] Cf. (tr. L. P. Smith and E. Huntress), *Jesus and the Word* (New York: Scribner, 1934).

[30] Cf. E. Fuchs (tr. A. Scobie), *Studies of the Historical Jesus: Studies in Biblical Theology* 42 (Naperville: Allenson, 1964).

[31] Cf. *A New Quest for the Historical Jesus and Other Essays* (Philadelphia: Fortress, 1982).

[32] Cf. *A Future for the Historical Jesus. The Place of Jesus in Preaching and Theology* (Nashville: Abingdon,

other arena in which Jesus as an object of faith, in consequence of the Gospels, rather than Jesus as the subject of faith, informing the Gospels, is the principal concern. In other words, "the new quest" became -- and remains -- so utterly bound up with ideological programs, that it would be truer to say that it has never really been tried, than to say it has failed. Be that as it may, the period since the war has arguably brought no significant advance in the study of Jesus.

The suggested itinerary of "the new quest" may someday be revived; whether or not it is, something needs to be done about the question of Jesus. For our present purpose, however, that question is not to be investigated in its properly historical or theological dimensions, since the essentially literary issue of how the Gospels unfolded, and how the meaning of a particular phrase evolved, is our purview. It is no doubt the case that one's address of the literary issue will influence one's historical and/or theological judgment, and vice versa, but such influence is not our interest here; certainly, such questions can only be confused by muddling them, as they tend to be in "the new quest." Our concern is simply: what do we need to posit, as performed meaning within early Judaism, in order to explain how the Gospels

---

1971).

came to say what they do? The answer to that question is
the literary figure called Jesus, insofar as that figure
can be known. (Once that figure is collated with
historical evidence and reason, it may itself be claimed
to be historical. But any such claim is not part of our
present inquiry.) To a significant extent, that figure is
a cipher, an inference from texts. And yet the inference
is not idle, since without that figure, the texts have no
center, and cease to mean anything: they point to Jesus,
not only denotatively, as their necessary precedent, but
implicitly, as the informing source of what they mean. To
this extent, it is sensible to speak of Jesus as a figure
of literary history, whatever one might think of "the
historical Jesus."

If Jesus' performance of the saying concerning foxes,
birds, and "the son of the man" itself focused on the
twin issues of christology and discipleship, that would
certainly seem to explain the presentations of Matthew
and Luke. But two considerations make that apparently
straightforward explanation appear improbable. First,
although there is a consensus between Matthew and Luke
that the saying issues a call to discipleship grounded in
christology, their respective understandings of both
discipleship and christology are -- as we have seen --
distinctive. Another, less probative, consideration
within the same vein is that the context of *logion* 86 in

the *Gospel according to Thomas* is somewhat different.[33]
Were Jesus' performance explicitly geared to specific
views of such central matters, greater fidelity to his
perspective might be expected. Second, the reference to
"the son of the man," cognate with that of Simeon ben
Yoḥai, contrasts the genre of humanity with animate
creation; such a usage is scarcely a straightforward
vehicle of christology (or of messianic claims). The
point of the imagerial contrast pivots around the axis
which separates people from animals, not disciples from
rabble.

The performance of Jesus seems rather to have focused on
how people are more rootless than animals. It inverts the
logic of Simeon, his near contemporary. Where Simeon
invoked the contrast between people and birds to show how
much more God would care for humanity, and therefore
Simeon himself, Jesus used the same contrast to show how

---

[33] Smith (1988) 84-86. Smith (p. 85) sees the Thomaean
context purely in terms of human mortality. I have argued
elsewhere, however, that *Thomas* is framed by means of an
interlocutory structure (cf. "The Gospel according to
Thomas as a Source of Jesus' Teaching," *Gospel
Perspectives* 5 [ed. D. Wenham; Sheffield: JSOT, 1985]
155-175, 161). That structure makes discipleship the
leading theme since *l.* 61b, so that I would not agree
with Smith's description of "Thomas' haphazard logic,"
nor would I characterize the Thomaean context as
radically different from the Synoptic context.

much more difficult life was for people, and therefore
for Jesus himself, than it was for animals. The point and
purpose of the saying, of course, is found among those
who commit themselves to the rootlessness of Jesus,[34] and
to that extent the transition to the issue of authority
and discipleship in the Synoptics is predictable. But the
transformation of that performance in Matthew and Luke
only makes sense if (a) "the son of the man" is taken
christologically, and (b) rootlessness is related to
discipleship in particular. In other words, their
transformation of Jesus' aphorism, a generalizing -- if
somewhat cynical -- epigram, is only tenable within the
confessional and sociological environment of early
Christianity.

The recovery of Jesus' performance, as an inference from
and within the Gospels, is perfectly practicable,
provided certain criteria are observed. To justify a
characterization as "performance," a saying must proceed
from an initiating figure of literary history, such as
Simeon or Jesus, and that speaker must use the language
of his milieu distinctively. In the present instance,
their statements about "(the) son of (the) man" must be
mutually intelligible, as they indeed are, but not merely
repetitious. A remarkably obtuse school of criticism,

---

[34] Cf. Casey (1985) 10-13, 15.

represented recently by P. S. Alexander, complains that *any* attempt to describe Jesus' creativity is a veiled conspiracy to abstract him from Judaism.[35] Alexander would apparently revert to the school of pseudo-history, whose mantra is that there is nothing new under the sun: all is a matter of permutations and combinations within some classic core of meanings. Yet the very existence of texts attests that significantly literary figures are held by the literature which refers to them to say and do things which are understood to be notable. They say and do surprising things, which influence the perceived course of events and traditions, and neither the performers nor what they performed would be recalled otherwise. Of course Jesus performed within early Judaism, as did Simeon; but neither can be reduced to a repetition of the other. And the irony is, that neither performance is accessible directly from a source of early Judaism, although both are located in tributaries thereof: Jesus' saying is conveyed in Gospels, Simeon's in Talmud and Midrash. There is much that is new under the sun.

The particular innovation which lies to hand concerns "(the) son of (the) man," and the appearance that Jesus' usage is to be distinguished from that of Simeon. That

---

[35] Cf. his review of *A Galilean Rabbi and His Bible*, *Journal of Jewish Studies* 36 (1985) 238-242.

impression is strengthened when one takes into consideration Luke 12:8, 9. It has already been observed that 12:6, 7 are striking in their non-use of the idiom, at least when the story of Simeon is read comparatively. In vv. 8, 9, however, that non-use becomes not only striking, but also seems to be part of a conscious understanding of the meaning of the phrase.[36] In the latter two verses, "the son of the man" is manifestly not a generic person, but an angelic figure, who is in a position to muster the angels of the heavenly court.[37] Such a figure, of course, is reminscent of the one like a son of man in Daniel 7:13; 10:16, 18 and Enoch 46:2, 3, 4; 48:2; 60:10; 62:5, 7, 9, 14; 69:27, 29; 71:17.[38] The

---

[36] Again, it is probably necessary to stress that, in referring to a conscious meaning, confusion with Jesus' meaning is best avoided.

[37] Cf. D. R. Catchpole, "The Angelic Son of Man in Luke 12:8," *NvT* 24 (1982) 255-265, 260. Catchpole himself argues against a legal construction (pp. 256-250), but his remarks are too limited to philological concerns (in respect of ὁμολογέω, ἀρνέομαι, and ἔμπροσθεν) to be fully convincing. It is the son of man's *confession or denial before the angels of God* which invokes the imagery of the divine court, not the usage of any particular words. See also F. H. Borsch, *The Christian and Gnostic Son of Man*: Studies in Biblical Theology 14 (Naperville: Allenson, 1970) 16-18, and his exegetical and conceptual comments in *The Son of Man in Myth and History* (Philadelphia: Westminster, 1967) 353-364.

[38] Cf. E. D. Burton, *A Source Book for the Study of the Teaching of Jesus* (Chicago: University of Chicago Press,

Danielic imagery is taken up within the New Testament, in order to refer to Jesus' future coming in an anticipated apocalypse, but within Daniel itself, the figure is essentially an agent of redemption and disclosure within the heavenly court.

Since the contribution of Rudolf Bultmann, the tendency has been to take Luke 12:8, 9 as referring to an apocalyptic figure, expressed in language redolent of Daniel 7.[39] The transition Bultmann postulated was from Jesus' expectation of a distinct "messiah" to the belief of the early Church that Jesus spoke of his *own* παρουσία.[40] In his recent study of the influence of Daniel 7 upon the New Testament,[41] Maurice Casey concludes that Jesus' use of "(the) son of (the) man," generically understood,[42] prompted the use of Daniel 7 as a reference

---

1924) 222, 223.

[39] Cf. M. Black, "Jesus and the Son of Man," *JSNT* 1 (1978) 4-18, 7.

[40] Bultmann (tr. K. Grobel), *The Theology of the New Testament* (New York: Scribner, 1951) 26-32.

[41] Cf. *Son of Man: The Interpretation and Influence of Daniel 7* (London: SPCK, 1979).

[42] Cf. Mark 2:10, 28; Matthew 8:20/Luke 9:58; Matthew 11:19/Luke 7:34; Matthew 12:32/Luke 12:10; Luke 22:48; Mark 10:45; 14:21a, b, and (to a less straightforward extent) Luke 12:8b; Mark 8:38; Mark 8:31/9:31/10:33-4.

to his parousia.[43] It may be accepted that Casey's redefinition of the Bultmannian consensus, chiefly in order to better account for the Aramaic evidence, is a satisfactory explanation of most types of idiom within the New Testament. The Jesus of literary history, as here characterized, would therefore speak generically, while his followers -- after his resurrection -- would construe his speech in reference to his present authority and/or his future coming.[44] Such a solution, although commendably neat, fails to account for two sorts of evidence.

The first sort of evidence has already been indicated: the simple fact of the matter is that Jesus' use of "(the) son of (the) man," even when it is generic, is not to be understood, without qualification, as identical with that of Simeon ben Yoḥai. The dominical usage is both applied and not applied distinctively, in a manner which tends to emphasize the negative predicament of ordinary humanity, and of Jesus as one of its number.

The second sort of evidence, which casts doubt upon the consensus in its neatest form, is of quite a different nature. As the saying in Luke 12:8, 9 stands, Jesus is

---

[43] Pp. 234-5; cf. Mark 13:26; 14:62 and Mark 8:38; Matthew 10:23; 16:26; 24:44/Luke 12:40; Matthew 25:31; Luke 18:8, and the review of W. O. Walker in *JBL* 100 (1981) 643-5.

[44] As in the Matthean parallel (Matthew 10:32) to Luke 12:8.

presented as invoking "the son of the man" in the context
of angelic advocacy. It fits neatly neither with those
sayings which refer to Daniel 7 in a parousial construal,
nor with those which are generic. Of course, it might be
taken as simply invoking *Jesus'* authority as "the son of
the man," and therefore classed as secondary; it is
possible to avoid the manifest sense of the passage by
collapsing the meaning of "the son of the man" into a
merely Lukan designation of Jesus.[45] But if the community
responsible for the formation sanguinely conceived of
Jesus' authority as invoked by the use of the phrase, why
should there be the added paraphernalia of the heavenly
court? No matter whether Luke 12:8, 9 be seen as
dominical or ecclesial; the odd phenomenon, so far
unaccounted for, is the emphatically angelic aspect of
the usage.

The reader of Daniel 7:13 is scarcely perplexed by the
association of angelic imagery with בר אנש(א).[46] One who
is described as כבר אנש is presented (by angels,
presumably) to the ancient of days within the heavenly
court. The natural understanding of Daniel 10:16, 18
(כדמות בני אדם and במראה אדם) would link that figure with

---

[45]Cf. D. R. A. Hare, *The Son of Man Tradition*
(Minneapolis: Fortress, 1990) 62.

[46]Cf. Catchpole (1982) 262–265.

the angelic interpreter of chapter 10, who struggles with the angel Michael on behalf of Daniel's people (vv. 20, 21, cf. vv. 12–14). Some modern critics have tended to read Daniel, and therefore those of Jesus' sayings which refer to Daniel, as referring symbolically to a pattern of humiliation and exaltation *on the part of God's people.*[47] That overtly literary apprehension does no justice to the obviously angelic construal of the language in 1 Enoch, 4 Ezra 13, and the Revelation 1:13; 14:14. Side by side with the generic usage, an angelic reference is also possible.

---

[47] Cf. C. F. D. Moule, *The Birth of the New Testament* (New York: Harper and Row, 1962) 63. Moule elsewhere refers to such analysis as a "British school of thought," "Neglected features in the problem of the Son of Man," *Essays in New Testament Interpretation* (Cambridge: Cambridge University Press, 1982) 75–90, 76–77, 79, 89. On pp. 80–81, Moule attempts to refute the angelic reading here defended; he can only do so by taking chapter seven in isolation from chapter 10. As a matter of fact, Moule appears *not* to exclude an angelic reading later in his article, when he states, "then it is also conceivable that he (sc. Jesus) applied it (sc. the phrase) not only to some transcendental figure, but to his authority wherever it was exercised in his capacity as the focus of God's dedicated people" (p. 84). He explicitly proceeds to affirm that "on occasion, he used it, as *though* of someone other than himself, when he wished to stress the ultimate, eschatological character of the final vindication" (p. 84). A more adequate understanding of Daniel seven in its literary and historical context would remove the italicized qualification.

Indeed, the generic usage and the angelic usage are complementary. כבר אנש in Daniel is no technical reference, or title, but a descriptive designation of an unusual, human angel. The generic usage is the best background to presuppose in that development. Moreover, it would greatly ease our appreciation of the arthrous phrase, ὁ υἱὸς τοῦ ἀνθρώπου, in the Gospels, to see in the definite article prior to υἱός (after which the second articular usage follows naturally) that a reminiscence of a specific figure (not a title) was in mind. To see the redundantly arthrous usage merely as an echo of the determined state in Aramaic is problematic: why should the article appear *consistently*, if an occasional mistranslation is at issue?[48] Moule has suggested that the arthrous usage is a deliberate reminiscence of the Danielic figure: although his corporate (rather than angelic) reading of that figure has been questioned here, that Daniel's image is evoked may be confirmed.[49] In other words, the arthrous usage,

---

[48] Cf. Casey (1987) 31-34. He argues that some of the usages are the result of literal rendering, and others introduce articles "to make clear that a particular person was referred to" (p. 32). The absence of an exception, however, may be said to vitiate such inherently probabilistic arguments.

[49] Cf. Moule (1982) 77, 82-85, 89; cf. *The Origin of Christology* (Cambridge: Cambridge University Press, 1977)

which has long been seen as at the center of the dilemma, may be taken to support the argument that בר אנש(א) in Jesus' teaching is ordinarily generic, but sometimes angelic in application (as the specific link with Daniel would suggest). The angelic reference was formalized by the usage of the article in Greek during the course of transmission.

Generally speaking, scholarly discussion has tended to distinguish three categories of the usage, "the son of the man," within the Gospels. Sayings of Jesus are viewed as referring to his present authority (as a special envoy

---

14. To an extremely limited extent, an analogy may be posited between a reference to Daniel 7 in "the son of man" and the reference to Ezekiel 1 in "the chariot" (מרכבהא) and the reference to Exodus 3 in "the bush" (הסנה). What limits such an analogy is that the rabbinic phrases are generally used to refer to the *passages*, not figures in the passages. Cf. M. Jastrow, *A Dictionary of the Targumim...* (Brooklyn: Shalom, 1967).
Another usage constitutes a closer analogy, in terms of both substance and chronology, when the figures of a man in 4 Ezra 13 harkens back to Daniel 7, without special qualification. The anarthrous usage (in the predicative position) in John 5:27 may permit us to see that the phrase בר אנש(א) alone, without specifically Danielic associations, might have referred to an agent of angelic judgment under some circumstances. But the more common, arthrous usage is more plausibly taken as a conscious, titular reference to Daniel 7:13 (which -- in itself -- is not titular; cf. Fitzmyer [1979] 154, 155).

or as a human being),[50] to his suffering,[51] and/or to his advent as an eschatological judge.[52] Reliance upon an Aramaic approach to the phrase has helped us to see that there is a sense in which the phrase might be used generically, and that has enriched our understanding of Jesus (as presented within the Gospels).

A more comprehensively Aramaic approach would help us to see that Jesus is also distinctive in his non-use of the phrase, a non-use which reinforces the innovation of placing, side by side with the generic meaning, reference to "(the) son of (the) man" as an angel of advocacy in

---

[50] A list might include Matthew 8:20/Luke 9:58; Matthew 9:6/Mark 2:10/Luke 5:24; Luke 6:22; Matthew 11:19/Luke 7:34; Matthew 12:8/Mark 2:28/Luke 6:5; Luke 9:56; Matthew 12:32/Luke 12:10; Matthew 12:40/Luke 11:30; Matthew 13:37; Matthew 16:13; Matthew 17:9/Mark 9:9; Matthew 18:11/Luke 19:10; Matthew 20:28/Mark 10:45. For an argument for a wider understanding of the category, somewhat as is also reflected here, cf. C. M. Tuckett, "ThePresent Son of Man," *JSNT* 14 (1982) 58-81.

[51] A list might include Mark 8:31/Luke 9:22; Matthew 17:12/Mark 9:12; Matthew 17:22, 23/Mark 9:31/Luke 9:44; Matthew 20:18, 19/Mark 10:33, 34/Luke 18:31-33; Matthew 26:2; Matthew 26:24/Mark 14:21/Luke 22:22; Luke 22:48; Matthew 26:45/Mark 14:41; Luke 24:7.

[52] A list might include Matthew 10:23; 13:41; 16:27, 28; Mark 8:38/Luke 9:26; Luke 12:8; 17:22; Matthew 24:27/Luke 17:24; Luke 18:8; Matthew 24:30, 31/Mark 13:26, 27/Luke 21:27; Luke 21:36; Matthew 24:37/Luke 17:26; Matthew 24:39/Luke 17:30; Matthew 24:44/Luke 12:40; Matthew 25:31; Matthew 26:64/Mark 14:62/Luke 22:69.

the divine court. These two dominical performances of meaning have fed the construals which resulted in three sorts of usage in the Gospels. The texts as they lie to hand, of course, thoroughly represent that transformation which is characteristic of the Synoptic catechesis, but relatively few usages appear *purely* christological.[53] More usually, the sayings of Jesus reflect a generic בר (אנשׁ)א,[54] its angelic analogue,[55] and possibly both.[56] It is a matter of course that the present categories are provisional, since they evolve out of a somewhat fresh perspective of analysis.

The present discussion can close with no more than a

---

[53] So Luke, perhaps, 6:22 (if it is not generic); 9:56; Matthew 12:40/Luke 11:30; Matthew 13:37; Matthew 16:13; Matthew 17:9/Mark 9:9; Matthew 18:11/Luke 19:10.

[54] Cf. Matthew 8:20/Luke 9:58; Matthew 11:19/Luke 7:34; Mark 8:31/Luke 9:22; Matthew 17:12/Mark 9:12; Matthew 17:22, 23/Mark 9:31/Luke 9:44; Matthew 20:18, 19/Mark 10:33, 34/Luke 18:31-33; Matthew 20:28/Mark 10:34; Matthew 26:2; Matthew 26:24/Mark 14:21/Luke 22:22; Luke 22:48; Matthew 26:45/Mark 14:41; Luke 24:7.

[55] Matthew 9:6/Mark 2:10/Luke 5:24; Matthew 10:23; 13:41; Mark 8:38/Luke 9:26; Matthew 16:27, 28; Luke 12:8; Matthew 19:28; Luke 17:22; Matthew 24:27/Luke 17:24; Luke 18:8; Matthew 24:30, 31/Mark 13:26, 27/Luke 21:27; Luke 21:36; Matthew 24:37/Luke 17:26; Matthew 24:39/Luke 17:30; Matthew 24:44/Luke 12:40; Matthew 25:31; Matthew 26:64/Mark 14:62/Luke 22:69.

[56] Cf. Matthew 12:8/Mark 2:28/Luke 6:5; Matthew 12:32/Luke 12:10.

hypothesis, which a systematic exegesis of the relevant
passages might confirm or refute.[57] But the hypothesis,
for what it is worth, would posit that the literarily
historical Jesus performed sayings in which (א)אנש בר
features as a generic and/or angelic reference.[58] The
angelic reference is predicated upon the understanding of
a close analogy between people and angels, which is well
established within the Hebrew Scriptures (cf. Genesis 18;
Joshua 5:13, 14; Judges 13:2-20; Zechariah 1:7-11), and
is still discernible in Matthew 9:6/Mark 2:10/Luke 5:24;
Matthew 16:27/Mark 8:38/Luke 9:26; Luke 12:8; Matthew
19:28; 25:31; Matthew 26:64/Mark 14:62/Luke 22:69; John
1:51; Acts 7:56. Subsequently, both types of reference
were transformed within the literary construals of the
Synoptic Gospels, so that ὁ υἱὸς τοῦ ἀνθρώπου referred to
Jesus as the disciples' authority, their paradigm of
suffering, and eschatological judge.

---

[57]Catchpole (1982) 260 refers to Luke 12:8, 9 and Matthew
18:10 by way of support, and cites Tobit 12:15; Enoch
104:1; Luke 1:19 as "an individualizing of the old idea
of an angelic ruler for each nation (cf. Dan. 10:12;
12:1; Sir 17:17)." On p. 261, he argues that his reading
"dovetails" with Matthew 24:27, 37, 39/Luke 17:24, 26,
30; Matthew 25:31-46. The thesis of an angelic meaning
might also illuminate Acts 7:56 (cf. P. Doble, "The Son
of Man Saying in Stephen's Witnessing," NTS 31 [1985]
68-84, 83, although Doble presupposes an identification
with Jesus), and -- of course -- John 1:51.

[58]Again, cf. Borsch (1967) 360.

Forgiving at and Swearing by the Temple

In *Redating the New Testament*,[1] John Robinson devoted an entire chapter to "The Significance of 70." He did so for the simple reason that the destruction of the Temple by fire, "the single most datable and climactic event of the period," which clearly influenced much of the presentation of the gospel concerning Jesus (both orally and in writing), "is never once mentioned as a past fact."[2] Threats of destruction against the Temple, especially those couched as prophetic, need to be evaluated against that background of silence, and in that context might be looked upon with particular skepticism. But Matthew 5:23-24; 23:15-24 need to be evaluated in a separate breath, because they appear to take it, as read, that the Temple is still standing.[3]

The first passage imagines a circumstance in which one is offering sacrifice, and then remembers that a brother has been offended: the direction is to leave the gift and

---

[1]John A. T. Robinson, *Redating the New Testament* (London: SCM, 1976) 13-30.

[2]*Ibid.*, 13.

[3]Cf. W. D. Davies and Dale C. Allison, *A Critical and Exegetical Commentary on the Gospel according to Saint Matthew* I: The International Critical Commentary (Edinburgh: Clark, 1988) 516.

depart to be reconciled, on the assumption that the sacrifice can wait. There are certain features of the passage which mark it out as reflecting more the concerns of the Matthean community than any program of Jesus'. The following verses (5:25, 26) append to the direction an imperative involving *juridical* practice,[4] which is quite out of keeping with advice concerning sacrifice. Indeed, the appendix is given separately in Luke 12:57-59, although the wording is distinct enough to call into question the assumption that "Q" is to be taken as a written source. The Matthean and Lukan contexts are also so distinctive that "Q" begins to look less a document than a collection of the halakhic teaching of Jesus, his mishnah, which later was domesticated within a more Hellenistic environment as the instructive sayings of a sage.[5] Be that as it may, the form of the teaching in Matthew conflates cultic and judicial imagery in 5:23-26. Moreover, the "altar" in Matthew before which one is to leave one's gift is specifically the altar of burnt

---

[4]Lachs suggests that the mention of only one judge specifies the allusion as to a Roman court, a more common forum of jurisprudence in Palestine after A. D. 70, cf. Samuel Tobias Lachs, *A Rabbinic Commentary on the New Testament: the Gospels of Matthew, Mark, and Luke* (Hoboken: Ktav, 1987) 93, 94 and Sanhedrin 1:1.

[5]Cf. Chilton, *Profiles of a Rabbi. Synoptic Opportunities in Reading about Jesus*: Brown Judaic Studies 177 (Atlanta: Scholars Press, 1989).

offering or of incense (θυσιαστήριον, twice mentioned). Such specificity makes the advice inapt for general use, since only priests offered at the altar, in either sense. But the vocabulary is at home within Christian usage, which referred to the θυσιαστήριον as an image of its own offering, after the destruction of the Temple.[6]

Elsewhere in Matthew, Jesus shows particular interest in

---

[6]The best examples are offered in the epistles of Ignatius of Antioch, a fact which tends to support the Syrian provenience of Matthew. Cf. *Ephesians* 5:2; *Trallians* 7:2; *Magnesians* 7:2; *Philadelphians* 4; *Romans* 2:2. See Johannes Behm, "θύω, θυσία, θυσιαστήριον," *Theological Dictionary of the New Testament* 3 (ed. G. Kittel, tr. G. W. Bromiley; Grand Rapids: Eerdmans, 1978) 180–190, and especially Brooke Foss Westcott, "Additional Note on xiii.10. On the history of the word θυσιαστήριον," *The Epistle to the Hebrews* (London: MacMillan, 1909) 455–463. Westcott shows that the term is "the habitual rendering of מזבח" (p. 455), and that a generalized usage, to refer to the court of the altar, if it can be established within Judaic usage, would be characteristic of hellenistic Judaism (cf. 1 Maccabees 1:59; Ecclesiasticus 50.11–14 and Westcott, p. 456). In neither case does it appear to me that the meaning is even as general as Westcott suggests it might be. Such generalization may appear, however, in *Christian* characterizations, cf. Revelation 11:1; 1 Clement 41, also cited by Westcott, p. 456, cf. p. 461). (Although Davies [p. 516] cites it for quite another argument, *Didache* 14:1, 2 is probably also to be taken within that category.) In any case, there does not seem to have been a sufficiently general usage within the Judaism of the first century to make sense of the saying in Matthew as it now stands, as a norm for ordinary worship.

cultic arrangements (cf. 17:24-27), and I have argued that he was opposed to the collection of the half shekel in particular.[7] And Jesus' occupation of the Temple, in which he prohibited the sale of animals in the southern court, rather than Ḥanuth, the traditional location, is one of his best attested acts.[8] Moreover, forgiveness appears to have been linked in his teaching to being pure enough to eat with him and/or to sacrifice (cf. Matthew 8:2-4/Mark 1:40-44/Luke 5:12-14; Matthew 9:9-13/Mark 2:13-17/Luke 5:27-32; 15:1, 2; Matthew 15:11/Mark 7:15; Matthew 6:12, 14, 15; Mark 11:25; Luke 7:34; 10:8; 11:4; 18:9-14; 19:1-10).

Matthew 5:23, 24 contains one feature which, although it may appear absurd at first sight, may permit us to see a glimmer of Jesus' own teaching. Matthew's Jesus instructs his follower to deposit his sacrifice and to seek reconciliation prior to the actual offering. Such an arrangement may appear impractical, and does not appear

---

[7] Cf. "A Coin of Three Realms: Matthew 17:24-27," *The Bible in Three Dimensions. Essays in celebration of forty years of Biblical Studies in the University of Sheffield*: Journal for the Study of the Old Testament, Supplement 87 (ed. D. J. A. Clines, S. E. Fowl, S. E. Porter; Sheffield: JSOT, 1990) 269-282.

[8] Cf. Victor Eppstein, "The historicity of the Gospel account of the Cleansing of the Temple," *Zeitschrift für die neutestamentliche Wissenschaft* 55 (1964) 42-58.

directly to reflect the eucharistic practice of the Church,[9] but it does have certain analogies in Rabbinic practice, where a lack a fitness on the part of a person or his offering might result in a sacrifice for a feast being deferred for some days or longer.[10] In the sense that there is a systemic link between forgiveness, purity, and actual sacrifice, we may find that Jesus' program is dimly reflected in the passage as it stands.

Matthew 23:15-24 also fits comfortably within the world of Christian rhetoric. Just how comfortably it does so is

---

[9]Nonetheless, the practice of exchanging the Lord's peace entered the liturgy early, and may have been related to the passage; cf. Cyril of Jerusalem, *Mystagogical Lectures* 5:3 (cited under Cyril's *Catechesis* in Davies [p. 517]).

[10]Rosh Hashannah 4a-6b deals with a delay within a feast, while Sanhedrin 11a deals with the more substantial delay provided by intercalation; cf. John Lightfoot (tr. J. Strype), *A Commentary on the New Testament from the Talmud and Hebraica* (London: Oxford University Press, 1859) 115. A different line is taken in H. L. Strack and P. Billerbeck, *Das Evangelium nach Matthäus*: Kommentar zum Neuen Testament aus Talmud und Midrasch 1 (München: Beck, 1922); they misleadingly claim that a practice such as is envisaged in Matthew is unknown in the halakhah. But they quite correctly go on to show that reconciliation was demanded by the rabbis in advance of sacrifice, as Leviticus 5 would lead us to expect. Cf. Baba Kamma 9:11, 12 and 110a-111a, where sacrifice is linked to the duty of restitution; C. G. Montefiore, *Rabbinic Literature and Gospel Teachings* (London: MacMillan, 1930) 46.

suggested by its attraction in some authorities of v. 14, which blames the hypocritical scribes and Pharisees for consuming widows' houses and extending their prayers for effect. "Family 13" gives that attack as v. 14, while it appears prior to v. 13 in the Textus Receptus. The vagrancy of the verse, as well as its relatively late attestation, demonstrate that it should not be considered part of the received text of Matthew, but as an instance of fashionable sayings in the early Church finding their way into Matthew. The fashion which is evidenced, however, is notable: scribes and Pharisess, which are quite distinct groups in early Judaism, are conflated in the general category of "hypocrites," because Christianity is now viewed as a separate entity, and no longer as part of the synagogues of Judaism. "Hypocrisy" is also the general category of Judaism in *Didache* 8, which closes with no less a dominical tradition than the Lord's Prayer. It seems clear that there was a tendency in Syria towards the close of the first century to recast the sayings of Jesus within an anti-Judaic program of instruction. Chapter 23 of Matthew, in its pronouncement of woe upon hypocritical scribes and Pharisees (vv. 13, 15, 23, 25, 27, 29) and its rejection of "rabbi" as a title (v. 8), probably reflects such a program.

The particular charge the scribes and Pharisees sought proselytes, (v. 15) is, of course, exaggerated, although it is the sort of complaint we might expect of a community in competition with thriving synagogues in Syria (cf. also 23:2, 3). That provenience would explain the presence of the Semitism "son of Gehenna," without recourse to an argument for the authenticity of the saying.[11] Exaggeration also appears to be the order of the day in vv. 16-19, in that, although it is true the rabbis are said in their own literature to have sworn by the "place" of the Temple,[12] the valuation of money over divine sanctification which is ascribed to them is absurd. It is the sort of thing an enemy of a distinct social group might say, but as a saying of Jesus it is most implausible.

Greater plausibility attaches, however, to vv. 20-22. They amount to an injunction not to swear at all,[13] on the grounds, not of the precedence of sanctification over money, but of God's presence in the place of sacrifice, and in heaven. Matthew 5:33-37 attributes substantially the same position to Jesus, within an entirely different form of material (cf. also James 5:12). The insistence

---

[11]Cf. Alan Hugh McNeile, *The Gospel according to St. Matthew* (London: MacMillan, 1957) 333.

[12]Cf. Strack--Billerbeck, 335, 931, 932.

[13]Nonetheless, there is not evident here the formal exclusion of oaths as in the later formation at Matthew 5:33-37.

within the tradition of Jesus that he taught against oaths is consistent with a stream of opinion within early Judaism (cf. Ecclesiasticus 23:9-13; Philo, *On the Decalogue* 17 @ 84 Josephus, *The Jewish War* 2.8.6 @ 135 [on the Essenes]),[14] but sufficiently distinctive from general, rabbinic/Pharisaic practice to be considered characteristic of Jesus.

The final verses (vv. 23, 24) blame the hypocritical scribes and Pharisees for doing precisely what must be done to sustain the Temple whose sanctity has just been asserted: tithing. Of course, they, as distinguished from the priesthood, only become the obvious authority of the institution after A. D. 70, so that the entire setting may be said to be more Matthean than dominical. As Lachs points out, biblical tithing relates to grain, wine, and oil, which was commonly ancient practice;[15] the rabbinic teaching included extensions into herbs (cf. Maaseroth 1:1; Demai 2:1).[16] Micah 6:6-8 offers the sort of principle on which one might criticize such an extension, but -- once again -- the rhetoric of the Matthean woe

---

[14]Cf. Lachs, 101-103, who also cites Rabbinic sources.

[15]Lachs, p. 370, cf. Gary Anderson, *Sacrifices and Offerings in Ancient Israel. Studies in their Social and Political Importance*: Harvard Semitic Monographs 41 (Atlanta: Scholars, 1987) 77-90.

[16]Cf. Lightfoot, pp. 298, 299.

appears to reflect the stance of an outsider to the debate. On the other hand, the warning (v. 24) against gulping down a camel (*gamla*) while being on the alert for a gnat (*kamla*) works especially well in Aramaic, and might be held to be typical of the vivid imagery for which Jesus was reputed as a teacher.[17] Any skilled teacher of epigrams might coin it, but as the point of generation of an attack upon punctilious practice focused on the issue of purity in what is ingested, it commends itself as likely.

On the whole, the verses in question would look best in black, since they appear to reflect the social situation of the community which produced Matthew. But it is not necessary, or even plausible, to imagine that they are an example of *creatio ex nihilo*. Jesus' position regarding the forgiveness which purity required generated Matthew 5:23, 24 within a community which regarded itself as a replacement of the destroyed Temple. The same community, meeting the challenge of Pharisaic or Rabbinic Judaism with overt hostility, turned Jesus' warning about gulping down camels (Matthew 23:24) into woes against scrupulous tithing (v. 23), and his counsel against oaths (vv. 20-22) into a vindictive attack on their opponents greed

---

[17]Cf. Matthew Black, *An Aramaic Approach to the Gospels and Acts* (Oxford: Clarendon, 1967) 175, 176 (citing the suggestion of A. T. Olmstead).

for money (vv. 16-19) and people (v. 15). Such an evaluation leads me to recommend:

5:23, 24 -- grey (tending towards black)

23:15-19 -- black

23:20-22 -- gray (tending towards pink)

23:23 -- black

23:24 -- pink.

Bibliography

Gary A. Anderson, *Sacrifices and Offerings in Ancient Israel. Studies in their Social and Political Importance*: Harvard Semitic Monographs 41 (Atlanta: Scholars, 1987).

Johannes Behm, "θύω, θυσία, θυσιαστήριον," *Theological Dictionary of the New Testament* 3 (ed. G. Kittel, tr. G. W. Bromiley; Grand Rapids: Eerdmans, 1978) 180-190

Matthew Black, *An Aramaic Approach to the Gospels and Acts* (Oxford: Clarendon, 1967)

Bruce D. Chilton, "A Coin of Three Realms: Matthew 17:24-27," *The Bible in Three Dimensions. Essays in celebration of forty years of Biblical Studies in the University of Sheffield*: Journal for the Study of the Old Testament, Supplement 87 (ed. D. J. A. Clines, S. E. Fowl, S. E. Porter; Sheffield: JSOT, 1990) 269-282

----------------, *Profiles of a Rabbi. Synoptic Opportunities in Reading about Jesus*: Brown Judaic Studies 177 (Atlanta: Scholars Press, 1989)

W. D. Davies and Dale C. Allison, *A Critical and Exegetical Commentary on the Gospel according to Saint Matthew* I: The International Critical Commentary (Edinburgh: Clark, 1988)

Victor Eppstein, "The historicity of the Gospel account of the Cleansing of the Temple," *Zeitschrift für die neutestamentliche Wissenschaft* 55 (1964) 42-58

Samuel Tobias Lachs, *A Rabbinic Commentary on the New Testament: the Gospels of Matthew, Mark, and Luke* (Hoboken: Ktav, 1987)

John Lightfoot (tr. J. Strype), *A Commentary on the New Testament from the Talmud and Hebraica* (London: Oxford University Press, 1859)

Alan Hugh McNeile, *The Gospel according to St. Matthew* (London: MacMillan, 1957)

C. G. Montefiore, *Rabbinic Literature and Gospel Teachings* (London: MacMillan, 1930)

John A. T. Robinson, *Redating the New Testament* (London: SCM, 1976)

H. L. Strack and P. Billerbeck, *Das Evangelium nach Matthäus*: Kommentar zum Neuen Testament aus Talmud und Midrasch 1 (München: Beck, 1922)

Brooke Foss Westcott, "Additional Note on xiii.10. On the history of the word θυσιαστήριον," *The Epistle to the Hebrews* (London: MacMillian, 1909) 455–463

"Do Not Do What You Hate": Where There Is Not Gold, There Might Be Brass, The Case of the Thomaean "Golden Rule" (6.3)[1]

"Do not do what you hate" appears to be sound advice, particularly coming as it does, in *Thomas* 6.3, after an injunction not to lie. It is compact and aphoristic; indeed, its apparent simplicity would seem to make it a candidate for inclusion in a collection of authentic sayings of Jesus. Especially in the wake of the contribution of John Dominic Crossan,[2] the simplest, most direct aphorisms have been seen as the most likely to be Jesus'. Word for word, *Thomas* 6.3 is tighter than the Matthaean and Lukan versions of the "Golden Rule:" might it be the case that *Thomas* gives us the most primitive form of that teaching which is available?

The very fact that the question should arise is indicative of the commanding influence of certain systemic assumptions in the study of Jesus today, particularly in North America. All of those assumptions are understandable, and at least partially justifiable, but none of them can be commended willy-nilly as

---

[1]Freda M. Dorsey In Memoriam.

[2]*In Fragments: The Aphorisms of Jesus* (San Francisco: Harper & Row, 1983), cf. the discussion of Bernard Brandon Scott, "Picking Up the Pieces," *Forum* 1.1 (1985) 15–21.

instruments for the recovery of historical information about Jesus. The purpose of the present article is to identify some of those assumptions, and to develop critical principles, while addressing the question to hand.

Matthew 7:12 presents the well known, positive version of the "Golden Rule" as the fulfillment of "the law and the prophets," and to that extent appears more a theological device than an instance of ethical teaching. Indeed, the immediate, surrounding context in Matthew (vv. 7-11, cf. vv. 13, 14) concerns divine gifts, rather than human behavior. One of the few, reliable guides to the analysis of Jesus' teaching is that the present structure of discourses attributed to him is synthetic. Even those whose approach to the Gospels is highly literary acknowledge that, prior to the activity of the "authors," a definite tradition, with its own logical structure, had taken shape.[3] A better model is one in which each of the Synoptic Gospels is understood as the paradigm of catechesis in a particular part of the Mediterranean world, Rome (Mark), Antioch (Luke), and Syria (Matthew).[4]

---

[3]Cf. David Aune, *The New Testament in Its Literary Environment* (Philadelphia: Westminster, 1987) 19, 20, 53, 53, 65, 66.

[4]Cf. Chilton, *Profiles of a Rabbi. Synoptic Opportunities in Reading about Jesus*: Brown Judaic Studies 177

The deceptive simplicity of the Synoptic presentation should not deceive us: we are dealing with the Apostolic, narrative symbol of the faith of the early Church, not with history, and by "symbol" we refer to the meaning of the term in the first two centuries of the common era, as a meaningful recapitulation of what is believed.[5] If we wish to know what, as candidates for baptism, followers of Jesus in Rome or Antioch or Edessa were expected to know, the Gospels are a useful guide. If we wish to think constructively about Jesus, we need to draw inferences, by postulating the sort of thing an early rabbi might have said and done in order for the claims made on Jesus' behalf in the Hellenistic world to have become possible.

Matthew 7:12 occurs in the midst of the great, Syrian symbol of Jesus' teaching known as the "Sermon on the Mount." Its fundamental structure, from the opening in chapter five, concerns how disciples' actions merit divine reward, and how such actions are to be motivated

---

(Atlanta: Scholars Press, 1989).

[5] In the early Church, two sorts of symbol predominated. The first, the narrative symbol or Apostolic reminiscence, came to be crystallized in the Synoptic Gospels. The second, the credal symbol, was more amenable to the discursive reason which prevailed during the Hellenistic period of the Church, and for that reason the creed of the second century (or "Apostles' Creed") was successively reformulated from the fourth century, as the "Nicene," "Chalcedonian," and "Athanasian" Creeds.

and regulated. The section in which the "Golden Rule" appears opens with the injunction, "Ask, and it shall be given to you; seek, and you shall find; knock, and it shall be opened to you" (7:7). There is no doubt but that the gravamen of the passage is that God, as a father. gives good things to those who know enough to ask for them (7:11). When, therefore, we are told that whatever we wish people should do for us, we should do for them (v. 12), the apparent meaning is that God will, under those conditions, see that we get our reward; "for this," we are reminded, "is the law and the prophets." The Golden Rule in Matthew is first of all a theological, rather than an ethical norm, because it is the standard by which it is claimed God metes out his favor; as the following parable has it, the Rule is a narrow gate, by which alone one might enter life (vv. 13, 14). Although popular usage fundamentally presents the Rule as a moral standard, separable both from Scripture and from Jesus' teaching, the Matthean context is precisely and rigorously rooted in an understanding of divine reward and retribution.

The synthetic nature of the Matthean presentation becomes all the more apparent in comparison with the Lukan environment of the Golden Rule (6:31). In a sense, that environment is ethical, because the issues which frame the passage concern the love of enemies (vv. 27-30,

32-35). Notably, such concerns are also addressed in Matthew's Sermon on the Mount, but in a different context (5:38-48; part of the late device known as the "Antitheses," which punctuate Jesus' teaching by means of a formal opposition to the Hebrew Scriptures). The apparently ethical focus of the Rule in Luke is, however, only superficial. Here as well, the emphasis ultimately falls on the question of divine reward (vv. 32-35), and in a peculiarly negative way. The complex of imperatives concerning love, of which the Rule is the centerpiece, immediately follows a series of "Woes" (6:24-26), the flip side of the beatitudes (6:20-22). Love, in the Lukan sermon "on the plan" (as it is known, in deference to 6:17), is a strategy designed to distinguish the disciples from "sinners" (vv. 32-34), and thereby to win a great reward as "sons of the most high" (v. 35). On analysis, then, the Lukan context no is less narrowly catechetical than the Matthean.

If the canonical Gospels are synthetic in their contextualization and wording of the Golden Rule, perhaps a more vigorous aphorism, such as is conveyed in *Thomas*, is its nucleus. Logically speaking, of course, the possibility that *Thomas* (or any other source of antiquity which is in demonstrable touch with the tradition of Jesus' teaching) most accurately conveys Jesus' position must be considered. But the date of the emergence of any source, including *Thomas* (see below) needs to be included in any such consideration, and -- even more importantly -- the tendencies or programs of the communities and individuals which produced those sources must be taken into account. An aphorism, as an apparently simple form of communication, need not be the most original form of a given communication. At any stage, a statement might be "simplified," in order to make it more readily accessible and/or transmissible. The result will be what might be called a synthetic aphorism, a conscious attempt to streamline a more complicated dictum. The evidence is overwhelming that, in antiquity, those trained even at a relatively elementary level in the literary transmission of materials were adept at transforming longer into shorter epigrams, and *vice versa*.[6] Even if, therefore, we were to find that *Thomas* 6.3 were aphoristic in form, that would be no guarantee -- despite the criterion derived from Crossans' work -- that the teaching was "primitive."

The diction of *Thomas* may to some extent claim a greater affinity (as compared to Matthew and Luke) with Shabbath 31a, the nearest analogy to the Golden Rule within Rabbinica (ascribed to Hillel). To that extent, an

---

[6]Cf. Vernon Robbins, "Picking Up the Fragments," *Forum* 1.2 (1985) 31-64; "Pronouncement Stories From A Rhetorical Perspective," *Forum* 4.2 (1988) 3-32.

aphoristic aspect (whether synthetic or not) may be claimed for the Thomaean version of the Rule, although it needs to be remembered that the Rabbinic teaching appears with a major indication of how care for one's neighbor is to be understood and enacted:

> What you hate, do not do to your fellow. That is the whole the Torah, while all the rest is commentary. Go and learn it!

Hillel's version of the Rule is therefore framed within an imperative to learn the Torah: the injunction to love one's neighbor *is* the whole of the Torah, which one must master in order to love one's neighbor.

Skillfully, "Hillel" (or whoever originated the dictum) manages to defend dedication to the Torah as a form of the ethical norm of love. That achievement is all the more striking within the context of the haggadah in which Hillel's Rule appears. A proselyte has just asked Shammai (Hillel's paradigmatic disputant) to teach him the entire Torah while he (the proselyte) stands on one foot. Shammai's reaction is to drive the proselyte away with a measuring rod. Hillel's distinctive response therefore comes as a double trump of Shammai's claim to authority. First, he keeps the proselyte -- who, in turn, keeps the Torah -- where Shammai was likely to have lost him; second, he points out for the proselyte just the aspect of the Torah, its articulation of love, which shows why learning the Torah cannot be reduced to a moment, but is by identity the entire movement of love which God demands. Hillel has the better of both Shammai and the proselyte.

Negatively formulated, as an imperative against doing what one finds loathsome, the maxim commonly known in the modern period as the Golden Rule appears to have circulated generally;[7] it has also influenced the form of the Golden Rule in the *Didache* (1:2, cf. Tobit 4:15 and Acts 15:20, 29 in Bezae):

> Whatever you wish not to be done to you, do not do to another.

Given that the proverbial form of the Rule (that is, in the negative) is the form that predominates in Christian antiquity, there is no question of attempting to argue that Hillel's version specifically influenced Jesus', which is best represented in *Thomas*. The negative form of the Rule is as common in the Christian tradition as in many others; there is no need or reason to posit some specific source (such as Hillel's dictum) for a conventional statement (such as *Thomas* 6.3). Indeed, the conventional, proverbial form of the saying in *Thomas*

---

[7]Cf. A. Dihle, *Die goldene Regel. Eine Einführung in die Geschichte der antiken und frühchristlichen Vulgärethik: Studienheft zur Altertumswissenschaft 7* (Göttingen: Vandenhoeck und Ruprecht, 1962).

will itself call for attention below, but a more pressing consideration, from the point of view of comparing *Thomas* 6.3 with Shabbath 31a, is contextual rather than formal.

The synthetic nature of the aphorism in *Thomas* becomes apparent when its present context, and therefore its actual meaning, is considered. The issue in play, as established by the question of the disciples in 6.1, regards fasting, prayer, alms, and diet. All such practices are qualified as lying and hateful according to 6.2, 3, and 6.4-6 even threatens (by contextual implication) that the Father will actively seek out any "hidden" or "covered" acts of that kind (cf. the quite different contexts of Matthew 10:26/Luke 12:2; Mark 4:22/Luke 8:17). Judaism is to be punished, whether its practice is overt or covert. Even if, then, and it is a big "if" (as we shall see), the wording of 6.3 is reminiscent of a proverbial form of the Golden Rule, such as we find in Tobit 4:15 and *Didache* 1:2, it has suffered a remarkably anti-Judaic distortion, which is in line with a major tendency within *Thomas* (cf. *ll.* 14, 27, 52, 53, 104). That distortion has been accomplished by bringing together the injunctions against lying and doing what is hateful with the warning about things hidden being revealed, all in response to a supposed question about fasting, prayer, alms and diet. It is evident that 6.3 is part of a synthetic aphorism designed to address a pressing concern of the Thomaean community, namely, the distinction of Jesus and his movement from Judaism.[8]

Other features of *Thomas* 6.3 will only strengthen our impression that it is, from the point of view of what it means, a creation of the document's community, but a moment must first be taken to reflect upon the implications of the anti-Judaism of *Thomas*. The position against prayer, fasting, and alms-giving in 14.1, 2 may reflect an argument within the Church, rather than against Judaism as such, but the dismissal of the "twenty-four prophets" in Israel as "the dead" in 52.1, 2 appears to be inescapably pointed, as does the prosaic argument against circumcision in *l.* 53. The close of that saying, commending a circumcision in spirit, coheres well with the notion of a true form of fasting and observing sabbath (*l.* 27), transcending the literal institutions (cf. *ll.* 6, 104).

The *logia* which have been cited not only articulate a coherent program in respect of Judaism, but do so within several of the discourses which mark out *Thomas* as a

---

[8] Apparently in all innocence, Philippe de Suarez (p. 255) accepts the program of *Thomas* implicitly:

> Comme le lexte le laisse clairement entendre, Jésus s'insurge contres des pratiques qui favorisent l'hypocrisie.

structured harmony of Jesus' sayings. *Thomas* is no mere hodge-podge of traditional materials, although association by catchword and topic is a feature of organization. Evidentially, the sayings were handed on orally within the community of *Thomas*, but the peculiar shape of the Thomaean tradition as we know it, in a documentary form, was achieved when an interlocutory structure was imposed upon the whole. The structure of interlocutions has disciples ask questions or make statements, to which Jesus is alledged to respond in the sayings which follow.[9] A governing context is thereby generated for each saying, shorne of any narrative context (such as in the canonical Gospels, to which the Thomaean *logia* are usually comparable).[10] Just these locutions of disciples target our attention as we read about the issues of the correct interpretation of Jesus' words (*l.* 1, with the superscription, and its reference to Didymos Judas Thomas), prayer, fasting, and

---

[9]Sometimes, as will readily be seen from the list of interlocutions which is given here, sayings are bracketed by interlocutions, rather than simply following them. Moreover, the interlocutory topics are sometimes taken up repeatedly.

[10]Cf. Chilton, "*The Gospel according to Thomas* as a Source of Jesus' Teaching," *Gospel Perspectives 5: The Jesus Tradition Outside the Gospels* (Sheffield: JSOT, 1985) 155–175, where the present analysis was first developed, and "Kingdom Come, Kingdom Sung. Voices in the Gospels," *Forum* 3.2 (1987) 51–75.

alms-giving (*l*. 6, 104), right leadership within the community (*l*. 12), the end of discipleship (*l*. 18), entering the kingdom and finding Jesus (*ll*. 20, 21, 22, 24, 113, 114), the identity of Jesus (*l*. 43, 61.2), the world to come (*l*. 51, 52, 53), human, especially physical relationships (*l*. 79, 99), and human government (*l*. 100). The interlocutory structure of the document makes it apparent that a community centered upon Jesus as an enduring, interpretative reality, separate (not merely distinct) from Judaism is the fundamental presupposition and aim of the whole. It is no accident that, when the disciples ask who Jesus is, he responds sarcastically that, in even posing the question, they have come like "the Jews" who cannot understand the whole of revelation (*l*. 43). *L*. 6 therefore belongs within an identifiable program of *Thomas'* ideological structure, and contributes directly to the shape of that structure.

By a curious coincidence of events, *Thomas* was discovered at a time when scholarship was prepared to entertain, and even to encourage, the thought that its Jesus is the most authentic which can be known. The fact that it is a collection of sayings helped such a consensus to develop; *Thomas* has even been compared with "Q," which -- if it did actually exist -- was the earliest such collection. Helmust Koester championed that comparison, and also stressed the importance of Thomas' identity as a person named Judas who was also a "twin," "Didymos" (Greek) or "Thomas" (Aramaic). *The Acts of Thomas*, composed during the third century, unequivocally makes out Judas, the literal brother of Jesus, to be his twin, and Koester accepts that identification as "primitive."[11]

As such, of course, the claim is problematic. *The Acts of Thomas* uses the device that Judas is the twin of Jesus in order to buttress its peculiarly ascetic version of Christianity which Judas is portrayed as advocating. The name Judas was common in the period, and need not have referred to Jesus' brother. "Judas Thomas" could refer to anyone named Judas, and the cognomen "Thomas" might have meant "twin" literally, but Jesus was known to have

---

[11]Cf. Helmut Koester, "ΓΝΩΜΑΙ ΔΙΑΦΟΡΟΙ: The Origin and Nature of Diversification in the History of Early Christianity," *Harvard Theological Review* 58 (1965) 279-318, also available in *Trajectories through Early Christianity* (with James M. Robinson; Philadelphia: Fortress, 1977) 114-157; "One Jesus and Four Primitive Gospels," *HTR* 61 (1968) 203-247, *Trajectories*, 158-204. Koester's position has been popularized, but not strengthened, in Stevan L. Davies, *The Gospel of Thomas and Christian Wisdom* (New York: Seabury, 1983). It is startling that, on p. 153, Davies has "the scribe" fill in the material at *l.* 14 which should have been inserted at *l.* 6 because he did not wish to go back and copy his material properly. Such arguments are typical of the scholarly tendency during the recent period to attribute *Thomas'* structure to "primitive" accidents, when the ideological program of the document is ready to hand.

called other disciples names such as "rock" (Cephas) and "thunderers," apparently with some lightness of touch. Why Koester, a fully critical scholar, should see historical accuracy in the combination of a common name, a quirky sobriet, and a late legend, is not apparent. A few years after he wrote, it might be remembered that Irving Wallace published a novel, entitled *The Word*,[12] in which another brother of Jesus was alleged to have written a Gospel. Novelist and scholar together seem correctly to have read their times; their construal of the ancient documents is another matter.

Fashion has prevailed over analysis in the study of *Thomas* for too long. Loose comparisons with "Q" are misleading; the anti-Judaic and christological program of the document is obvious; the document itself is to be dated within the fourth century and its generation within the second century.[13] Even its final saying, which requires females to become male in order to enter the kingdom, has not been enough to alert some researchers to the reality that they are dealing with a Christian text from an age in which sexaulity, and especially

---

[12](New York: Simon & Schuster, 1972).

[13]Cf. Fitzmyer and M. Marcovich, "Textual Criticism and the Gospel of Thomas," *Journal of Theological Studies* 20 (1969) 53-74.

femininity, was regarded as a curse.[14] The time has come to acknowledge that what some of us hoped to see, and what we have actually found, are two quite different things.[15]

But the fundamental proof that *Thomas* is, at best, a secondary source in respect of the Golden Rule is that, in its present form, the document does not invoke a basic term of the rule. The folk commendation of neighborliness in Shabbath and the *Didache* shares with *Thomas* a negative formulation; the one, crucial element which *Thomas* does *not* convey is that it is to *one's neighbor* that what is hateful is not to be done. What in the other sources is a matter of love is for the Thomaean version a matter of integrity. It may be doubted whether the Golden Rule in any substantial form stands behind *Thomas* 6.3, although the *wording* of some form of it might conceivably be

---

[14]Cf. Elaine Pagels, *The Gnostic Gospels* (New York: Random House, 1979). The ideological bias implicit in Pagels's work has been ably demonstrated in a recent project at Bard College by Katherine H. Maloy, *Critique of Teleological Textuality: Wisdom Literature in Late Antiquity, a Comparison of Gnostic and Judaic Texts* (Annandale: Bard College, 1990).

[15]Cf. Francis T. Fallon and Ron Cameron, "The Gospel of Thomas. A Forschungsbericht and Analysis," *Aufstieg und Niedergang der römischen Welt* II.25.6 (Berlin: de Gruyter, 1988) 4195–4251.

alluded to within *Thomas*.[16] Especially when not doing what you hate is coupled with not lying, the aphoristic genre appears synthetic, more Polonial than proverbial or primitive. Indeed, it may be that the form, "Do not do what you hate," originated with the Coptic version of *Thomas*. In the Greek fragment from Oxyrhynchus, which is to be dated within the third century, the reading is, "Do not do what *is hated*" ([ὃ τι μισ]εῖται μὴ ποιεῖτ[ε]). The normal understanding has been that "is hated" (μισεῖται) is a miswriting of "you hate" (μισεῖτε).[17] "Do not do what is hated" is hardly a version of the Golden Rule, and it is interesting that the editors of the most commonly cited version of the Coptic text of *Thomas* refer to the

---

[16]The case, however, can not be made any stronger than that, since the actual wording of the New Testament in Coptic, whether Sahidic or Bohairic, and whether the text is from the Gospels or Acts, is quite distinctive. ⲘⲞⲤⲦⲈ appears as the verb for "hate" in *Thomas*, whose normal dialect is Sahidic (with Subachmimic elements); it appears in Acts 15:20 in neither version of the Coptic New Testament. MPA appears as the verb "to do" in the Boharic version of Acts 15:20 (for ⲰⲰⲠⲈ in Sahidic), but that similarity is scarcely sufficient to argue for any genuine connection. The possibility therefore emerges that the similarity with the Golden Rule is an artifact, not of any ancient influence, but of the modern attempt to find in *Thomas* the most "primitive" version of one saying of Jesus or another. Wolfgang Schrage notes a similarity only with Luke 8:17; 12:2 (pp. 35, 37).

[17]Cf. Philippe de Suarez, p. 168; Fitzmyer, pp. 385, 386.

Rule as a parallel only "in one sense."[18]

If the gist of *Thomas* is that one is not to do what *God* hates, parallels are not difficult to discover. Ecclesiasticus 15:11b expressly reads, "for what he (sc. God) hates, you shall not do" (ἃ γὰρ ἐμίσησεν οὐ ποιήσεις).[19] If such were the formulation in the tradition of *Thomas*, the deletion of an open reference to God, and of any allusion to the Hebrew Scriptures, would not be difficult to explain, since such tendencies are programmatic within *Thomas.* But an accommodation (conscious or not) to some of the wording of the Golden Rule, as in the Synoptics, and more especially in its negative form, as in Romans 13:10, Acts 15:20, 29 (in the "Western" witnesses), the *Didache* 1:2, Tobit, Philo, and — for that matter — Confucius, is not difficult to imagine.[20]

---

[18] Cf. Guillaumont *et al.*, p. 59.

[19] The rendering is according to the most reliable Greek manuscripts, although in the RSV it has been revised to "for he will not do what he hates."

[20] Cf. Tobit 4:15; Eusebius, *Praeparatio Evangelica* 8:7 (for its citation of Philo); Confucius, *Analecta*, 15.23, all of which are cited in John Martin Creed, p. 94. Cf. also the *Testament of Naphtali* 1:6; 2 Enoch 61:1, 2; Sextus, *Sententiae*, 89 (and 210b) cited by Davies and Allison, p. 686.

The notion that there is an accommodation to the ancient wisdom of various cultures in the Golden Rule has been pressed to the utmost in the analysis of Ulrich Luz. In his commentary on Matthew, he argues that the formulation is an attempt to domesticate Jesus' radical demand for love, in order to make it tenable within a worldly vision of morality.[21] On such an understanding, the version in *Thomas* is no more secondary than any other form. But *Thomas* 6.3 in fact illustrates what is unsatisfactory in Luz's position: if the Synoptics are simply indulging in an echo of ancient wisdom, and attributing it to Jesus, why do they not allude to the usual, negative form? The attempt to claim that the positive form, attributed to Jesus, is in some way superior to all other versions, and unique in its formulation, is indeed exaggerated,[22] but the fact remains that the usual appearance of the maxim is in the negative, while the positive analogue is usually crafted to envisage particular conditions.[23]

---

[21]Cf. Luz, p. 393-394. Accordingly, Luz (p. 388) also emphasizes the appearance of the Rule in Hellenistic sources, such as Dio Cassius (52, 34.39), and Isocrates (*Nicocleam* 49).

[22]So Fitzmyer, pp. 639, 640, who cites Aristeas 207 and Herodotus 3.142, in addition to some of the other analogies here cited. Cf. the conclusions of Creed, p. 94, Plummer, p. 186, Marshall, p. 262

[23]Examples of the positive formulation would include 2 Enoch 61.1, 2:
    And now, my children, keep your hearts from every

The particular paradox posed by the form of the Golden Rule in Matthew and Luke is indicative of the general problem of "the historical Jesus," and of its general solution. What occasioned awareness of the "problem" was an aknowledgement that the sources available, whether canonical (and from the first century) or not (and from from second century and later) were tendentious, and composed from the point of view of a culture far removed from the one which produced Jesus. But there was a critically flawed tendency during the last century to suppose that the earliest source must be the most reliable, and that supposition has gone hand in hand with the assumption that simplicity, primitivity and reliability are somehow to be identified. Just that bundle of specious axioms has given us the consensus that, whatever the date of its manuscripts and the direction of its program, *Thomas* must be considered as a source whose value equals that of the Synoptics. But even

---

injustice which the Lord hates. Just as a man asks for his own soul from God, so let him do to every living soul..."
It is notable that the positive formulation is only invoked where a direct analogy with God's love is involved; when the saying concerns ethics, the avoidance of injustice (as in most formulations of the Rule) is the idiom. Moreover, the first part of the saying represents the sort of speech which may be reflected in the fragment from Oxyrhynchus.

a cursory awareness of the specific form of the versions of the Rule available in antiquity makes it plain that the principal, literary issue is: how did the maxim come to be attributed to Jesus in its positive form?

One possible answer to the question is that Jesus taught the Rule, which was generally acknowledged within his culture, in its positive form. But if so, the context of his teaching must necessarily have differed from that envisaged in the Synoptics, which is catechetical, and that envisaged in *Thomas,* which is apologetic. Elsewhere in the Gospels, Jesus is held to articulate a principle of pre-emptive forgiveness (cf. Matthew 5:23-26; 6:12, 14, 15; 18:15-18, 23-35; Mark 11:25[, 26]; Luke 6:37; 11:4; 17:3, 4); such a context would make sense of a programmatic conversion of the maxim into the positive idiom of the Gospels. There is no sense in which it can be convincingly argued that Jesus *originated* the positive form, but -- if we need to posit a reason for which the positive form was associated with his tradition and not Hillel's (or another's) -- the answer lies near to hand that forgiveness in advance of any requirement to forgive was characteristic of his teaching.

The conclusions to which we are drawn may by now be obvious, but they are of a general application, and therefore will bear emphasis:

1) *Thomas* 6.3 is in substance not a form of the Golden Rule. The suggestion that it is such is an artifact of the simplistic assumption that what appears "aphoristic" is "primitive."

2) "Aphorisms" may be synthetic, as may any form recognizable in antiquity. Specifically, the harmonizing "aphorisms" of *Thomas*, which unite Synoptic and non-Synoptic traditions of dominical *logia*, and express an anti-Judaic program of ecclesiastical order, must never be assumed to be "pre-canonical" on formal grounds alone.

2) *Thomas* 6.3 may invoke the wording of the Golden Rule within its pastiche of dominical *logia*, but if it does so, the form of the Rule is proverbial, the negative version of Eccleisiases 15:11b; Tobit 4:15 and *Didache* 1.2.

3) Jesus might, of course, have cited the proverbial form of the Rule (after all, Confucius might have as well), but if he did so, it would not have been with the antinomian meaning devised in *Thomas*.

4) If Jesus had anything new to contribute to the literary shape of the Rule (and that is by no means

evident), the Matthaean and Lukan versions represent it better than *Thomas* from a formal point of view, although their discursive contexts are as interpretative as the Thomaean device of the synthetic aphorism. Insofar as Jesus' position is recoverable, the exercise is not a matter of invoking purely formal criteria, and ignoring the context in which meaning is articulated. On the contrary, "Jesus" is not a significant figure, except to the extent he is invoked by the literary witnesses to the faith which takes him to be its source. "Jesus" is -- critically speaking -- a cipher: what must be supposed to lie at the origin of the documents, communal and cumulative in nature, which refer back to him. He is only historical to the extent he is literarily historical, an intelligent inference from the texts which lie to hand. Their meaning is only comprehensible when due attention is paid to the context in which words and actions unfold, because such contexts are the exclusive matrices of meaning available to any reader, in any time.

5) *Thomas* 6.3 tells us nothing useful about the Golden Rule in either its proverbial or dominical forms, although it is immensely informative of the Thomaean milieu.

6) Black is too light a color to print the "aphorism" in.

Bibliography

David Aune, *The New Testament in Its Literary Environment* (Philadelphia: Westminster, 1987)

Bruce Chilton, "*The Gospel according to Thomas* as a Source of Jesus' Teaching," *Gospel Perspectives 5: The Jesus Tradition Outside the Gospels* (Sheffield: JSOT, 1985) 155-175

--------------, "Kingdom Come, Kingdom Sung. Voices in the Gospels," *Forum* 3.2 (1987) 51-75

--------------, *Profiles of a Rabbi. Synoptic Opportunities in Reading about Jesus*: Brown Judaic Studies 177 (Atlanta: Scholars Press, 1989)

John Martin Creed, *The Gospel according to St Luke* (London: Macmillan, 1930)

John Dominic Crossan, *In Fragments: The Aphorisms of Jesus* (San Francisco: Harper & Row, 1983)

W. D. Davies and Dale C. Allison, *A Critical and Exegetical Commentary on the Gospel according to Saint Matthew*: The International Critical Commentary (Edinburgh: Clark, 1988)

Stevan L. Davies, *The Gospel of Thomas and Christian Wisdom* (New York: Seabury, 1983)

A. Dihle, *Die goldene Regel: Eine Einführung in die Geschichte der antiken und frühchristlichen Vulgärethik:* Studienheft zum Altertumswissenschaft 7 (Göttingen: Vandenhoeck und Ruprecht, 1962)

Francis T. Fallon and Ron Cameron, "The Gospel of Thomas. A Forschungsbericht and Analysis," *Aufstieg und Niedergang der römischen Welt* II.25.6 (Berlin: de Gruyter, 1988) 4195-4251.

Joseph A. Fitzmyer, *The Gospel According to Luke (I-IX):* The Anchor Bible (Garden City: Doubleday, 1981)

A. Guillaumont, H.-Ch. Puech, G. Quispel, W. Till and Yassah ʿAbd Al Masîḥ, *The Gospel according to Thomas* (New York: Harper and Brothers, 1959)

G. Horner, *The Coptic Version of the New Testament in the Northern Dialect* (vols I and II; Oxford: Clarendon, 1911)

--------, *The Coptic Version of the New Testament in the Southern Dialect* (vols I, II [1911], and VI [1922]; Oxford: Clarendon)

Helmut Koester, "ΓΝΩΜΑΙ ΔΙΑΦΟΡΟΙ: The Origin and Nature of Diversification in the History of Early Christianity," *Harvard Theological Review* 58 (1965) 279-318, also available in *Trajectories through Early Christianity* (with James M. Robinson; Philadelphia: Fortress, 1977) 114-157

--------------, "One Jesus and Four Primitive Gospels," *HTR* 61 (1968) 203-247, *Trajectories*, 158-204.

Ulrich Luz, *Das Evangelium nach Matthäus 1*: Evangelisch-Katholischen Kommentar zum Neuen Testament (Benziger and Neukirchener: Zürich and Neukirchen-Vluyn, 1985)

Katherine H. Maloy, *Critique of Teleological Textuality: Wisdom Literature in Late Antiquity, a Comparison of Gnostic and Judaic Texts* (Annandale: Bard College, 1990)

I. Howard Marshall, *The Gospel of Luke*: The New International Greek Testament Commentary (Grand Rapids: Eerdmans, 1978)

M. Marcovich, "Textual Criticism and the Gospel of Thomas," *Journal of Theological Studies* 20 (1969) 53-74

I. Howard Marshall, *The Gospel of Luke*: New International Greek Testament Commentary (Grand Rapids: Eerdmans, 1978)

Alfred Plummer, *A Critical and Exegetical Commentary on the Gospel according to St Luke*: The International Critical Commentary (New York: Scribner, 1898)

Vernon Robbins, "Picking Up the Fragments," *Forum* 1.2 (1985) 31–64

--------------, "Pronouncement Stories From A Rhetorical Perspective," *Forum* 4.2 (1988) 3–32

Wolfgang Schrage, *Das Verhältnis des Thomas-Evangeliums zur synoptischen Tradition und zu den koptischen Evangeliunübersetzungen. Zugleich ein Beitrag zur gnostischen Syntoptikerdeutung*: Beihefte zur Zeitschrift für die neutestamentliche Wissenschaft 29 (Berlin: Töpelmann, 1964)

Bernard Brandon Scott, "Picking Up the Pieces," *Forum* 1.1 (1985) 15–21

Philippe de Suarez, *L'Evangile selon Thomas. Traduction, Présentation et ommentaires* (Marsanne: Métanoïa, 1974)

R. McL. Wilson, *Studies in the Gospel of Thomas* (London:

Mowbray, 1960)

[ὡς] φραγέλλιον ἐκ σχοινίων (John 2:15)

Ernst Bammel contributed a study to a notable volume he edited, in honor of C. F. D. Moule, which offers a critical perspective upon the Johannine material, suitably rearranged, as offering data of primary interest within the reconstruction of the ministry of Jesus.[1] The argument is characteristically elegant: style, erudition, and fresh insight make up a powerful challenge to the bland presumption that the Synoptic Gospels hold the key to all we might know about Jesus. The present contribution is largely complementary of Dr Bammel's argument; although in one central matter, to which the title alludes, it takes a different course. In so doing, however, it only confirms my teacher's insight, that John -- correctly read -- provides data every bit as important for the understanding of Jesus as the Synoptics.

The consultation of John 11:47, in which the high priests and Pharisees gathered in council (συνήγαγον... συνέδριον), is read by Dr Bammel as a formal proceeding, which makes the hearing before Annas in chapter eighteen

---

[1] "*Ex illa itque die consilium fecerunt...,*" *The Trial of Jesus. Cambridge Studies in honour of C. F. D. Moule*: Studies in Biblical Theology (London: SCM, 1970) 11-40.

a purely tactical session.[2] The necessary conclusion of
such an approach is that the telescoping of events into a
"holy week" is more radical in the Synoptics than in
John, and specifically that the decision to execute Jesus
was taken considerably in advance of the dénouement
before Pilate. The question naturally arises: what sort
of place would the occupation of the Temple (in John,
2:13-17) have in such a scheme? Dr Bammel himself answers
that question, with reference to the textual history of
the pericope. He observes that Tatian (at least according
to certain witnesses), Celsus' Jew (as Origen would have
it, cf. contra Celsum 1.67), and Papyrus Egerton 2 place
the story later in Jesus' ministry, and most likely
associated it with with Tabernacles in chapter 7,[3] and

---

[2]Cf. Bammel, pp. 29, 30. It might be mentioned that such
a reading is supported by John 12:10, where ἐβουλεύσαντο
δὲ οἱ ἀρχιερεῖς ἵνα καὶ τὸν Λάζαρον ἀποκτείνωσιν employs
the same verb (with postpositive καί) in order to
identify the plot against Lazarus with the proceeding
against Jesus. In addition, the later passages makes it
apparent the high-priestly opposition was the crux of the
matter in the Johannine understanding: "the Pharisees" in
11:47 may be a stereotypical addition. On the other hand,
as we shall see, it may in fact be the case that the
construal of purity which Jesus acted upon (and acted
out) in his occupation of the Temple put him into
conflict with both priests and Pharisees.

[3]Cf. Bammel, pp. 17-20. It is the nature of the Egerton
Papyrus and contra Celsum that the precise location of
the story in narrative terms is inferential. In addition,

concludes that the occupation of the Temple and the resolution to execute Jesus occurred prior to the final Passover of his life.[4] Indeed, Dr Bammel sees an echo of that chronology in the disciples' awareness in John 11:7f., 16 that Judaea is for Jesus a place of mortal danger.

Dr Bammel argues for the earlier placement of the occupation against Dodd, the mediator of the claim of Johannine independence from the Synoptics to the world of modern, English-speaking scholarship. As has already been indicated, his opinion has both plausibility and, to a certain degree, some textual tradition on its side. But Dr Bammel was perhaps a little too quick to view some of the Johannine deviations from the Synoptic story of the

---

of course, certain traditions of the *Toledoth Jesu* would support the sort of solution Dr Bammel advocates.

[4]Raymond E. Brown, *The Gospel according to John* 1: Anchor Bible (London: Chapman, 1978) 118 suggests "that on his first journey to Jerusalem...Jesus uttered a prophetic warning about the destruction of the sanctuary....it seems likely that Jesus' action of cleansing the temple precincts took place in the last days of his life." Brown also agrees with Bammel that the story of Lazarus has been so introduced as to cause a displacement; cf. also Robert Tomson Fortna, *The Gospel of Signs. A Reconstruction of the Narrative Source Underlying the fourth Gospel*: SNTSMS 11 (Cambridge: Cambridge University Press, 1970) 145-147.

occupation as secondary; considered from a different angle, they may appear to be part and parcel of a distinctive, and more accurate, construal of what Jesus was doing in the Temple.

An approach such as Dr Bammel's reads τὰ τε πρόβατα καὶ τοὺς βόας in v. 15 as "an interpolation;" the thought is that the preceding πάντας can only have referred to the men who were trading in animals, as in Matthew 21:12 (cf. Mark 11:15; Luke 19:45).[5] The motivation of the addition is "an anti-cultic tendency,"[6] and there can be no doubt but that there is a programmatic portrayal in the fourth Gospel of antipathy between Jesus and the Temple, or at least between Jesus and the administration of the Temple. From the first chapter, "the Jews" send out a delegation of "priests and Levites" in order to interrogate John (1:19), and similar personnel become involved in proceedings against Jesus (7:32, 45; 11:47f.; 12:10; 18:13f., 19f., 35). Feasts become pre-eminent as settings of controversy between Jesus and "the Jews," usually in connection with his signs (cf. 5:1f.; 6:4f.; 7:2ff.; 10:22f.; 11:55f.; 12:1f.), and the Temple in particular is potentially a place of violence against him (7:14f.;

---

[5]Bammel, p. 16 nn. 23, 27 citing Wellhausen and E. Hirsch.

[6]Bammel, p. 16.

10:23f.; 11:56f.). All such passages might indeed be characterized as anti-cultic, but it is not at all evident that the mention of sheep and oxen in 2:15 is a matter of the same sort of polemic.

At just this point, we must return to the stylistic oddity of v. 15. As Barrett points out, if the mention of the animals were "a merely epexegetical phrase, we should have had πάντα, not πάντας. "[7] Barrett's conclusion was resisted, however, by Ernst Haenchen, who argued that τοὺς βόας has determined the gender of πᾶς.[8] Although Haenchen's objection is noteworthy, and although his suggestion concerning the purpose of the φραγέλλιον will be accepted below, his resistance to Barrett's analysis is not compelling. The difficulty of πάντας is not only its gender, but its position. Once, the personnel τοὺς πωλοῦντας βόας καὶ πρόβατα καὶ περιστερὰς καὶ τοὺς κερματιστὰς καθημένος are mentioned in v. 14, πάντας is naturally taken of them, with the reference to the animals as appositive. That was certainly the decision embodied in two notable renderings, the Authorized Version and Luther's Bible. But if the position of πάντας

---

[7]C. K. Barrett, *The Gospel according to St John* (London: SPCK, 1978) 198; cf. also Barnabas Lindars, *The Gospel of John*: New Century Bible (London: Oliphants, 1972) 138.

[8]In *Das Johannesevangelium. Ein Kommentar* (Tübingen: Mohr, 1980) 200.

appears to make its reference plain, why ever did the peculiar construction, employing τε and καί, follow? That construction, ἅπαξ λεγόμενον in the fourth Gospel, is what makes the phrase seem odd as in apposition, with the result that the sense of the passage has appeared problematic.

If the phrase concerning the animals in v. 15 appears to be an aporia, it is naturally associated with another, involving the merchants of pigeons in v. 16. The claim is sometimes made, and has been made as recently as in Brown's commentary,[9] that Jesus is portrayed as treating such vendors, as providers to the poor (cf. Leviticus 5:7), in a kindlier fashion than he treated the others, substituting words for a whip. Why Jesus should be cast in the role of defending those whose wealth is derived from the poor is not explained. (In any case the supposition is implicit that the different groups of vendors and animals are part of John's tradition, and not a theological illustration. To that extent, the observation is incisive.) With Westcott, it seems wise not to attribute any commercial preference to Jesus,[10] but that only excites our curiosity: why the concatenation of

---

[9] Brown, p. 115.

[10] Cf. Brooke Foss Westcott, *The Gospel according to St. John* (London: Murray, 1908).

sellers, changers, and animals, one mentioned after and interrupting another, in vv. 14-16?

Absent any substantial indication that the aporia is not to be explained in respect of the Johannine attitude toward the Temple generally, the possibility that sources are conflated in the pericope should obviously be considered.[11] The accessibility to John of an account of Jesus' occupation of the Temple along the lines of the passage in the Synoptics may be taken for granted. Mark's version (11:15b-16) and Matthew's (21:12) have Jesus cast out those selling *and* buying in the Temple, and overturning the tables of the money-changers and the seats of the pigeon-sellers. The additional statement in Mark (as compared to Matthew and Luke), that Jesus did not permit anyone to carry a vessel through the Temple is, as we shall see, a probably correct inference or datum, but its uniqueness excludes it from the commonly Synoptic material.[12] If we assume that such a story was

---

[11]Cf. Brown, p. 120, who concludes that "an independent tradition" is reflected here.

[12]Similarly, Luke's brevity is such as practically to make it seem superfluous, although it *might* be notable that, just as in John 2:14, Luke 19:45 refers only to sellers, not to buyers. That may be an indication of the circulation of the material incorporated in John at the time Luke was composed. The approach to the relationship among the Gospels which I have come to prefer is one in which Matthew, Mark, and Luke are taken to be independent

available at the time John 2:13-16 was written, the existence *and the order of mention* of the sellers, the money-changers with their tables, and the pigeon-vendors are entirely explicable. The deviation of the pericope from the commonly Synoptic version, and especially its additions, would then be taken as reflecting another version of the story. It would include reference only to sellers, not buyers, of sacrificial animals, specified as oxen and sheep, not only pigeons. It would also refer to a group called κερματισταί καθήμενοι, and to the incident of the φραγέλλιον ἐκ σχοινίων. Each of these elements should be considered seriously as historically relevant to what Jesus did in the Temple.

The claim of historicity just made is, of course, consonant with Dr Bammel's evaluation of much that is contained in the fourth Gospel.[13] In addition, the claim is only sustainable by virtue of recourse to a principle of analysis he has developed considerably. He has resisted the fallacy of portraying Judaism as a

---

documentations of apostolic catechesis, along with a collection of Jesus' mishnah (which we have come to call "Q"), and John is taken as a deliberate, meditative supplement to such catechesis. Cf. *Profiles of a Rabbi. Synoptic Opportunities in Reading about Jesus*: Brown Judaic Studies (Atlanta: Scholars, 1989).

[13]Bammel, p. 35.

"background" of the Gospels, as if Judaic sources were merely a frame around a portrait which in fact defined its own points of reference, and has spoken instead of the "atmosphere" of the Gospel as illuminated by those sources.[14] Each of the elements specified as possibly belonging to a second source of John is better appreciated, and seen as more vividly historical, within its Judaic environment. Indeed, the passage illustrates the general proposition that the fourth Gospel breathes the atmosphere of early Judaism so deeply, it cannot live outside that environment.

Why should sellers be referred to alone? Buyers of any commodity are, after all, part of the merchandising a market is designed to serve. For that reason, the mention of both groups in Mark (11:15) and Matthew (21:12) is natural, and the build-up to the charge that the merchants have made God's house a "den of thieves" (Mark 11:17; Mark 21:13) follows more easily. But why should the buyers be omitted in John, given its anti-cultic tendency? Any criticism of cultic commercialism would obviously be more pointed if, as in the Synoptics, buyers could be mentioned, but the second source of John knew

---

[14]Bammel, p. 36. Of course, he is speaking at this point of the *Toledoth Jesu*, a body of material he has long specialized in, but the perspective is applicable more generally.

better than to put them there, and even omitted to
mention Jesus' citation of Jeremiah 7:11; both
exclusions, for all that they would have been useful
within the Johannine apologetic, are honored in the
received text of the fourth Gospel. The normal place of
trade in sacrificial animals was not the Temple at all,
but Hanuth on the Mount of Olives.[15] The very innovation
of selling animals in the Temple was potentially
scandalous, implying -- as one might have thought -- a
reversal of the prophecy in Zechariah 14:21c, and seems
specifically to have scandalized Jesus.[16]

David Flusser comes to the reasonable conclusion that the
setting up of vendors at the Temple was unusual, and that
the practice did not last.[17] Joachim Jeremias is able to
show that "in the Court of the Gentiles, in spite of the
sanctity of the Temple area, there could have been a
flourishing trade in animals for sacrifice."[18] But

---

[15]Cf. Victor Eppstein, "The historicity of the Gospel
account of the Cleansing of the Temple," *Zeitschrift für
die neutestamentliche Wissenschaft* 55 (1964), 42-58, 48.

[16]Cf. Richard H. Hiers, "Purification of the Temple:
Preparation for the Kingdom of God," *Journal of Biblical
Literature* 90 (1971) 82-90, 83.

[17]Cf. David Flusser (tr. Ronald Walls), *Jesus* (New York:
Herder and Herder, 1969) 108-109.

[18]Jeremias (tr. F. H. and C. H. Cave), *Jerusalem in*

Jeremias is unable to produce a single passage from early Judaic or rabbinic literature which actually states that there was such a trade in so many words. Normal traffic, as Jeremias himself shows was focused on the Mount of Olives,[19] although other sites in Jerusalem were also involved. His best piece of supporting evidence for his supposition of trade in the Temple,[20] the importation of cattle by Baba b. Buta (cf. Yerushalmi Betzah 2:4), does not illustrate ordinary, commercial activity, but rabbinic interest in *how* animals were to be sacrificed, in that Baba b. Buta is said to have brought the cattle into the Temple so as to encourage the offering of animals in accordance with the teaching he supported.[21]

---

the *Time of Jesus* (London: SCM, 1969) 49.

[19] Jeremias, *Jerusalem*, 48.

[20] Jeremias, *Jerusalem*, 49.

[21] The relevant passages read as follows, as given in H. L. Strack, P. Billerbeck, *Kommentar zum Neuen Testament aus Talmud und Midrasch* 1 (München: Beck, 1922) 851–852; the first is the mishnaic discussion at issue, the second the Gemara:

> Die Schule Schammais sagte: Man darf Friedenopfer (an einem Feiertage) darbringen, aber nicht die Hände auf sie austemmen; dagegen darf man (der einzelne) keine Ganzopfer (an einem Feiertage) darbringen; die Schule Hillels sagte: Man darf Friedensofper u. Ganzopfer darbringen u. die Hände auf sie austemmen.
>
> Es war daselbst Baba b. Buṭa (Zeitgenosse Herodes des Grossen) von den Schülern der Schule Schammais:

Given that the vending of animals was itself problematic, the notion that they should be available in the Temple for purchase elsewhere or resale was, in all likelihood, unthinkable.

Victor Eppstein has suggested that the presence of vendors in the Temple should be associated with a specific innovation of Caiaphas, which Talmud places forty years prior to the destruction of the Temple (cf. Aboda Zara 8b; Shabbath 15a; Sanhedrin 41a). The sources refer to the exile of the Sanhedrin from the Chamber of Hewn Stone in the Temple to Hanuth: Eppstein suggests

---

der wusste, dass die Halakha war wie die Meinung der Schule Hillels. Einmal betrat er den Vorhof u. fand ihn verödet (weil niemand mehr auf Grund der schammaitischen Lehrmeinung an einem Feiertag ein Opfer darbrachte). Da Sprach er: Mögen veröden die Häuser derer, die das Haus unseres Gottes verödet haben! Was tat er? Er liess 3000 Stück Kleinvieh vom Kleinvieh Qedars kommen u. untersuchte sie betreffs (etwaigen) Leibesfehler u. stellte sie auf dem Tempelberg auf. Er sprach zu den Israeliten: Höret mich, meine Brüder, Haus Israel: wer will, bringe Ganzopfer, bringe sie u. stemme seine Hände auf...

Quite evidently, we are not dealing here, as Jeremias would have it, with a reference to a commercial arrangement. Indeed, the present passage is rather illuminating from another point of view: Jesus was also concerned to foment a certain understanding of sacrifice. He promulgated his teaching by excluding animals, where Baba b. Buṭa had provided them; such, in any case, is the argument of the present contribution.

that, in turn, the merchants at Hanuth were permitted to sell within the precincts of the Temple.[22] The presence of money-changers there can have surprised no one,[23] and Eppstein attempts to explain the overturning of their tables as an inadvertent result of the mêlée over the vendors.[24] That anything accidental or inadvertent could have taken place with furniture as massive as was used in the Temple seems implausible (cf. Sheqalim 2:1; 6:5); more probably, the quotation from Jeremiah 7:11 (the saying of Jesus in the Synoptic version, cf. Matthew 21:13; Mark 11:17; Luke 19:46) was applied to the money-changers in the course of the increasingly

---

[22]Eppstein, pp. 42–55.

[23]As the mishnaic tractate Sheqalim 1:1, 3 makes abundantly clear, the changers were particularly prominent during of Adar (the month immediately prior to Nisan), when the half-sheqel was collected both in Jerusalem and the provinces. But Bekhoroth 8:7 specifies that Tyrean currency is to be used for the sacrifices of Numbers 18:16; Exodus 21:32; Deuteronomy 22:29; Exodus 22:16, 17 and Deuteronomy 22:19. Such payment was so standard that one recent handbook can claim that "all sacred dues" were payable in Tyrean coinage (E. Schürer [M. Black, F. Millar, G. Vermes], *The History of the Jewish People in the Age of Jesus Christ [175 B.C. - A. D. 135]* II [Edinburgh: Clark, 1979] 272), although at least one passage in the literature (Mark 12:41–44; Luke 21:1–4) renders that generalization suspect. The surcharge involved in the exchange of currency for cultic purposes was fixed and its application limited, cf. Sheqalim 1:6, 7.

[24]Eppstein, p. 57.

anti-cultic transmission of the story.[25]

Of course, the specific reference to oxen and sheep does play into the hands of the anti-cultic tendency of the early Church, but there is no sense in which they need to be regarded as an invention of that tendency. Indeed, *any* major feast required the sacrifice of both oxen and sheep (cf. Numbers 28:11-29:38). Of course, the especially high number of animals prescribed in Torah for Sukkoth (Numbers 29:12-38) would make that time of year as striking for trade in the Temple as Passover, and the number of sheep would not entirely dwarf the number of oxen, as at Passover. In addition to Dr Bammel's argument for putting Jesus' occupation at Sukkoth, not Passover, an argument based upon the fourth Gospel, it might also be mentioned that Jesus' entry into Jerusalem, with its attendant singing of the Hallel, the cries of Hosanna, festal boughs, and its reference to the Mount of Olives, is more immediately reminiscent of Sukkoth than of

---

[25]An additional factor, which might have influenced the shape of the Synoptic version, is that Jesus did protest the requirement that he pay the half sheqel as a tax. Cf. Chilton, "A Coin of Three Realms (Matthew 17:24-27)," *The Bible in Three Dimensions. Essays in celebration of forty years of Biblical Studies in the University of Sheffield*: Journal For the Study of the Old Testament 87 (Sheffield: JSOT, 1990) 269-82.

Passover.[26]

The scandal involved in trading on the sacred mount obviously had nothing whatever to do with the presence of animals. By definition, they were appropriate victims, pure and unblemished. If they were not, they could not have been sold, much less brought into the cultic area of slaughter, north of the altar.[27] Indeed, there would have been a certain advantage to the buyer and to the cult in Caiaphas' innovation: any damage an animal might suffer between Hanuth and the Temple, under the prevalent arrangement during the first century, would be at the buyers' cost, and -- if undetected or overlooked -- would result in sacrificial invalidity.[28] The scandal of the arrangement was not the animals, but the money being paid for them in the precincts of the Temple. For that reason, the uniquely Johannine, "Do not make my father's house a

---

[26]Cf. Chilton, "The Transfiguration: Dominical Assurance and Apostolic Vision," *New Testament Studies* 27 (1979) 115-124; T. W. Manson, "The Cleansing of the Temple," *Bulletin of the John Rylands Library* 33 (1951) 271-282; C. W. F. Smith, "No Time for Figs," *Journal of Biblical Literature* 79 (1960) 315-327; Smith, "Tabernacles in the Fourth Gospel and Mark," *New Testament Studies* 9 (1963) 130-146; W. L. Lane, *The Gospel according to Mark*: the New London Commentary on the New Testament (London: Marshall, Morgan & Scott, 1974) 390, 391.

[27]Cf. Zebaḥim 5:1-5, and contrast 5:6-8.

[28]Cf. Keritoth 6:8; Sheqalim 4:9; Gittin 56a.

house of trade" (2:16b), is precisely to the point. At first sight, however, the center of the controversy may seem to be absent from the story: where are the proceeds of the trade in animals? John's second source may provide reference to the money, as well as the animals, in the κερματισταί καθήμενοι of v. 14. Those figures have naturally been associated with the money-changers of v. 15, and the Synoptics, but there are problems with that identification. Κερματιστής is rare in documents contemporaneous with the New Testament,[29] and it appears only here within the New Testament, along with κέρμα, from which it derives. Translators generally suppose that the κερματισταί are synonymous with the κολλυβισταί of v. 15.[30] From the perspective of the received form of John's Gospel, they are undoubtedly correct: it is precisely the κέρμα of the κολλυβιστῶν which is dumped over by Jesus. But it is just what John intends to say which does not make perfect sense. The coins collected for exchange into

---

[29]Cf. J. H. Moulton and G. Milligan, *The Vocabulary of the Greek Testament Illustrated from the Papyri and other Non-literary Sources* (London: Hodder and Stoughton, 1930) 342; Barrett, p. 197.

[30]Cf. Brown, p. 115. With characteristic care, however, M.-J. Lagrange showed how inferentially and narrowly based that supposition is, cf. *Evangile selon Saint Jean*: Etudes Bibliques (Paris: Gabalda, 1925) 65. Lagrange also allows that the κολλυβιστοί have been provided by the Synoptic tradition (p. 66).

a half sheqel were not such as could easily be described as κέρμα; the collection was rather of the δίδραχμον, as at Matthew 17:24, and the amount was commonly paid for two, with the στατήρ (cf. Matthew 17:27). The στατήρ was a silver coin; the δίδραχμον was worth two Attic drachmae, and there were periods in which a δραχμή alone could buy a sheep.[31] Clearly, by the period of the Gospels, δραχμαί were not regarded as extraordinarily valuable; ten would not be entirely out of place in a widow's house (cf. Luke 15:8, 9).[32] The coins involved in the collection of the half-sheqel, however, were clearly not κέρμα, when it is borne in mind that sheqel was the equivalent of four δραχμαί or denarii.[33] Of course, were one paying for sacrificial animals, or changing money for

---

[31]Cf. W. Bauer (tr. W. F. Arndt and F. W. Gingrich, augmented by Gingrich and F. W. Danker), *A Greek-English Lexicon of the New Testament and Other Early Christian Literature* (Chicago: University of Chicago Press, 1979) 192, 206, 764

[32]A more likely possession would be a two λέπτα or a κοδράντης (cf. Mark 12:42; Luke 21:2). Within the period of our concern, a quadrans was worth 32 silver denarii, and 64 denarii, according to C. H. V. Sutherland, *Coinage in Imperial Roman Policy, 31 B. C. - A. D. 68* (London: Methuen, 1951) 199. In relation to the sheqel, such coins would indeed be κέρμα.

[33]The value of the sheqel is given by Josephus, *Antiquities* 3.8.2 @ 195. Sheqalim 2:1 refers to the changing of coins into the even larger denomination, the daric, for the purposes of transport.

that purpose, small change would be generated.[34] The
appearance emerges, then, that in the received text of
John, the Synoptic story of the money-changers has been
cross-bred with the story of the second source, in which
the cashiers of the animal-vendors had their small change
poured off their tables, and the tables themselves were
overturned.

The φραγέλλιον ἐκ σχοινίων, finally, clearly establishes
the target of Jesus' action in John's second source. Just
that point was recognized by Westcott, who recognized the
σχοινία as ropes used to tether the oxen and sheep (but
not, obviously, the pigeons).[35] Staffs and objects not

---

[34]In Sheqalim 5:3-5 a scheme is laid out, in which money
for sacrifice was paid in the Temple in exchange for a
seal. The seal was then good for drink offering. It may
be that Caiaphas' innovation involved such an
arrangement. In any case, money found near cattle-dealers
(wherever located) could be deemed to be second tithe
(Sheqalim 7:2). Clearly, there was a felt affinity
between money paid for sacrifice and the sacred currency.

[35]Westcott, 91. Barrett's suggestion that the *flagellium*
directly refers to "a whip for driving cattle," although
theoretically possible, is not plausible here in that
(a) it is made ἐκ σχοινίων, and (b) even P[66,73] -- among
other witnesses -- describe the resulting object as ὡς
φραγέλλιον, not directly *as* a *flagellium*. Quite
evidently, the text is not simply referring to a common
object. Amongst more recent commentators, Ernst Haenchen
may be mentioned as supporting Westcott's interpretation.
Indeed, Haenchen states the point far more plainly (p.

suited to the practice of sacrifice were forbidden in the Temple,[36] but Jesus is here portrayed as using the very objects which would need to be there in order to control the animals, so as to expel them and their vendors.[37] As Brown rightly observes, in v. 19 "Jesus is insisting that they (sc. the merchants) are destroying the Temple," and Jesus' act amounts to an attempt to prevent that destruction.[38] Far from being an attempt to prophesy the ruin of the Temple,[39] Jesus' aim was purification, along

---

200), "Da man Tiere nicht mit den blossen Händen treiben kann, macht sich Jesus «eine Art Geissel» (lies mit P66 und P75 ὡς φραγέλλιον) aus Stricken, mit denen die Tiere angebunden gewesen waren."

[36]Cf. Berakhoth 9:5. It is notable that the same mishnah proscribes entry with a money-belt.

[37]Cf. Lagrange, pp. 65, 66. His comment is not the less lucid for its acerbity, "Les hommes comprennent et s'enfuient les premiers, mais Jésus expulse aussi (en plus des synoptiques) les brebis et les boeufs plus lents à s'ébranler, ce que Loisy, attentif à un certain idéal de style et indifférent à la réalité, regarde comme surajouté."

[38]Brown, p. 122. Brown sees v. 19 as "originally an eschatological proclamation," because he has been influenced in his reading by the markedly different Synoptic versions of the saying. But within John's second source, the issues are purity and decadence, not eschatology. For the use of the imperative, cf. Lagrange, p. 94, and his citation of Isaiah 37:30; Matthew 23:32; John 13:27, and Bultmann, p. 125 n. 4, and his citation of Amos 4:4; Isaiah 8:9; Jeremiah 7:21.

[39]So, recently, E. P. Sanders, *Jesus and Judaism* (London:

the lines of stopping illicit trade (Cf. Zechariah 14:21b[40]). His act did not merely illustrate a reality, it accomplished it:[41] he and his followers occupied the

SCM, 1985) 75. Sanders's article has found a particularly lucid rejoinder in a contribution from Craig A. Evans, "Jesus' Action in the Temple and Evidence of Corruption in the First-Century Temple," *Society of Biblical Literature 1989 Seminar Papers* (ed. D. Lull; Atlanta: Scholars, 1989) 522-539. The especial strength of Evans's work is that it points out the paucity of evidence for the messianic scheme of the destruction and rebuilding of the Temple which Sanders takes as axiomatic. I am grateful to Prof. Evans for sending me a copy of the manuscript of the article prior to its publication. Cf. also Evans, "Jesus' Action in the Temple: Cleansing or Portent of Destruction?" *Catholic Biblical Quarterly* 51 (1989) 237-270. PP. 265-267 provide a fine, critical appraisal of Eppstein's contribution.

[40]Cf. Brown, p. 119.

[41]Cf. C. H. Dodd, *The Interpretation of the Fourth Gospel* (Cambridge: Cambridge University Press, 1953) 301, "...Jesus is not promising a significant event yet to come, but inviting his questioners to see in the actual occurrence of the Cleansing of the Temple the σημεῖον they desire." Dodd unfortunately goes on to give Jesus' act a quasi-Platonic twist, "The purging of the temple -- that is, the expulsion of the sacrificial animals from its courts -- signifies the destruction and replacement of the system of religious observance of which the temple was the centre: a new 'temple' for an old one" (cf. Lindars, p. 137). Historically speaking, it is preferable not to see an act in respect of purity as metaphorical of anything else, be it eschatology (as in Sanders) or religious observance (as in Dodd): systemically, purity obviously has a value all its own in early Judaism.

Temple in order to stop the sale of animals there, as well as the transit of vessels (Mark 11:16, cf. Zechariah 14:21a).[42] What Jesus was doing in the Temple was preventing the sacrifice of animals whose trade made them ritually impure in his eyes, and the focus of his action is marked by the φραγέλλιον ἐκ σχοινίων.

Of course, it is one thing to discover the focus of Jesus' action, and quite another to hone the lenses through which it should be viewed. But at least, by knowing the point of focus, we have some idea of the appropriate orientation of our perspective. The φραγέλλιον ἐκ σχοινίων is an object which ill comports with Sanders's theory, that Jesus wished to prophesy the destruction of the Temple. Even more emphatically, it rules out the easy Platonism of making Jesus' object generally to the religious system of sacrifice, as in Dodd's reading.[43] *Faute de mieux*, it might seem wise to

---

[42]The vessels, it should be observed, might indeed have been used to carry the blood of slaughtered animals, cf. (for example) Zebaḥim 5. Cf. Chilton, *A Galilean Rabbi and His Bible: Jesus' Own Interpretation of Isaiah* (London: SPCK, 1984) 17, 18.

[43]Cf. H. Stegemann, "Some Aspects of Eschatology in Texts from the Qumran Community and in the Teaching of Jesus," *Biblical Archaeology Today: Proceedings of the International Congress of Biblical Archaeology. Jerusalem, April 1984* (ed. A. Biran; Jerusalem: Israel Exploration Society, 1985) 408–426.

return to the theory of the Synoptic Gospels, and portray
Jesus as objecting to priestly corruption, as in Evans's
suggestion. But John -- or rather, the second source of
John -- suggests we have a tighter focus to achieve, a
focus not on commercialism as a whole, but on the
specifics of trading for sacrifical animals in the
precincts of the Temple. To imagine him as attacking
commercialism is appealing,[44] as the development of the
Synoptic tradition would indicate, but such a
characterization of Jesus is simply too general to fit
the particular nature of his activity.

Scholarship has persistently provided us with reading
glasses, when our actual problem is that we suffer
astigmatism. Studies seek to specify the alleged occasion
upon which Jesus is said to have attacked the very notion
of sacrifice, or its administration in the Temple, or the
building where it took place. The result is that we
comfortably read Jesus' entire ministry as an anti-cultic
enterprise, conveniently think of him in prophetic,
didactic, and/or messianic terms, and subsume any
appearance of interest in sacrifice *per se* within some
combination of those categories. How else can Jesus be
conceived of in an age in which "sacrifice" is only

---

[44]Cf. *Thomas l.* 64 (end).

positively meaningful as a metaphor, within the realm, say, of war, sport, or parenthood? That very question is a symptom that our vision is, historically speaking, astigmatic. The tradition of Jesus' theology, as reflected in all four Gospels, is simply too redolent of concern for the institutions of sacrifice to be consistent with the implicitly or explicitly anti-cultic portraits of him which are current.

Matthew represents Jesus as insisting that sacrifice should be offered -- in the Temple -- after one is reconciled with one's neighbor (Matthew 5:23, 24), as as commissioning his followers with an authority to forgive (16:19;[45] 18:18). The cleansing of lepers, an emphatically priestly function, is a persistent theme within the Synoptics at various levels (cf. Matthew 8:1-4/Mark 1:40-45/Luke 5:12-16, [cf. Matthew 10:8]; Matthew 11:5/Luke 7:22; Luke 17:14, 17), and purity is also presented as a global issue (Matthew 15:1-20/Mark 7:1-23; Luke 11:37-44; Matthew 23:23-27). The practical matter of how money is to be raised for the Temple and sacrifice is

---

[45]The priestly aspects of this saying, which become apparent under comparison with Targum Isaiah 22:22, are investigated in Chilton, "Shebna, Eliakim, and the Promise to Peter," *Targumic Approaches to the Gospels. Essays in the Mutual Definition of Judaism and Christianity*: Studies in Judaism (Lanham: University Press of America) 63-80.

also reflected as a concern of Jesus in the Synoptics (Matthew 17:24-27; Mark 12:41-44/Luke 21:1-4; Matthew 23:23/Luke 11:42). Throughout, the essential stance of Matthew 23:16-22, which portrays the Temple as the source of santification, rather than the gifts within it, is clearly maintained. Jesus is consistently portrayed in the Synoptic Gospels as construing purity in terms of what the worshipper willingly does in respect of God's presence in the Temple, rather than as characteristic of or inherent within objects. That stance is so closely associated with Jesus, it is also adduced in the controversy concerning the sabbath (Matthew 12:1-8/Mark 2:23-28/Luke 6:1-5).

The Synoptic portrayal has obviously been conditioned by the thinking of early Christianity, but it is not within our present purpose to discuss the extent to which that is the case. Even absent from such discussion, the data must make it seem odd in the extreme to suppose that Jesus was not characteristically concerned with what and who was fit for sacrifice. Such a supposition is the astigmatism we need to correct. The geographical references within the narrative of Jesus' passion in all four Gospels make it highly probable that Jesus' concern for the traffic in the Temple was not an incidental or symbolic flash in the pan, but part of a programmatic intention to assure the fitness of sacrifice. He stays in Bethany,[46] on the east side of the Mount of Olives, and is therefore in a position to know of the arrangements for selling sacrifical animals. Indeed, the Mount of Olives itself features prominently, as the starting point of the triumphal entry,[47] as the location of his discourse against the Temple,[48] and as the place of his arrest.[49] Jesus takes up a position in all four Gospels which is cognate with his occupation of the Temple: he dwells where fitting sacrifices may be acquired. That is where the authorities who resented his incursion tracked him down. His trail had been marked by a πραγέλλιον ἐκ σχοινίωαν.

---

[46]Cf. Matthew 21:17 (and the reference to nearby Bethpage in v. 1); 26:6; Mark 11:1, 11, 12; 14:3; Luke 19:29 (and, after the resurrection, 24:50); John 11:1, 18; 12:1.

[47]Matthew 21:1; Mark 11:1; Luke 19:29.

[48]Matthew 24:3; Mark 13:3, cf. Luke 21:37.

[49]Matthew 26:30; Mark 14:26; Luke 22:39. Of course, reference to Gethsemane (Matthew 26:36; Mark 14:32) and to the Johannine garden (18:1) should be associated with the same complex of material.

Typologies of Memra and the fourth Gospel

The remarks of G. F. Moore in respect of the term *memra* in the Targumim have been taken as of virtually canonical status in recent discussion; scholars have generally accepted that "nowhere in the Targums is *memra* a 'being' of any kind or in any sense," and that the term is "purely a phenomenon of translation, not a figment of speculation."[1] But it is frequently overlooked that Moore did not close his inquiry with those observations. *Memra* does indeed render particular passages, conveying such senses as "utterance," "command," or "word." But why is

---

[1]G. F. Moore, *Judaism in the First Centuries of the Christian Era. The Age of the Tannaim* I (Cambridge: Harvard University Press, 1927) 419; cf. "Intermediaries in Jewish Theology," *Harvard Theological Review* 15 (1922) 41-85, esp. 53, 54. Moore's approach is accepted in W. E. Aufrecht, *Surrogates for the Divine Name in the Palestinian Targums to Exodus* (Toronto: Ph. D., 1979) and Andrew Chester, *Divine Revelation and Divine Titles in the Pentateuchal Targumim*: Texte und Studien zum Antiken Judentum (Tübingen: Mohr, 1986). Chester refutes the arguments of Domingo Muñoz Leon, *Dios-Palabra. Memra en los Targumim del Pentateuco*: Insitución San Jerónimo 4 (Granada: Santa Rita-Monachil, 1974) and C. T. R. Hayward, *Divine Name and Presence: The Memra*: Oxford Centre for Postgraduate Hebrew Studies (Totowa: Allanheld, Osmun and Co., 1981); cf. the description in Chilton, "Recent and Prospective Discussion of *Memra*," *From Ancient Israel to Modern Judaism. Intellect in Quest of Understanding. Essays in Honor of Marvin Fox* II: Brown Judaic Studies 173 (eds J. Neusner, E. S. Frerichs, N. M. Sarna; Atlanta: Scholars, 1989) 119-137.

it used in some places, and not in others (where, for example פתגמא might appear, instead of מימרא, or no like usage is employed)? And with what policy or purpose is it introduced into certain passages, apparently without immediate reference to the Hebrew text which is rendered? Those who stop reading Moore when he speaks of memra as a phenomenon of translation, as if it were merely a matter of representing a given in the texts rendered, miss the most productive aspect of his analysis.[2]

Moore in fact recognized that a definable spectrum of usages characterizes the distribution of memra in the Targumim, and that there are evident patterns of meaning within that spectrum. He identified types of usage which include the notions of command,[3] the obedience of command,[4] the acceptance of a command,[5] divine speaking,[6]

---

[2] That is precisely the difficulty in Chester's work (op. cit., pp. 308, 309, 313. He says that memra is "translational," and that it "portrays one main mode of God's activity," apparently without recognizing that in the first case he speaks of a linguistic phenomenon, and in the second of a theologoumenon (cf. Chilton, op. cit., pp. 122, 123).

[3] Moore, "Intermediaries," p. 47.

[4] op. cit., pp. 47, 48.

[5] op. cit., p. 48.

[6] op. cit., pp. 48, 49.

divine meeting with others,[7] oracles,[8] oaths made by God,[9] his fighting for Israel,[10] his protection,[11] and his establishing covenant.[12] Moore's categories were developed on the basis of his reading of Onqelos; in a work published in 1982, the present writer offered a typology of *memra* in the Targum of Isaiah, based upon Moore's approach, and applied it to new material.[13] In that study, however, the refinement was introduced that the order of categories was determined by the order of appearance of the first instance of each category. The types present *memra* as an occasion for rebellion,[14] an agent of punishment,[15] a demand for obedience,[16] an edict,[17] a

---

[7]*op. cit.*, p. 49.

[8]*op. cit.*, pp. 49, 50.

[9]*op. cit.*, p. 50.

[10]*op. cit.*, pp. 50, 51.

[11]*op. cit.*, pp. 51.

[12]*op. cit.*, p. 51.

[13]*The Glory of Israel. The Theology and Provenience of the Isaiah Targum*: Journal for the Study of the Old Testament Supplement Series 23 (Sheffield: JSOT, 1982) 56-69.

[14]*op. cit.*, pp. 57, 58.

[15]*op. cit.*, pp. 58-60.

[16]*op. cit.*, p. 60.

[17]*op. cit.*, p. 61.

voice,[18] divine protection,[19] an eternal witness,[20] and an intermediary of prayer.[21] The overlap with Moore's categories is evident, but not complete. His typology, on the basis of Onqelos, included categories and a precedence of categories not found in Jonathan's Isaiah, and vice versa. The possibility emerges that the Targum of Isaiah is distinctive in its usage of *memra*, precisely by virtue of its focus upon Israel's disobedience, and God's demand for a reversal on the basis of his election of his people. In other words, literary variation needs to be built into our characterization of the usage of *memra*, rather than obscured by a general reference to translational technique.

A comparative investigation of the usage was recently undertaken, by typing occurrences in Neophyti I and Pseudo-Jonathan, two of the so-called Palestinian Targums

---

[18] *op. cit.*, pp. 61, 62.

[19] *op. cit.*, pp. 62, 63.

[20] *op. cit.*, p. 63.

[21] *op. cit.*, pp. 63, 64 (cf. n. 31, pp. 143, 144). It must be understood that I cited the observation of V. Hamp, that use of the term "intermediary" need not imply a hypostatic entity, cf. *Der Begriff "Wort" in den aramäischen Bibelübersetzungen. Ein exegetischer Beitrag zur Hypostasen-Frage und zur Geschichte der Logos Spekulation* (München: Filser, 1938) 204.

to the Pentateuch.[22] Because the order of appearance of the first instance of each category is not a practical criterion for sequencing types of usage when more than one document is involved, it was determined to order the types according to the *frequency* of their occurrence. What is immediately striking is how the types vary from book to book within each Targum. In Neophyti's Genesis, *memra* appears as (1) speaking, (2) involved in worship, (3) influencing people and events, (4) involved in covenant, and (5) creating. In Exodus, on the other hand, Neophyti's *memra* is presented as (1) being with others, (2) influencing, (3) deliberating, (4) involved in worship, and (5) demanding obedience. The shift in emphasis may not be explained on the basis of the contents of Genesis and Exodus alone, because Pseudo-Jonathan gives us a different take on *memra* in each case. *Memra* is (1) aiding, (2) deliberating, (3) involved in covenant, and (4) influencing in Pseudo-Jonathan's Genesis, but (1) acting, (2) demanding obedience, (3) being with others, (4) involved in worship and (5) influencing in Pseudo-Jonathan's Exodus.

Indeed, a comparison of Neophyti and Pseudo-Jonathan can be developed, by identifying distinctive emphases within

---

[22]Cf. "Recent and Prospective Discussion of *Memra*," pp. 125ff. Full citations are provided in the article, and are omitted here for reasons of space and clarity.

each as we move from book to book. Such a procedure has Neophyti's *memra* speaking, involved in worship, and creating in Genesis, while deliberating in Exodus. Meanwhile, Pseudo-Jonathan's *memra* is aiding and deliberating in Genesis, and acting in Exodus. By comparing what is distinctive in each book of each Targum, a clear pattern emerges.

Neophyti portrays the *memra* as involved in worship in Genesis, and it emerges as the distinctive emphasis in Leviticus; Neophyti's Numbers has the *memra* deliberating, as in Exodus, while in Neophyti's Deuteronomy, the *memra* is essentially a voice. Neophyti's pattern of distinctive usage is therefore chiastic, with vocal associations predominating in Genesis and Deuteronomy, deliberation the emphasis in Exodus and Numbers, and Leviticus presenting an involvement with worship. Pseudo-Jonathan, on the other hand, moves from the emphasis upon the *memra* as deliberating in Genesis, to its acting in Exodus, and thence to giving the law (Leviticus), demanding obedience (Numbers), and occasioning revolt (Deuteronomy). The pattern of distinctive usages, then, appears more sequential -- and even consequential -- in Pseudo-Jonathan, as compared to Neophyti.

Of course, it must be recollected what we are comparing in the cases to hand. There is no question of a deliberate patterning of the usage of *memra*: neither Neophyti nor Pseudo-Jonathan appears to have been composed with a view to developing consciously distinctive linguistic profiles. But the fact that the profiles are distinctive invites the consideration that *memra* should not be considered as a word of fixed meaning, whose use may be explained simply on the basis of the exigencies of translation. That מימרא is to be related to the verb אמר, the ordinary verb of speaking, and assumes a divine subject as the origin of the address, is indeed a necessary occasion of such usages, but the patterns of types manifest within Neophyti and Pseudo-Jonathan suggest that the association is not the sufficient condition of the usages. Rather, the immediate inference from the patterns of distinctive usage observed is that God is portrayed as speaking in different ways and at different points within Neophyti and Pseudo-Jonathan. In other words, *memra* is not simply a metonym for God, or even for God understood as speaking, but is the term which conveys the sense of God's distinctively vocal, deliberative and worshiped aspects in Neophyti, and his distinctively active, demanding, and resisted aspects in Pseudo-Jonathan.

In general terms, one may infer that *memra* is the Targumic reference to God's activity of commanding. Within that activity, a meturgeman might think of commanding as what is ordered, as the response to the order, or as what is behind the order. There are a range of emphases, both interior to the act of commanding, informing the decision of command, and exterior to the act, devolving from it, which *memra* might theoretically convey. There is no warrant for saying that there is such a thing as a *concept* of God's *memra*, certainly not as personal being or hypostasis, nor even that there is a systematic idea that is consistent from Targum to Targum. What links the Targumim, in their distinct usages of *memra*, is not a theological thought, but a theological manner of speaking of God in terms of divine commanding. *Memra* is not invoked haphazardly when some verb of speaking happens to be used of God in the Hebrew text which is rendered. The Targums to hand suggest that the usage of the term reflects the manner in which given meturgemanin conceive of God's intention in the command, or the human response to what is effected (or affected) by the command.

Within the history of each Targum's development, the typologies of usage vary, and the principal variables at issue are (1) the notion of how God commands (and what response his command elicits), and (2) the complex of ideas triggered by a given book and passage. *Memra* might therefore be understood as covering the conceptual field[23] of divine speaking, inclusive of the deliberation behind, and the results of, that speaking. The term performs taxonomically, invoking the possibility that a range of terms within the appropriate lexical field might be employed.

Within the study of the fourth Gospel, commentators in recent years have largely dismissed the hypothesis that *memra* might be a precedent for the usage of *logos*.[24] That dismissal, however, is produced by a misconception of both terms. First, it is assumed by students of the New Testament that the issue turns on whether *memra* refers to a hypostasis or is purely translational. Such an

---

[23]Cf. Georges Mounin, *Les problèmes théoretiques de la traduction* (Paris: Gallimard, 1963) 71–112.

[24]Cf. C. K. Barrett, *The Gospel according to St. John* (Philadelphia: Westminster, 1978) 153, who refers to *memra* as "a blind alley in the study of the biblical background of John's logos doctrine." A more judicious appraisal is offered by Raymond E. Brown in *The Gospel according to John (1-xii)*: The Anchor Bible (Garden City: Doubleday, 1966) 524, who grants that the meaning of *memra* may have influenced the fourth Gospel. Nonetheless, he holds that the "personification of the Word would, of course, be part of the Christian theological innovation;" cf. the remarks which follow immediately. The principal counter-argument has been made by Martin McNamara in *Targum and Testament. Aramaic Paraphrases of the Hebrew bible: a Light on the New Testament* (Grand Rapids: Eerdmans, 1972) 101-104.

understanding did indeed characterize discussion in the time of Moore, when his argument for the latter characterization prevailed, but it takes no account of the impact of more recent work, much of it based on more adequate linguistic and exegetical categories. Second, most modern commentators on John, writing from the perspective of Christian tradition (and, more often than not, from the perspective of their own Christian faith) assume that *logos* in John also refers to a hypostasis, namely to Jesus conceived of as personally existent prior to his incarnation.[25] The present argument holds that the Targumic theologoumenon of the *memra* as God's activity of commanding has influenced the sense of *logos* in the fourth Gospel, and that logos in that Gospel is not fundamentally a christological term, as contemporary discussion has assumed.

In order to develop the argument, references to *logos* in the body of the Gospel will first be considered, in that

---

[25]A significant, perhaps disproportionate, influence upon commentators has been exerted by Kittel's remark in the *theologisches Wörterbuch* that "all attempts to explain the λόγος statements of Jn. 1 in terms of the Targumic מימרא have failed, since this is never a personal hypostasis, but only a substitute for the tetragrammaton" (G. Kittel, "λέγω. D. Word and Speech in the New Testament," *Theological Dictionary of the New Testament* 4 [ed. Kittel, tr. G. W. Bromiley; Grand Rapids: Eerdmans, 1967] 100-136).

its prologue is, by critical consensus, to be approached as a separable entity.[26] It is interesting that the initial pattern of usage refers, not to God's word in the first instance, but to Jesus'. His disciples are said to believe his word concerning the Temple after his resurrection (2:22); large numbers of Samaritans are attracted to Jesus' own discourse (4:40-42); a royal official accepts Jesus' word that his son is healed (4:50). The *logos* of Jesus is said to be hard (6:60) or difficult to understand (7:36, cf. v. 40). No particular background in Aramaic may be said to be manifest in such usages, and even within that language, מימרא is not notably more appropriate than, say, פתגמא or מלתא as an analogue of λόγος. [27]

Then, however, as we follow the pattern of presentation of the body of the Gospel itself, the claim is made that those who hear Jesus' word and believe in the one who sent him have eternal life (5:24). Implicitly, attending

---

[26]Cf. Ed. L. Miller, *Salvation-History in the Prologue of John*: Supplements to Novum Testamentum 60 (Leiden: Brill, 1989) 2-10.

[27]Indeed, one of the two latter terms would be the more natural analogue of the usage of λόγος in the plural, cf. 10:19, and the reading of the Codex Bezae at 15:20a. The usage in the Gospel where Pilate hears the "word" of "the Jews" (19:8, cf. v. 13), cannot be said to add to the particular meaning developed in the work.

to Jesus is equated with trusting in God. That equation is more than implicit in the usage which follows immediately (5:37, 38):

> The father who sent me has witnessed concerning me. You have at no time heard his voice, nor have you seen his form; you do not have his word remaining among you, because you have not believed the one whom he sent.

The relationship between 5:24 and 5:37, 38 merits attention. Two uses in such proximity are likely to have been coordinated, and both occur within what is presented as a single discourse of Jesus (beginning at v. 17, as a response to "the Jews"). The "word" which Jesus speaks in v. 24 is the occasion on which one might believe God and have eternal life. In vv. 37, 38 a failure to believe Jesus shows that God's word does not abide among those addressed by Jesus. Evidently, Jesus' word and God's word are held to be so closely related, that to fail to believe the former implies a rejection of the latter.[28]

---

[28]Ernst Haenchen's perplexity concerning vv. 37, 38 is incomprehensible, except on the supposition that his terms of reference are more dogmatic than exegetical. He writes in *John 1: A Commentary on the Gospel of John*: Hermeneia (tr. R. W. Funk and U. Busse; Philadelphia: Fortress, 1984) 263, 264: "To what does 'word' (λόγος) refer? To Jesus, the Logos of the Prologue, or to the OT?"

In stunning contrast, B. F. Westcott emphatically refers to "belief in the word of the Father who speaks through

That relationship between human discourse and God's discourse, both referred to as "word," is reminiscent of the position in the Targum of Isaiah, where *memra* may refer to what prophets are commanded to say, as well as to God's commanding message.[29]

Because Jesus' "word" and God's are correlates in the Johannine presentation, the notion that Jesus' disciples should "remain" in his λόγος (8:31, cf. vv. 37, 51, 52),[30] becomes explicable. Moreover, in the eighth chapter, a distinction is made between understanding Jesus' λαλίαν and hearing his λόγον, such that the latter makes the former possible (v. 43). Such a distinction is perfectly at home within Aramaic, in which מימרא refers more to message, פתגמא to word, and מלתא to saying. The most demanding statements in the chapter, that keeping Jesus'

---

the Son" in v. 24 (p. 87) and to God's word as "a power within man" in v, 38 (p.90); cf. *The Gospel according to St John* (London: Murray, 1890).

[29] Cf. 63:10 (and cf. 30:1; Targum Zechariah 7:12), and *The Glory of Israel*. pp. 56–69. For a translation of the Targum, cf. Chilton, *The Isaiah Targum. Introduction, Translation, Apparatus and Notes*: The Aramaic Bible 11 (Wilmington: Glazier, 1987). It might also be recalled that in John 2:22, Jesus' disciples believe in both the scripture and his "word."

[30] In that the issue in 5:38 is whether God's word is "remaining" in those addressed, the correlation between God's word and Jesus' is reinforced by verbal usage (μένω).

logos preserves one from death (vv. 51, 52), find their explanation in Jesus' own insistence that *he* knows the father and "keep(s) his word" (v. 55). It would be difficult to contrive a more lucid juxtaposition of Jesus' word and God's.

Although the coordination of the message of Jesus and God's discourse is the most striking pattern in the Gospel, there is also a willingness to speak quite directly of God's own address through scripture as his *memra* (10:34–36):

> Jesus answered them, Is it not written in your law, "I said, you are gods"? If those to whom the word of God came he called gods, and the scripture cannot be dissolved, can you say of the one whom the father sanctified and send into the world, "You blaspheme," because I said, "I am God's son"?

Evidently, a statement of a christological order is here being made, but the striking feature of the claim from the present point of view is that λόγος is used, as if routinely, of God's address to Israel by means of the scriptures, *not* of Jesus' own status as God's son. The understanding of a Targumic background would help to account for such usages, as if as a matter of course. The usages in respect of Isaiah's prophecy (12:38) and the book of Psalms (15:25) would seem to be associated with that category of meaning.[31]

In John's Gospel, the underlying perspective that the *logos* may be God's in particular, not only Jesus' or even God's in Jesus', turns out to be fundamental. It is precisely on that basis that Jesus can claim that the word which he speaks will judge anyone who rejects him and does not accept his utterances (12:48): it is neither Jesus himself, nor precisely what he says, which will judge such a person on the last day, but the *logos*. The *logos* spoken by Jesus is held to have a dynamic property here, as in 15:3, where it is held to have purified those who belong to Jesus.[32] But it is Jesus, and no other, who is understood to speak the *logos*, and the treatment of the disciples is to reflect people's response to him (15:20). But the underlying force of discipleship is that disciples have kept *God's logos*: in chapter 17, commonly known as the high priestly prayer,[33] Jesus addresses his father (v. 1) with the claim, "they have kept *your logos*" (v. 6). Moreover, Jesus' function is described instrumentally here (v. 14):

---

[31]Cf. Chilton, "John XII 34 and Targum LII 13," *Novum Testamentum* 22 (1980) 176–178.

[32]Cf. Westcott, p. 217.

[33]Haenchen, *op. cit.* (volume 2), 150 ascribes that designation to the sixteenth century work of David Chytraeus.

> I have given them your *logos* and the world hated
> them, because they are not from the world, just as I
> am not from the world.

Keeping the *logos*, the fundamental attribute of discipleship, makes the disciple one with the son who speaks, and with the father who frames, that *logos* (vv. 20-23). Indeed, that dynamic extends even to those who believe in Jesus as a result of his disciples' "word" (v. 20): because the power of the *logos* concerned is God's, it is not diluted by repetition or extension. That sense is perhaps inherent in subsequent usages in the Gospel which are certainly less redolent of the meaning of *logos*, but which reflect the conviction that Jesus' word is to be fulfilled (18:9, 32), just as scripture is (cf. 15:25), and that even what disciples repeat as Jesus' promise must be in some way be vindicated, even if that is possible only by means of qualification (21:23).

The fundamental perspective of the body of the Gospel, then, appears plain. Jesus speaks, and uniquely speaks, God's message, such that keeping that "word" makes the disciple one with son and father. The way is therefore open to identify the son with the *logos*, as indeed occurred during the second century, in the theologies of Irenaeus and Clement, for example.[34] But that

---

[34]Cf. Anathon Aall, *Geschichte der Logosidee in der*

identification does not yet take place in the Gospel according to John, which simply makes of Jesus the speaker of the divine logos.

The only exegetical obstacle which may prevent commentators from acceding to the last assertion is the prologue of the Gospel, to which we must now turn. Because that is held to reflect a doctrine of Jesus' personal pre-existence as the *logos*, that conviction has been read into the Gospel as a whole. That procedure is methodologically flawed, in that the prologue is held to be separable from the Gospel, in view of its history in the tradition.[35] Even more crucially -- as will now be argued -- the prologue itself does not impute personal pre-existence to Jesus as the divine *logos*. The reading which holds that it does so is unduly influenced by the subsequent theology of the early Church.

The first usage of *logos* in the Gospel simply establishes its identity with God (not with Jesus, 1:1, 2)[36] as the

---

christlichen   Litteratur   (Leipzig: Reisland,   1899) 354-369, 405-427.

[35]Cf. Miller, *op. cit.,* Haenchen, pp. 101, 102.

[36]Haenchen, pp. 108, 109, suggests that, in the absence of the definite article, we should take θεός here to mean "divine," as in Philo, *De Somniis* 1.229, 230 and Origen's *Commentary* 2.2.12-18.

creative source of what exists (1:3), in a way quite consistent with the association of *memra* and creation.[37] The development of a theology of the *logos* by Philo of Alexandria provided a precedent of a personal image of the "word" as the initial reason of God, the plan of the architect who created the world.[38] But the startling point in any comparison of the prologue and Philo is what is *not* in the prologue: the *logos* is simply said to be divine, not to be personal, or the plan of divine reason.

The notion that the *logos* is to be identified with Jesus in the prologue is to some extent based upon a reading of the text in Greek which does not attend adequately to its obviously deliberate sequence. God's *logos* is said to be

---

[37]Westcott's remark (pp. 2, 3, cf. pp. xiv–xix), "The theological use of the term appears to be derived directly from the Palestinian *Memra*, and not from the Alexandrine *Logos*," is apposite.

[38]Cf. *De Opificio Mundi* 17–25. Cf. David Winston, *Logos and Mystical Theology in Philo of Alexandria* (Cincinnati: Hebrew Union College, 1985); Chilton, "Commenting on the Old Testament (with particular reference to the pesharim, Philo, and the Mekilta)," *It is Written: Scripture Citing Scripture. Essays in Honour of Barnabas Lindars* (ed. D. A. Carson and H. G. M. Williamson; Cambridge: Cambridge University Press, 1988) 122–140, esp. 130–133. For the devloping identification of "word" and "wisdom," and the tendency to personify that divine activity in Hellenistic Judaism, cf. Robert L. Duncan, "The Logos: from Sophocles to the Gospel of John," *Christian Scholar's Review* 9 (1979) 121–130, esp. 125f.

the place where "life" is, and that life is held to be the "light" of all humanity (v. 4). Insofar as a directly christological category is developed in the prologue, that category is "light," not "word."[39] It is the "light" which shines in the darkness (v. 5), which enlightens every person (v. 9). Most crucially, the "light," a neuter noun in Greek (τὸ φῶς), is identified as masculine and singular in v. 10:

> In it was the world, and the world came into existence through it, and the world did not know him.

From that moment, the usage of pronouns and the summary reference to Jesus' ministry (vv. 11-13, cf. vv. 6-8) makes it clear we are dealing with a person, not an entity. But, from the present point of view, the telling factor is that Jesus has been presented, precisely and grammatically, as the light which takes its origin in the *logos*, not as the *logos* itself.

We then come to the clause which has dominated the reading of the fourth Gospel, and which has been taken as the cornerstone of a christological construction of the *logos* in Christian theology from the second century (v. 14a):

---

[39]It is striking how Brown, normally a cautious exegete, conflates the two, *op. cit.*, p. 10.

And the *logos* became flesh and dwelt among us...
Once *logos* has been identified with Jesus, as it is for
Clement and Irenaeus, the reference of the clause can
only be to the incarnation.[40] Indeed, the Latin text of
the clause, *et verbum caro factum est*, is conventionally
taken in association with the credal assertion that the
"son," understood as the second person of the Trinity,
became incarnate (*incarnatus est*). But all such readings
and construals are possible, only on the assumption that
the *logos* and Jesus are one; then he is a pre-existent,
personal entity come down from heaven. The problem with
such an exegesis of the Johannine text is the care with
which Jesus is *not* directly associated with the *logos* in
vv. 1–13.

If v. 14 is not read as asserting a christological
incarnation, what else can it be saying? The present
proposal is that an approach to that question, guided by
our discussion of the *memra* in the Targumim, suggests an
answer. *Memra* is essentially God's mighty command,
vindicating and warning his people; v. 14 refers to the
logos as becoming flesh, and then explains that assertion
by saying it "dwelt among us" (ἐσκήνωσεν ἐν ἡμῖν). The
verb σκηνόω, it is often observed, relates naturally to
שׁכן in Hebrew and Aramaic, from which *Shekhinah*, the

---

[40]Cf. Brown, pp. 30f.

principal theologoumenon of God's presence in the cult, is derived.[41] Little can be gathered by the usage in itself, but it may suggest that the vocabulary of the prologue has been influenced by an awareness of Targumic theologoumena. In any case, to describe the *logos*, understood as *memra*, as dwelling among us such that we might behold its glory, is not in the least surprising.

The "glory" beheld is subjected to a precise qualification at the end of the verse; it is "glory as of an only one with a father, full of grace and truth" (1:14c). At this point, elementary misreadings have obscured a complex statement. The assertion is *not* "we beheld his glory, glory as of the only Son from the Father," as in the Revised Standard Version; still less is it "we have seen his glory, the glory of the only Son, who came from the Father," as in the New International Version. The definite articles are conspicuously absent from the text in Greek; the glory spoken of is as of an only child, not "the only Son." The comparison is straightforwardly metaphorical, not doctrinal. Now, however, comes the element of complexity: the glory of the *logos* is "as of an only one" (ὡς μονογενοῦς), and we know, as readers of the Gospel, that Jesus is God's son.[42]

---

[41]Cf. Westcott, pp. 11, 12.

[42]The Gospel is intended for a synchronic reading, by

Indeed, we know explicitly that Jesus, as God's "son," speaks his "word," and that the reaction to the one is congruent with the reaction to the other. The inference that the glory as the *logos* was "as of" Jesus is therefore precisely consonant with the presentation of the Gospel as a whole.

The remainder of the prologue reflects the maintenance of the distinction between the *logos* and Jesus which has been posited, and suggests the sense in which we should understand that the *logos* "became flesh." John, we are told, witnessed "concerning it" (περί αὐτοῦ, that is, the word), by saying of Jesus, "This was he of whom I said, 'He that becomes after me...'" (v. 15). Fundamentally, the *logos* is still more the object of the prologue's attention than Jesus, and that continues to be the case in v. 16:

> For from the fullness αὐτοῦ we have all received, even grace upon grace.

Αὐτοῦ, whether taken of the *logos* or of Jesus, is a masculine pronoun, but the statement seems a resumption of what has been said in vv. 3–5: we live from devolutions of the *logos*, the dynamic structure of word,

---

those who have already passed through catechesis, cf. Chilton, *Profiles of a Rabbi. Synoptic Opportunities in Reading about Jesus*: Brown Judaic Studies 177 (Atlanta: Scholars Press, 1989) 180, 181.

light and life.

The understanding that God's "word" is still the essential issue in play makes the transition to the next topic straightforward (v. 17):

> For the law was given through Moses, grace and truth came through Jesus Christ.

The connection of *logos*, taken as *memra*, to the revelation through Moses is evident. Moreover, the syntax and logic of v. 17 coheres with that of v. 16; the coordination of God's activity in creation with his donation of the law through Moses is established as a Targumic *theologoumenon* by our discussion in the first part of the present paper.

The link between the verses is literal, as well. The "grace" (ἡ χάρις) which came through Jesus Christ (v. 17) is akin to the "grace upon grace" (χάριν ἀντὶ χάριτος) we have all received (v. 16). There is a constant and consistent activity of God's *logos* from the creation and through the revelations to Moses and to Jesus. The *logos* in John is simply a development of conventional notions of the *memra* in early Judaism. *At no point and in no way does the prologue present the revelation through Jesus as disjunctive with the revelation through Moses: any such disjunction is an artifact of imposing an anachronistic christology upon the text.* V. 17 also provides guidance in regard to the reading of v. 14. The statement that grace and truth "came" (ἐγένετο) through Jesus Christ is comparable to the assertion that God's word "became" (ἐγένετο) flesh; in both cases, the underlying contention is that Jesus is the actual person in whom God's "word," his activity in creating and revealing, is manifest.

The last verse of the prologue is also the last word of the present argument. V. 18 makes an assertion which makes any formally incarnational reading appear nonsensical:

No one has at any time seen God; an only begotten, God, who was in the bosom of the father, that one has made him known.

The first clause makes no sense whatever, if the prologue means to say that Jesus *is* the *logos*. If the *logos* is God (v. 1:1), and Jesus is that "word," v. 18 is more than paradoxical. But v. 18 makes eminent sense on just the reading we have here suggested: no one has at any time seen God, provided the reader has followed the logic of his revelation as the prologue outlines it. Jesus, as an only begotten (again, without the article) has made God known (ἐξηγήσατο). Just as we would expect on the basis of our reading of passages which refer to *logos* in the body of the Gospel, Jesus is presented as the exegesis of God, the one who speaks his word. In that role, the fourth Gospel can refer to Jesus as θεός just as Philo so refers to Moses:[43] not to make any ontological assertion, but to insist that the instrument of God's word is to be taken as divinely valued.

---

[43]Cf. *Legum Allegoria* I.40; *De Sacrificiis Abelis et Caini* 9; *Quod Deterius Potiori insidiari soleat* 161, 162; *De Migratione Abrahami* 84; *De Mutatione Nominum* 19; *De Vita Moses* I.158; *Quod Omnis Probus Liber sit* 43.

Romans 9-11 as Scriptural Interpretation and Dialogue with Judaism

Paul is, arguably, never more himself than in these famous chapters of Romans, and -- for just that reason -- they have caused exegetes great perplexity. The main lines of Paul's argument seem reasonably clear, but the form of his argumentation, with its many references to scripture and deductions from scripture, strike most readers as both foreign and convoluted. Why is a basically simple idea wrapped up in an esoteric package? As we shall see, that question will itself require refinement as we encounter Paul's thinking, but it will serve us well as we first approach our text.

I. What is the idea, and how is it packaged?

An observant student could sketch out a précis of Paul's thought in Romans 9-11, without reference to the scripture he cites. The result would be a reasonable, self-contained address, which could be succinctly delivered:

> Although I am distressed that my people have not accepted the gospel (9:1-5), their failure is not God's: it is just that he has, as always, chosen freely whom he wills (9:6-13). That might seem hard, but God is sovereign in the matter of choice

(9:14-23), and he has simply decided to call both Jews and Gentiles (9:24-33).[1]

There is now no distinction between Jew and Greek in the matter of salvation: if you confess the Lord Jesus and believe God raised him from the dead, you will be saved (10:1-21, v. 9). Those who are believers must not, however, imagine that God has rejected his people. After all, Jews do believe in Jesus (11:1-10), and even those who do not believe have, in their lack of faith, provided an opportunity for Gentiles (11:11-24). Once the fullness of the Gentiles is accomplished, *all* Israel, including both Jews and Gentiles, will be seen to be saved (11:25-36).

There are, of course, crucial facets within each of the statements in the above précis which remain to be explored, but they are subsidiary to the main lines of the argument. What becomes unmistakably clear, when we boil Paul's ornate speech down to its essentials, is that he is making a cogent case for a particular view of how God's saving activity in Christ Jesus is consistent with

---

[1]A break at 9:24 is more plausible in Greek than in English; cf. the twenty-sixth edition of *Novum Testamentum Graece* (eds. E. Nestle, K. Aland; Stuttgart: Deutsche Bibelstiftung, 1979).

his election of Israel. Once it is clear that Israel is
elected, not sovereign, that divine choice is operative,
rather than divine right, Paul's observations follow
logically.

Paul's design at this point comports well with the
purpose of his letter to the Romans as a whole, and makes
sense within the Hellenistic environment in which he
functioned. In a recent book, Stanley Stowers has
explained that the writing of letters, whether at the
common level of incidental discourse, or with a refined
standard of rhetoric, was conventional within the culture
of the Mediterranean Basin and is a natural context in
which to understand much of the New Testament.[2] That
convention also influenced ancient Judaism, which --
despite the impression of an isolated phenomenon which
some writers give -- was itself a lively constituent
within the cultural life of its time.[3] But Stowers is

---

[2]*Letter Writing in Greco-Roman Antiquity*: Library of
Early Christianity (Philadelphia: Westminster, 1986) 25.

[3]Stowers, pp. 41-2. Within the Hebrew Bible, Stowers
cites 2 Samuel 11:14, 15; I Kings 21:8-10; 2 Kings
10:1-6; 19:9-14; Ezra 4-5. The last two passages, of
course, relate Assyrian and Persian letters (and the
second should be extended to 6:12). Moreover, all of the
passages cited concern royal, official, or military
communication, rather than the sort of cultural activity
which is reflected in the New Testament. Stowers's
references to Philo, Josephus, and 1, 2 Maccabees are

well within the scholarly consensus when he concludes that Judaism did not actively appropriate the convention and transmit it directly to Christianity.[4] Specifically, Paul in Romans appears to be writing a "protreptic letter," by which Stowers means a work designed to convert the reader to Paul's set of teachings. Stowers is able on the basis of a comparison with Greco-Roman convention to argue that the entire letter is designed to present Paul's gospel of salvation for Gentiles, and to defend it against the charge that it means the loss of Israel's salvation.[5] The analysis of Romans according to its function within its most plausible social setting therefore helps us to resolve the main lines of its purpose. Indeed, the clarity of function which emerges

more on target.

[4]Stowers does not, however, make reference to the letters of Bar Kokhba and to the evidence of correspondence between Antioch and Palestine; both sorts of letter are of direct pertinence to his theme. Cf. J. A. Fitzmyer, "Aramaic Epistolography," *A Wandering Aramean. Collected Aramaic Essays*: SBL Monograph Series 25 (Chico: Scholars Press, 1979) 183-204; W. A. Meeks and R. L. Wilken, *Jews and Christians in Antioch in the First Four Centuries of the Common Era*: SBL Sources for Biblical Study 13 (Ann Arbor: Scholars Press, 1978).

[5]Stowers, pp. 113, 114. Cf. also M. L. Stirewalt, "Appendix: The Form and Function of the Greek Letter-Essay," *The Romans Debate* (ed. K. P. Donfried; Minneapolis: Augsburg, 1977) 175-206 and Donfried, "False Presuppositions in the Study of Romans," *The Romans Debate,* pp. 120-148.

from such an approach may appear curiously at odds with the convoluted character of Paul's argument.

Whenever an exegete discovers that his or her explanation of a text is dramatically more homogeneous than the text itself, it is time to consider the possibility that over-simplification has crept in. Even if Romans be a "protreptic letter," the involved argument from scripture in chapters 9-11 is obviously the result of a dynamic not evidenced by the letter as a whole. Of course, scripture does play a crucial role in Romans generally (as it does normally in Pauline thought), but the consistency of recourse to textual argument makes our chapters appear distinctive.[6]

Before we consider why Paul's form of argumentation in Romans 9-11 is exegetical in a way most of the letter is not, we must first appreciate how the simple, discursive case Paul makes is enhanced by means of reference to scripture. At each major point in the argument, well known passages of scripture are cited.

A crucial bridge is provided by narratives concerning

---

[6]Cf. R. Badenas, *Christ the End of the Law. Romans 10:4 in Pauline Perspective*: Journal for the Study of the New Testament Supplement Series 10 (Sheffield: JSOT, 1985) 90-92.

Isaac. In Romans 9:7, Paul quotes Genesis 21:12, "After
Isaac shall your seed be named."[7] Now that reference may
appear to be an instance of using a "proof-text," chosen
pretty much at random from a much larger number of those
that might have been cited. But the quotation comes at
the climax of a story in which God tells Abraham to
accede to Sarah's demand, and cast out Hagar and Ishmael,
"for the son of this slave woman shall not inherit with
my son Isaac" (Genesis 21:10). The analogy with the
situation Paul believes he addresses is striking. He
spells the analogy out in Romans 9:8, "That is, these
children of flesh are not children of God, but children
of the promise are reckoned as the seed." Of course, that
finding requires that Isaac correspond to the promise,
and Paul makes out just that correspondence. In Romans
9:9, he quotes Genesis 18:14 (or perhaps v. 10), "At this
time (next year) I will come, and Sarah will have a son."
That verse, of course, is resonant, since it caps the
story of God's visitation at Mamre: Sarah laughs (v. 12),
and is blessed with Isaac, whose name means "he laughs,"
because it is God's joke in the end.

The pattern established in Romans 9:6–9 is followed
consistently in the chapters we are concerned with. At

---

[7]Throughout the present paper, the translations are the
author's.

first, Paul does not cite a specific scripture in what follows, but he does invoke the general case of Rebecca and Isaac (vv. 10, 11). She conceived twins, and before they did anything, or were even born, Rebecca was told, "The greater will serve the lesser" (Romans 9:12 and Genesis 25:23). At issue, of course, is the rivalry between Esau and Jacob, which is a major motif of Genesis. Paul sums it all up with a quotation from Malachi, "I loved Jacob and hated Esau" (Romans 9:13 and Malachi 1:2, 3). That Paul can draw upon Malachi's appropriation of the motif in Genesis is especially compelling: he implicitly claims that his analogy has prophetic warrant. The fundamentals of his scriptural reasoning are drawn from the Torah, but the nature of his reasoning, he claims, is in line with that of the prophets.[8]

It is indicative of the consistency of Pauline rhetoric that he now moves from Genesis to Exodus. That shift in scriptural foundation, at 9:14f., corresponds precisely

---

[8]Paul appears to have operated with the conventional categorization of the Hebrew Bible in Judaism. That categorization recognized divisions of the canon into the Torah (the Pentateuch), the Prophets (including the Former Prophets, from Joshua through 2 Kings, and the Latter Prophets, more familiarly considered prophetic in English), and the Writings (an essentially miscellaneous category).

to the development of Paul's argument (see the précis):
having rejoiced in God's sovereign choice as the
fulfillment of promise, Paul now defends God's
sovereignty against the charge that it is unjust or
arbitrary (v. 14). God said to Moses, "I will have mercy
on whom I have mercy, and I will show compassion to whom
I will show compassion" (Exodus 33:19; Romans 9:15).
Notably, that statement occurs when God is revealing his
glory and his name to Moses (cf. Genesis 33:12-23): what
is at issue is the very nature of God. A particular case
in Exodus of God deciding *not* to have mercy, as Paul says
(9:18), is that of Pharaoh, of whom scripture says, "For
this purpose I have raised you up, that I might display
my power over you, and that my name might be announded in
all the earth" (Romans 9:17; Exodus 9:16).[9] God's "name"
is at issue in both passages, and their association
betrays Paul's almost midrashic logic (see below, part
II), in which scripture is held to address issues
coherently. The assumption of that coherence is carried
over to the prophets: Isaiah (29:16; 45:9 in Romans 9:20)
and Jeremiah (18:6 in Romans 9:21) are used to
demonstrate that it is misguided for a vessel of

---

[9]Generally, Paul's text is practically identical with the
emerging text of the Septuagint, but he may have been
influenced occasionally (as here) by Targumic
interpretations, and by the original Hebrew (cf. Chilton,
God in Strength. Jesus' Announcement of the Kingdom: The
Biblical Seminar (Sheffield: JSOT, 1987) 267, 273, 274.

punishment to answer back to its maker. Consideration of Isaiah 29:16; 45:9; Jeremiah 18:6 within their literary contexts shows that Paul is still attending carefully to the sense of the passages he cites. In all, the paramount issue is the fate of Israel, as determined by a sovereign God.

The next development of Paul's argument, at 9:24f. (again, cf. the précis) also corresponds to a shift in canonical focus. It is demonstrated by citing Hosea and Isaiah that we who are called by God are from both Jews and Gentiles (9:24). First, Hosea shows -- at least, to Paul's satisfaction -- that Gentiles are to be included among God's people (9:25, 26). Paul garbles the quotation from Hosea, drawing first from 2:23, and then from 1:10, and here is stretching to make a point. Hosea is contextually concerned with the restoration of Israel, not the inclusion of Gentiles; Paul reads what he takes to be a general truth of scripture into a passage in which that meaning has no literary place. He returns to his usual, more acute interpretation in 9:27-29 when he cites passages from Isaiah by way of arguing that Jews as such are not chosen, but that a remnant from their ranks is to be saved (Isaiah 10:22; 28:22 and Isaiah 1:9). Moreover, he cites a curious and creative mixture of Isaiah 28:16 and 8:14 in Romans 9:33, in order to show that the principle of selecting from the elect places a

stone of stumbling and a rock of offense in the midst of
Israel (Romans 9:30–32).

Paul's exegetical method is never more complex than in
Romans 9, and we need to pause for breath before
proceeding further. Although the details of the Pauline
execution may dazzle us (as they were no doubt intended
to), the fact is that certain characteristic traits are
plain. Paul argues from the Torah that (1) God operates
by fulfilling promises (vv. 1–13), and that (2) those
promises are kept for those chosen by God (vv. 14–23). He
then purports to demonstrate from the Prophets that God
has chosen his people from among Jews and Gentiles (vv.
24–33). On the whole, but for two exceptions, Paul cites
his passages with care and contextual sensitivity, which
means that any reader will better appreciate the argument
if he or she is familiar with the scriptures of Israel.
The two exceptions to Paul's care and sensitivity are
instructive. He reads Gentiles into Hosea (vv. 25, 26),
and splices together two verses of Isaiah (v. 33). As we
will see shortly, these are not mere lapses on Paul's
part. To his mind, the entry of Gentiles among the ranks
of God's chosen, and the coming of Christ as a rock of
offense to many in Israel, are facts of experience which
co-exist with and interpret facts of scripture. Paul's
"text" is not merely scripture, but his awareness, and

others' awareness, that Jesus is God's son.[10]

Once these interpretative characteristics of Paul's argument are appreciated, Romans 10 and 11 may more briefly be summarized from the point of view of their reference to scripture. In chapter 10, Paul makes his famous, daring assertion that, in Deuteronomy 30:11-14, when Moses refers to the nearness of the commandment, he means not any precise instruction, but the presence of Christ, who can neither be brought down from heaven, nor brought up from the abyss, except by God's power (Romans 10:6-8). How does Paul know the scriptures, properly understood, adduce Christ? He has just told us in v. 4, "Christ is the point of the law, for the righteousness of every believer."[11] By again citing Isaiah 28:16, in v. 11, Paul may betray his own awareness that he is invoking Christ, rather than deducing Christ, at this point. The other usages in chapter 10 -- of Leviticus 18:5[12] in 10:5,

---

[10]Comparison may be invited with the approach of Jesus to scripture, in which the kingdom is held to be the hermeneutical center of the scriptures (cf. Chilton, *A Galilean Rabbi and His Bible. Jesus' Use of the Interpreted Scripture of His Time*: Good News Studies 8 [Wilmington: Delaware, 1984]). For Paul, Christ is that center (cf. Romans 10:4).

[11]Cf. Badenas, pp. 144-155. Badenas himself does not render τέλος as "point," but such a rendering would be consistent with his case.

[12]Notably, this command, in its context, requires

of Joel 3:5 in 10:13, of Isaiah 52:7 in 10:15, of Isaiah
53:1 in 10:16, of Psalm 19:4[13] in 10:18, and of Isaaiah
65:1, 2 in 10:20, 21 -- fall within the more usual
Pauline range, of texts which illustrate a coherent
principle.

Chapter 11 may be surveyed even more summarily, because
the usages of scripture are all illustrative. There are
no special invocations of Christ or of the motif of the
inclusion of the Gentiles. Until this point, the bulk of
Paul's references have come from the Torah and the Latter
Prophets. Now he brings balance to his case scripturally,
by citing the instance of Elijah from the Former
Prophets. Again, attention to the contexts of the
scriptures Paul cites richly rewards itself. The
assertion that God has not rejected his people in 11:2,
drawn from 1 Samuel 12:22, comes in a context in which
the prophet Samuel assures Israel that, despite their
wickedness, God's choice is constant (1 Samuel 12:19-25).
The close of that passage, however, does threaten, "But
if you act wickedly, you shall be swept away, both you
and your king" (I Samuel 12:25). In other words, the

---

separation from the Gentiles, which supports the
understanding that, as in Galatians 3:12, Paul cites the
passage in order to overturn it with a principle of
inclusion.

[13]Psalm 18:5 in the Septuagint and 19:5 in the Masoretic Text.

thought of the remnant, which has been an explicit part of the argument since 9:27, 28 (by means of the citation of Isaiah 10:22, 23), has remained with Paul throughout. For that reason, the reference to Elijah in vv. 2b-5 (cf. 1 Kings 19:1-18, and vv. 10, 14 & 18 in particular) is apposite: there is a prophetic analogy of the circumstances Paul finds himself in, where only a radical minority has kept faith. Once it is established that the residue of the remnant can be deliberately hardened in their rebellion (cf. Deuteronomy 29:3[14] in 11:8 and Psalm 69:22, 23[15] in 11:9), there is no further need of scriptural warrant for what Paul argues. He does, however, offer a final citation of Isaiah (59:20, 21 and 27:9) in 11:26, 27, by way of making his comprehensive assertion that "all Israel" -- but a chastened, forgiven Israel, not a claimant as of right -- is to be saved.[16] At this crucial moment, he must again splice scriptures, not merely cite them, to achieve the dual stress on deliverance and forgiveness which is the apogee of his argument.

---

[14]With reverberations with Isaiah 6:9, 10; 29:10.

[15]Psalm 68:23, 24 in the Septuagint, and 69:23, 24 in the Masoretic Text.

[16]For the present purpose the scriptural allusions in the closing hymn in chapter 11, vv. 33-36, are excluded from consideration. The principles of interpretation at work there are nonetheless consistent with those elucidated by the present treatment.

Conclusion of Part I

We may set out mentally, as it were side by side, two analyses of Romans 9-11. Followed along one track, the chapters instance protreptic discourse, in which Paul appeals to his readers to follow his way of thinking. He wishes to convince them that God's inclusion of believing Gentiles with Jews who accept Jesus as Christ represents a fulfilment of the promise to Israel. Followed along the second track, the same chapters represent a carefully orchestrated argument from all the main sections of the Hebrew canon, cited in translation, which is designed to sweep readers up in the promise that all Israel -- forgiven Jews and Gentiles -- are to be saved (11:26, 27). It is obvious that the two tracks of analysis are complementary, and neither alone would adequately account for the chapters as a whole. But it is equally obvious that the chapters are crafted *as* a whole: the references to scripture are not only keyed to major developments of the argument, they contribute those developments. It is not a matter of discursive thought merely being illustrated scripturally (although illustration is one function of scripture in Romans). Rather, logic and interpretation here interpenetrate to a remarkable degree, and give Romans 9-11 a unique character within the Pauline corpus.[17] The questions therefore emerge, What is Paul doing here, which makes the chapters distinctive, and Why does he do it?

II. What is Paul doing, and why?

Our second, major question might be answered quickly, were we able to accept the suggestion -- developed in much recent scholarship -- that Paul is here providing his readers with a Midrash.[18] It has become conventional to observe that the noun "Midrash" is derived from the verbal form שׁרד, and therefore to infer that "Midrash" refers to any "searching out" of meaning on the basis of scripture within Judaism. It is fairly obvious that, if one is willing to work with such a free-wheeling definition, Romans 9-11 is indeed "Midrash." But such a

---

[17]Cf. Badenas, pp. 90-92.

[18]Cf. W. R. Stegner, "Romans 9:6-29 -- A Midrash," *Journal for the Study of the New Testament* 22 (1984) 37-52. Stegner's work is essentially based upon that of E. Earle Ellis, *Paul's Use of the Old Testament* (Edinburgh: Oliver and Boyd, 1957) and *Prophecy and Hermeneutic in Early Christianity* (Tübingen: Mohr, 1978). If recent discussion must qualify the description of Romans 9-11 as Midrash, there is nonetheless no doubt but that Ellis contributes signally to our understanding of Paul's manner of thinking scripturally. Indirectly, the Midrashim shed light on the sort of activity Paul was engaged in; it is only the direct equation of Pauline interpretation with the genre of Midrash which needs to be set aside.

description obscures more than it discloses.

When the rabbis produced the documents known collectively as Midrashim, the formal aim was -- on the whole[19] -- to produce commentaries on scripture. But the "commentary" was not, as in modern usage, an attempt strictly and historically to explain the meaning of a given document. Rather, the sense which the rabbis explored in their Midrashim was the meaning of scripture within their practice and liturgy and teaching, which were understood as of a piece with the Torah revealed to Moses on Sinai. That is, Midrash represents a synthesis of written text and rabbinic sensibility, in which both are accorded the status of revelation. Jacob Neusner has written the most compelling, systematic account of the development and character of the Midrashim.[20] Amongst other things, Neusner shows that a given Midrash may be composed of four distinct orders of interpretation:[21]

---

[19]In what follows, generalization has been necessary to a higher degree than would be acceptable if the exegesis of the Midrashim were primarily at issue, and it must be remembered that no generalization can replace familiarity with the literature involved.

[20]*Midrash in Context. Exegesis in Formative Judaism*: The Foundations of Judaism 1 (Philadelphia: Fortress, 1983).

[21]Neusner, pp. 82, 83. It should be noted that these are the modalities of interpretation which Neusner identifies in Talmud, and which he shows were then applied to the Bible in the Midrashim.

(1) close exegesis, or discussion by each word or phrase of scripture;

(2) amplification of the meaning of a passage;

(3) illustration of a particular theme by various passages;

(4) anthological collection around a general topic.

The result of the compilations of varying readings, involving different categories of interpretation, was the eleven distinct Midrashim (on various books of the Bible) which emerged by the end of the sixth century.[22]

When one sets out the Midrashim systematically, and provides precise examples (as Neusner does), the distance from Paul's activity in Romans in striking. His focus is no single biblical book, so that the general form of Midrash is not at issue. The categories of exegesis and amplification, which Neusner shows were most prominent in the earliest Midrashim (of the second century A.D.) simply do not obtain in the case of Paul. It *might* be said -- at a stretch -- that the third and fourth categories do characterize Pauline interpretation. But the stretch is considerable, because Paul does not merely illustrate by means of scripture (although illustration is among his techniques); he argues through it and with it towards a conclusion which scripture itself does not

---

[22]Neusner, p. 103.

draw, but -- at best -- is generally consistent with. And, of course, his over-arching theme, of Jesus Christ's completion of the Torah, the Prophets, and the Writings, could never be described as rabbinic. For all those reasons, to style Paul's interpretation as "Midrash" is misleading.

Having called attention to the inadequacy of any direct identification of Paul's method with the rabbis', a certain analogy remains. Both proceed synthetically, and the synthesis moves in two directions at once. First, both take scripture as a whole, as making a harmonious, common claim upon the mind.[23] Indeed, it should be pointed out that Paul specifies Torah first, and then the Prophets (by name) and the Writings, more punctiliously than the rabbis do. It appears that Paul wishes to make the point of scripture's unity, and also that he is making an inherently convoluted argument easier to follow than it would be if he were addressing genuine experts. Second, both Paul and the rabbis also synthesize

---

[23]For this reason, the procedures for associating disparate passages are important for both Paul and the rabbis. The famous rabbinic rules of interpretation might be regarded as an attempt to specify how the harmony of scripture may be defined; cf. A. Finkel, *The Pharisees and the Teacher of Nazareth:* Arbeiten zur Geschichte des Späjudentums und seiner Umwelt (Leiden: Brill, 1964) 123-128.

scripture with their own sensibilities. The last point is perhaps best illustrated by how differently the rabbis of Leviticus Rabbah took Genesis 21:12, where Abraham's seed is defined, without justification, as those who believe in the world to come.[24] What was for Paul obviously Christological was for the rabbis (of a later period) self-evidently a halakhah of eschatological belief. Just when the rabbis and Paul seem analogous, their conclusions are antipodal.

---

[24]The following rendering is that of H. Freedman (*Genesis: Midrash Rabbah* [eds H. Freedman and M. Simon; New York: Soncino, 1983]) at Genesis Rabbah 53.12:

AND GOD SAID UNTO ABRAHAM: LET IT NOT BE GRIEVOUS IN THY SIGHT...FOR IN ISAAC SHALL SEED BE CALLED TO THEE (21:12). R. Judah b. Shilum said: Not "Isaac," but IN ISAAC is written here. R. 'Azariah said in the name of Bar Ḥutah: The *beth* (IN) denotes two, i.e., [thy seed shall be called] in him who recognizes the existence of two worlds. R. Judah b. R. Shalum said: It is written, REMEMBER HIS MARVELOUS WORKS THAT HE HATH DONE, HIS SIGNS, AND THE JUDGMENTS OF HIS MOUTH (Ps. 105:5): [God says:] I have given a sign [whereby the true descendants of Abraham can by known], viz. he who expressly recognizes [God's judgments]: thus whoever believes in the two worlds shall be called "thy seed," while he who rejects belief in two worlds shall not be called "thy seed."

In order to appreciate the interpretation, which also appears in Talmud (Nedarim 31a), it is necessary to realize that ב (*beth*) in Hebrew may mean both "in" and "two."

Paul has also been compared to the sectarians of Qumran
and to Philo, in respect of his interpretation of
scripture. But the famous *Pesherim* of Qumran are designed
to relate scripture exactly to the history of the
community, and Philo is concerned to comment
systematically on scripture, so as to elucidate its
allegedly philosophical truth.[25] Both the *Pesherim* and the
Philonic corpus represent different activities and
settings from Paul's: his scriptural interpretation
strictly serves the protreptic function of Romans. He
shows no sustained interest in historicizing scripture
(as in the *Pesherim*) or in philosophizing with it (as in
Philo). Paul is driven by other motives, which is why
Romans 9-11 is neither Midrash, *Pesher*, nor philosophical
commentary.

Paul is arguing with all the Christians of Rome, both
Jews and Gentiles, in an attempt to promote unity. It is
true that Paul had no direct, personal acquaintance with
the community at Rome, and to that extent, there is an
abstract quality about the letter to the Romans which
sets it apart from other Pauline letters. Writing at a

---

[25]Cf. Chilton, "Commenting on the Old Testament (with
particular reference to the pesharim, Philo, and the
Mekilta)," *It is Written: Scripture Citing Scripture.
Essays in Honour of Barnabas Lindars, S.S.F.* (eds D. A.
Carson and H. G. M. Williamson; Cambridge: Cambridge
University Press, 1988) 122-140.

distance from a church known only at second hand, Paul approximates, more nearly than he ever does, to the presentation of his theology in a systematic fashion.[26] Nonetheless, the central, social issue in the church at Rome was known to Paul: there had been disturbances involving Jews in the city, and probably Christians as well, that resulted in their being expelled in A.D. 49 under the Emperor Claudius.[27] Their gradual re-integration

---

[26]Cf. E. P. Sanders, *Paul, the Law, and the Jewish People* (Philadelphia: Fortress, 1985) 31, 46, 59 n. 75, 97.

[27]Cf. Wolfgang Wiefel, "The Jewish Community in Ancient Rome and the Origins of Roman Christianity," *The Romans Debate,* 100-119. Wiefel attempts to harmonize the accounts of the New Testament, Suetonius, and Dio Cassius, and in so doing may be reasoning beyond the limits of certainty imposed by the evidence. He argues that Claudius first expelled Jews from Rome (so Suetonius and Orosius) and -- after many returned -- attempted to prohibit their meeting in public (so Dio Cassius). F. F. Bruce imagines the precisely opposite scenario: meetings were first banned, and expulsion followed (*New Testament History* [London: Pickering and Inglis, 1982] 279-283). But the fact of a disturbance involving Jews is well established; that it had an immediate impact upon Christianity is a sound inference (cf. Acts 18:2; Cassius Dio, *Roman History* 60.66; Suetonius, *Claudius* 25.4; Orosius, *Seven Books of History against the Pagans* 7.6). In any case, Wiefel is clearly correct in viewing Romans as an appeal for unity to a mixed church, in which Gentiles were in the majority. For further discussion, cf. E. Mary Smallwood, *The Jews under Roman Rule. From Pompey to Diocletian*: Studies in Judaism in Late Antiquity 20 (Leiden: Brill, 1976) 210-216 and Francis Watson, *Paul, Judaism and the Gentiles. A Sociological*

into a single church with Gentiles, which is Paul's goal, could only be accomplished by means of conveying a coherent vision in which both Jews and Gentiles had a place.

The letter to the Romans offers just such a vision, which is summed up under the slogan which appears here, and only here, within the Pauline corpus: salvation is for the Jew first, and then for the Greek (1:16; 2:9, 10 cf. 3:9, 29; 9:24; 10:12). Salvation is the possession of neither, but it is offered and granted to both, provided it is accepted by means of a willingness to be forgiven.

His letter to the Galatians presents Paul in such heated controversy with Jews who were also Christians, and with those who demanded that the conditions of Judaism be fulfilled by all followers of Christ (whether Jew or Gentile), that one might have expected Paul to have used the occasion of his letter to the Romans finally to argue that the gospel of Christ could rightly be severed from its Judaic roots.[28] Having written to the Galatians c.

Approach: Society for New Testament Studies Monograph Series 56 (Cambridge: Cambridge University Press, 1986) 91-94 (for positions in support of Bruce's).

[28]Yet even in his earlier letters, Paul's position in Romans may be regarded as adumbrated; cf. 1 Corinthians 1:21-25; 9:20-23; 10:32, 33; 12:13; Galatians 3:28.

A.D. 53, Paul went on in his Corinthian correspondence (c. A.D. 55-56) himself to appropiate scriptural stories of Israel's salvation directly for the Church (cf., for example, 1 Corinthians 10:1-4), and even to put believing Christians in the role of teachers comparable to -- and greater than! -- Moses (cf. 2 Corinthians 3:7-18). Here, in Rome (c. A.D. 57),[29] was a case in which Judaism had been weakened, to the point that Gentiles in the church were tempted to imagine that the divine right of Israel had been usurped definitively by the non-Jewish Church (cf. Romans 11:13-24). Paul's response is unequivocal: the rejection of many in Israel does not give latecomers any special privilege. Indeed, the implication of the remnant is that the essential promise to Israel is confirmed, although the rebellion of some in Israel demonstrates that no one, Jewish or not, can presume upon God's gracious election. When Paul insists throughout Romans that salvation is to Jews first, and then to Greeks, the implication is that the same dynamics of redemption, initially worked out in the case of Israel, are now available to all humanity by means of Jesus Christ. Romans 9-11 embody that leitmotif in the letter generally. The salvation effected in Christ is uniquely

---

[29]The dates here offered, which are well within the range of the scholarly consensus which has emerged, are those of Chilton, *Beginning New Testament Study* (Grand Rapids: Eerdmans, 1987).

comprehended by means of scripture, where "scripture" refers to the canon of Israel. When Paul turns to his Gentile readers alone in 11:13-24, he momentarily drops any reference to scripture, and argues from an agricultural image.[30] His message is clear: however weak the Jewish component may appear, they are root and you are branch. And it is all Israel, root and branch, which God is determined to save.

III. The Implications of Paul's Argumentative Interpretation

The salvation which God has effected in Christ Jesus is offered to all humanity, to whomever understands how rightly to appropriate it. To accept forgiveness for the wrath which rightly hangs over us all (Romans 1:18-2:16) demonstrates a humility greater than naturally comes to most of us, and implies a radical redefinition of how the promises of creation and of Abraham's election may be regarded as fulfilled (Romans 4-6). Paul is wrestling

---

[30]A. G. Baxter and J. A. Ziesler, "Paul and Arboriculture: Romans 11:17-24," *Journal for the Study of the New Testament* 24 (1985) 25-32. Their argument is especially telling, in that the purpose of the grafting -- which was not considered outlandish in antiquity -- was to re-invigorate the tree in which the scion was implanted. The authors cite a contemporary of Paul's, Columella (*De re rusticus* 5.11.1-15 and *De arboribus* 26-27); cf. pp. 27-29.

with sweeping issues in Romans. Romans 9-11 provide a precise and dynamic instrument for the understanding of God's offer of reconciliation in Christ: scripture and Christ together, the past experience of Israel and the present experience of the apostle, are held to be the two, complementary sources of a single revelation. Taken together, in a manner akin to longitude and lattitude, a careful reading of scripture and a critical reflection on the implications of faith in Christ are held to open a vision of a single, restored humanity.

The tragedy of Paul's deep and profoundly theological longing for a single Church, grounded in the promises to Israel and expressed by means of the Hebrew Bible, is that his letters -- particularly Romans -- have been plundered for rhetoric in order to fabricate an argument Paul never dreamed of making. In popular Paulinism, from the Fathers until our own day, there is a definite predilection for a supersessionist view of Israel: the Jews have been rejected, in order to make room for the newly chosen people of God. As we have seen, that is a conclusion Paul himself specifically rejected, and it has also been the occasion of a spurious argument in favor of anti-Semitism. Jews can be regarded, on this view, not merely as not saved, but as having rejected salvation.

The notion that Christians have   superseded Jews is in

many ways fomented by our traditional language. We
commonly call "the Old Testament" what Paul simply knew
as "scripture" (γραφή), and our own interpretation of
that corpus of books is often limited to historical
observations, as if it merely provided "background" for
the actual statement of faith, the New Testament.[31] To
meet the challenge of Romans 9–11, however, involves
reading the whole of the canon in the light of faith;
*particularly, it means becoming familiar with the
traditions of Israel as that which best articulates God's
action in Christ.*

As Paul demands that we articulate our faith in the terms
of reference of Israel, so he presses us on to a dialogue
with Judaism. Because we share a heritage with Judaism,
we are bound to agree and we are bound to disagree with
our Jewish contemporaries regarding the significance of
that heritage. Agreement and disagreement of that sort,
which is analogous to Paul's ambivalent relationship to
the Midrashim,[32] is irreducibly an aspect of our

---

[31]The designation "New Testament" by no means implies
necessarily that the Hebrew Bible is the "Old Testament."
On the principle that those who originate works have the
first call on naming them, "Hebrew Bible" and "New
Testament" can stand side by side without contradiction
or embarrassment.

[32]Cf. H. J. Schoeps (tr. H. Knight), *Paul. The Theology of
the Apostle in the Light of Jewish Religious History*

respective, religious identities.

The "Israel" whose salvation Paul sees accomplished in Christ consists of people whom Paul understands as identified by their union with Christ in baptism (Romans 6:1-11). Israel is not a people, in the sense of an ethnic entity, still less a land, and yet the simple fact Paul must acknowledge is that Christ is only manifest by means of the scriptures of a specific people, his people, who dwell by divine promise in a land which should be their own. For that reason, Abraham is a crucial figure in Paul's argument (Romans 4), in that the patriarch must be seen -- to function as a witness of Christ -- as opening the promise of faith to all, that the whole world might be possessed by means of the promise to Abraham (Romans 4:13). Circumcision must be seen as a seal of faith, not as its condition (vv. 9-12), and the land of Israel must be understood as the first installment of what is to come to all those who are to be included in Christ (vv. 16-25 and 11:25-27). Abraham is for Paul the paradigm of a univocal promise, of which earlier fulfillments were temporary affairs in the interim before Christ. Paul's account of faith, in other words, requires consistent recourse to, dialogue with, and

---

(Philadelphia: Westminster, 1961) 244.

re-interpretation of Judaism and its scriptures.[33]

The significance of such dialogue may be seen in historical, intellectual, and/or social terms; for considerations of that sort (as well as on religious grounds), Jews might welcome it. For Christians, however, dialogue is no mere option, which particular circumstances or dispositions might favor or disfavor. For those of us who attempt to follow in the steps of Paul, Judaism is not simply a potential field of mission,

---

[33]In just this sense, Watson's argument, that Paul is attempting here to show "the consistency of the Pauline view of God's activity with the OT Scriptures" (Paul, p. 162) is apposite. For Watson, however, that observation contributes to the finding that Romans was written in order to convince "the Jewish Christian congregation in Rome to separate themselves from the Jewish community, to accept the legitimacy of the Pauline Gentile congregation in which the law is not observed, and to unite with it for worship" (p. 173). A detailed consideration of Watson's views is merited, and cannot be provided here. Obviously, I would concur with the emphasis on Paul's desire for unity. But I do not believe Watson has adequately accounted for the relative flexibility of Roman Judaism (cf. Harry J. Leon, The Jews of Ancient Rome: The Morris Loeb Series [Philadelphia: the Jewish Publication Society of America, 1960]), where baptism in Jesus' name need not have implied automatic exclusion from the synagogue at the time Paul wrote, nor can I see Paul demanding the sort of separation from Judaism which is presupposed in Hebrews. Notably, Watson himself observes that Romans 11 is far more positive in respect of Judaism than his thesis would allow (pp. 170-173).

and still less some sort of embarrassment. Judaism represents an authentic (and relatively straightforward) reading of the Hebrew scriptures, and the gospel is to be grasped as the intersection between such a reading and our experience of Christ. Of course, as compared to a bland rejection of Judaism (or a condemnation of Christianity as overly complicated), that position will appear complex. But Paul was the apostle who never feared complexity in his battle to grasp, and to be grasped by, the truth of the gospel.

The Epitaph of Himerus
from the Jewish Catacomb of the Via Appia

In 1859, Raffaele Garucci began to catalog and transcribe inscriptions in a recently discovered catacomb, constructed for Jewish usage, which had been found in the vineyard of one Ignace Randinini.[1] Garucci worked under difficult circumstances. The irrigation of the Vigna Randanini caused the galleries of the catacomb to collapse, and pilfering was a severe problem. At one point, the inscriptions were largely removed, and then afixed to relatively secure walls, but without regard to their original locations.[2] During that period of confusion, the epitaph of Himerus disappeared.

In the absence of the artifact, the collections of

---

[1]Cf. Harry B. Leon, *The Jews of Ancient Rome*: The Morris Loeb Series (Philadelphia: Jewish Publication Society of America, 1960) 51 and Garucci, *Cimitero degli antichi Ebrei scoperto recentemente in Vigna Randanini* (Rome: 1862); *Dissertazioni archeologiche de vario argomento* (Rome: 1865 [volume II]). Apparently, the catacomb was also an object of the owner's investigation from 1857 (cf. A. T. Kraabel, "Jews in Imperial Rome: More Archaeological Evidence from an Oxford Collection," *Journal of Jewish Studies* 30 (1979) 41-58, 45 n. 18, citing O. Marruchi, *La catacombe romane* [Rome: 1905] 234).

[2]Leon, 51, 70, 71.

Jean-Baptiste Frey and Harry J. Leon had to proceed on the basis of criticism of Garucci alone, at least as far as inscription #239 (as it is conventionally known, after Frey's work) was concerned.[3] That situation changed on 22 February 1988, when the epitaph was brought to Bard College by Mr David Abel, a dealer in antiquities from Woodstock in New York. He had acquired the artifact from the sale of an estate in Millbrook, and brought it to the present writer for authentication.[4]

On the reverse side of the inscription, two identical legends (one written by hand, the other typed), both signed by Frank V. Burton, explain that the artifact was removed from the wall of a "vault" (presumably, a

---

[3] Cf. Jean-Baptiste Frey, *Corpus Inscriptionum Iudaicarum. Recueil des inscriptions juives qui vont du III*[e] *siècle avant Jésus-Christ au VII*[e] *siècle de notre ère*: Sussidi allo studio della Antichità Cristiana (Roma: Pontifico Instituto de Archeologia, 1936 [volume 1]), and the English rendering, with a "Prolegomenon" by Baruch Lifshitz, *Corpus of Jewish Inscriptions. Jewish Inscriptions from the Third Century B. C. to the Seventh Century A. D.* (New York: Ktav, 1975); Leon's work is cited above.

[4] After Mr. Abel's death, his executrix had the epitaph auctioned at Sotheby's in London. Further inquiries in regard to its current location have been fruitless. It might be mentioned that Mr Abel felt that the estate concerned did not include objects from the same period, or of the same interest.

loculus), on 21 January 1873.[5] The orthography and character of the inscription were consistent with its legend, and it was quickly determined that it corresponded to #239 in Frey's collection, an inscription from the Jewish catacomb of the Via Appia (as the discovery on the site of the Vigna Randanini has come to be called). Frey had dated the brickwork in which the inscription was probably set within the second century of our era, on the grounds of the stamps in the bricks themselves.[6] Professor Douglas Baz of Bard College was commissioned to prepare a photograph, which is here published. It is the purpose of this note to describe the inscription physically, and to discuss certain features of its transcription in the light of the artifact itself.

The epitaph is inscribed, in regular but badly aligned Greek characters, on a small slab of marble, one foot by 8 3/8" by 1/2".[7] The stone is smooth and well worked, but

---

[5]In autograph and typescript, the legend reads:
Found in Jewish Catacombs, Rome,
January 21st, 1873.
Taken from the wall of one of the
most ancient vaults.
Burton's address is given (in the letterhead of the typescript) as 384 Broadway, in New York City.

[6]Cf. Frey, 55.

[7]The thickness of the slab varies somewhat; at the top right, 9/16", 1/2" at the top left, 11/16" at the

for the right edge, which is jagged, not cut square, and the top, which is straight but ragged. Three of the corners are blunted, and the bottom corner, left was broken long ago.[8] The only sign of modern damage is at the bottom edge, in the middle.[9] The dark marks in the photograph appear to be stains of rust. A cleanly drilled hole towards the right bottom corner[10] is bisected by a

---

thickest point of the top edge (5 1/4" from the left). The effect of that variation is to create a nearly longitudinal bulge, just left of center. (The cognate measurements along the bottom edge are 9/16" at the right, 1/2" at the left, and 11/16" at the thickest point [4 1/4" from the left edge].) The thickness of the right edge is regularly 9/16"; that of the left is 1/2".
At the top, the length is 11 15/16", at the bottom, 12"; 2 5/8" from the bottom edge, the length reaches 12 1/8". (Cf. the next sentence of text, where the jaggedness of the right edge is mentioned.)
The width of the slab is regular.

[8]Fortunately, the break is small, and does not impinge on the working area of the inscription (see below). It reaches 15/16" upward, 3/8" to the left, and is 1/4" deep at the extreme point of the corner.

[9]The marks are consistent with the information that the inscription was forcibly removed from the setting to which it was attached (cf. the legend, described above). The comparatively fresh mark along the bottom edge is superficial. It is 1 1/8" wide and maximally 1/8" deep. It begins 5 7/16" from the left edge.

[10]The hole is 3/16" in diameter; its center is 2 5/8" from the bottom, 10 3/16" from the left edge. (The jagged condition of the right edge makes measurement from that side less convenient.)

guideline.[11] There are also guidelines on the left,[12] the top,[13] and the bottom.[14] The result of the guidelines is to produce a pristine area of working, roughly comparable to what is available on an ordinary piece of paper today.[15]

Some pains were taken, then, to align the inscription; but carelessness produced a flawed result. Only the last line of text, which virtually rests on the guideline, is straight and steady. The line above it dips slightly toward the right, and those above that rise increasingly upwards, as they proceed from left to right. All but the top line take up space to the *right* of the guideline on the right. Although the writing is plain, therefore, the whole work seems badly planned.

---

[11]The guideline runs constantly at 10 3/16" from the left edge (cf. the last note).

[12]The guideline on the left runs 9/16" from the left edge.

[13]It runs from a distance of 5/8" from the top (on the left), to one of 21/32" from the top (on the right).

[14]From the bottom edge, the line is 9/16" up, and there is a scratch below it, which evidently was entered from right to left. At first, it is straight, but then becomes uncertain, and dissipates.

[15]The area so defined is 9 5/8" in length, and 7 1/8" in width. (At the left, the latter measurement is 7 3/16".)

The lettering reads as follows:[16]

ΕΙΟΥΛΙΑΛΛΕ

ΞΑΝΔΡΑ ΦΗ

ΚΙΚΟΙΚΙΣΟΥΩ

ΕΙΜΕΡΩ ΒΕΝΕΒΕ

ΡΕΝΔΙΜΟΥΝΝΑ.

But for the last word, the epitaph makes perfect sense, as abbreviated and badly written Latin:[17]

Iulia Ale-

---

[16]The transcription represents the distribution of the letters on each line, and divides groups of letters only when a space appears clearly in the original. (Although the spacing in the fourth line is slight, the elevation of the Ω increases the impression of a break; the impression is represented here.) The overall pattern of distribution proves to be of interest, when the question of the intent of the third line comes into focus (see below).

In this transcription, Λ and Α are distinguished, although they are written in exactly the same way in the inscription. Previous editors, working without the benefit of seeing the inscription itself, or a photograph, have suggested the engraver confused the two letters (cf. Frey, #239, and Leon, 78 n. 1). Because the two letters are *always* written in the same way, occasional confusion seems to me to be ruled out as an explanation.

[17]Essentially, the suggested Latin text accords with that of Frey.

In this rendering, square-bracketed letters are restored in lacunae which resulted from abbreviation; round brackets surround letters which are present, but faulty as transcriptions of the underlying Latin.

xandra fe-

ci[t]^{18} co[n]i[u](g)i^{19} suo

Himero bene(m)e-

---

[18]Because *fecit* commonly appears in the inscriptions, and because its presence need only be alluded to, defective spellings are many and varied (cf. Frey, 653). The final *t* might also have been a revelation to the engraver, whose usual language (if he was Jewish) was probably Greek. The suggestion has been made, by William Adler (a reader for *The Jewish Quarterly Review*), that *feci* might be taken as the intended form, a first person, singular. But line three manifests a cramped set of letters, and heavy abbreviation; *fecit* should be understood, in accordance with Frey's demonstration of a pattern in the inscriptions. In respect of the probable language of the scribe, cf. Leon, 75-92 and "The Language of the Greek Inscriptions from the Jewish Catacombs of Rome," *Transactions and Proceedings of the American Philological Association* 58 (1927) 210-233.

[19]This particular abbreviation is unique, but the word is often shortened (cf. Frey, 651 and Leon, 90 n. 3). Adler (cf. the previous note) has offered a completely original and noteworthy explanation. He suggests that the last eight letters of the third line, ΟΙΚΙΣΟΥΩ, represent "a defective form of the dative singular of the Greek word οικοσόος(meaning: 'maintainer of the house')." The two instances of the adjective cited by Liddell and Scott, however, are considerably later than the period of the inscription (cf. *A Greek-English Lexicon* [Oxford: Clarendon, 1901] 1031). Moreover, the suggestion involves talking the third letter of the line, Κ, as an error for the *t* in *fecit* (but cf. the suggestion of the previous note). The relative crowding of letters in the third line makes it easier to suppose that a Latin epitaph has been hastily and faultily abbreviated.

ren(t)i.[20] MOYNNA.

The translation,[21] therefore, must be:

Julia Alexandra

set up [this stone]

to her husband Himerus

in grateful memory. *Mounna.*

The last word has generated considerable controversy during the history of discussion; we reserve comment until the close of this note.

It is interesting that the inscription follows the pattern that the husband bears a Greek name, and the wife a mixed Latin and Greek name.[22] That phenomenon accords with Leon's characterization that users of the Appian catacomb included the most Romanized congregations.[23] The number of inscriptions in marble there (rather than simply in the bricks and mortar which closed the *loculi*) also suggests the relative wealth (although not the literacy) of the families concerned. On the other hand,

---

[20]For other faulty representations, cf. Frey, 650 and Leon, 130, 131.

[21]No attempt is made here to make hyphenations in the English rendering correspond to breaks in the lines of the inscription. Cf. Leon, 298, 299. Leon inadvertently cites the wrong number of the inscription (cf. 90 n. 3).

[22]Cf. Leon, 102, 106.

[23]Cf. Leon, 77, 108-114.

the acquaintance of the users of the Appian catacomb with Hebrew and/or Aramaic phrases will need to be considered afresh,[24] if -- as is suggested below -- MOYNNA is most sensibly understood as a Semitic form.

MOYNNA in this inscription has long caused perplexity. Frey suggested that it might be a illuminated by usages from Asia Minor, but that would appear to be a most desperate expedient, when their sense and provenience are taken into account.[25] Frey himself restores אמונה in the inscription numbered 634, from Oria; that restoration opens the possibility that MOYNNA is a defective spelling of אמונה ("faith"), in which the initial א has been omitted. The phonological vagrancy of א in Aramaic, of course, is well known, so that the possibility -- which has not so far surfaced in the literature -- deserves consideration.

On analysis, however, Frey's restoration of the inscription from Oria may seem a dubious precedent for reading "Faith" in #239 from the Via Appia. אמנה (in the

---

[24]Cf. Leon, 77, 78.

[25]#239; Frey here cites Calder's *Monumenta Asiae Minoris* (1928) 37 n. 67. In fact, Calder knows the term only as a proper name or a term of respect in inscriptions which are not demonstrably Jewish.

phrase, "precepts of the faith") is clearly written (that is, without ו) in #634, the context differs from that in #239, and the inscription from Oria is dated to near the eighth century. (Even more remote is the usage of *fides* in the fulsome [albeit first century] Latin of inscription #476 from the Via Portuensis.) In the light of such dificulties, it is perhaps not surprising that Leon declared the problem insoluble, and complained about the transcriptional ineptitude of Raffaele Garucci.[26] Garucci's work, however, is faultless at this point, as we now know from direct access to the inscription.

Baruch Lifshitz, in his "Prolegomenon" to the English rendering of Frey's work, has taken Leon to task for not following a suggestion made by Moïse Schwabe.[27] As his suggestion would have it, MOYNNA represents "the initials of the Hebrew formula משכבו נוח נפש שׁ אמן."[28] But Lifshitz's estimation that Schwabe's proposal was "very satisfactory" is optimistic in the extreme. He himself accepts that "the most Romanized Jews were buried in the Via Appia catacombs," and is not inclined to the view

---

[26]Leon, 299.

[27] Cf. Schwabe's review of Frey's volume, which appeared in *Qiryat-Sepher: Bibliographical Quarterly of the Jewish National and University Library* XIV (1938) 498-513.

[28]Lifshitz, 32.

that Hebrew was used among them,[29] so that the supposition they would invoke a phrase of Hebrew by means of an acronym alone is problematic. Moreover, the closest analogy to the proposed phrase is at the close of a well written epitaph from the catacomb of Venosa (#611), which is dated later than those of Rome.[30] It seems much more straightforward to imagine that ‎[א]מונה has been rendered phonetically, a supposition which accords with the engraver's difficulties with spelling and abbreviating Latin. Initial ‎א, of course, often disappears in the pronunciation of Aramaic. (For that reason, the suggestion that a title such as ‎ממונא [in Mishnah, frequently found in tractate *Tamid*, for example] lies behind MOYNNA is less plausible.)[31] Dr Richard White, in a conversation, has suggested that the double v, followed by α, might have represented the prominal suffix ‎-נא in Aramaic (so that we would render the word, "our faith"). That possibility cannot be discounted, although the engraver's ear does not appear to have been markedly more acute than his eye, so that Dr White's refinement can be commended, but only by way of suggestion.[32] "Peace" (‎שלום)

---

[29]Lifshitz, 22.

[30]Cf. Leon, 122 n. 6.

[31]Cf.   Frey's   additional   comment   on   #239.

[32]Similarly, White's subsequent suggestion, that a participliar form of ‎נוה is involved, requires the

is quite often appended in other inscriptions, as well as "Amen" (אמן), from time to time, so that "Faith" is not surprising in the present position. And although the usages of #634 and #476 are not, strictly speaking, analogous to the proposed reading of #239, they do present certain similarities.

---

supposition that ה has disappeared; it is easier to imagine a vagrant א.

Prophecy in the Targumim

Consideration of the theme of prophecy in the Targumim for the purposes of a comparison with the Philonic corpus should commence with those documents, and strata within documents, recognized to be nearest in time to Philo. A generation ago, such an approach might reasonably have begun with "the Palestinian Targum," postulated by Paul Kahle as the *Vorlage* of the Targum Yerushalmi, the Fragments Targum, and the manuscripts from the Cairo Geniza, and claimed by Alejandros Díez Macho as the prototype of Neophyti I.[1] But the heady days which followed early discussion are now past, and the pretensions of a "Palestinian Targum" as early as the first century B. C. seem hollow. Even as keen a partisan of the hypothesis as Roger Le Déaut is left to define

---

[1] A fine, critical representation of the hypothesis is offered in M. McNamara, *The New Testament and the Palestinian Targum to the Pentateuch*: Analecta Biblica 27 (Rome: Pontifical Biblical Institute, 1966). Cf. his later work, *Targum and Testament* (Shannon: Irish University Press, 1972) and Paul Kahle, *The Cairo Geniza* (Oxford: Blackwell, 1959); Alejandro Díez Macho, "Le Targum palestinien," *Exégèse biblique et Judaïsme* (Strasbourg: Faculté de théologie catholique, 1973) 17-77; *Recherches de science religieuse* 47 (1973) 169-231; Roger Le Déaut (tr. S. F. Miletic), *The Message of the New Testament and the Aramaic Bible*: Subsidia Biblica 5 (Rome Pontifical Institute Press, 1982).

what is postulated as "a collection of exegetical
traditions, and not an *Urtext*, which never existed."[2]
Evidently, if what he is referring to is simply
exegetical activity of some sort in Aramaic, related
however tenuously to the Targumim which can be read
today, there is nothing exceptionable in his perspective;
but to call that activity "the Palestinian Targum," and
to treat it as part of the synoptic development of the
Targum,[3] is an instance of hypothesis slipping into
legerdemain.

The present essay is no occasion for repeating reference
to a debate which has been detailed and often heated,[4]

---

[2]*Targum du Pentateuque* I (Paris: Les éditions du Cerf,
1978) 22.

[3]That is precisely what Le Déaut proceeds to do on p. 42,
and he repeats his diagram, a hypostasis of "the
Palestinian Targum," in his article in *The Cambridge
History of Judaism.* The point requires emphasis, in that
students of the New Testament are likely to be misled
into believing that "the Palestinian Targum" continues to
be postulated by critical Targumists. It rather has the
appearance of the *arrière-garde* of Kahle's school.
Indeed, Le Déaut appears to defend the supposition of the
Palestinian Targum all the more trenchantly when he
addresses a non-specialist audience, cf. "The Targumim,"
The Cambridge History of Judaism 2 (eds W. D. Davies and
L. Finkelstein; Cambridge: Cambridge University Press,
1989) 563-590, as well as *The Message.*

[4]The debate is summarized in the introduction of Chilton,
The Glory of Israel. The Theology and Provenience of the

but we may generally observe that the Targumim once
called Palestinian are written in a dialect of Aramaic no
earlier than the third century, that they appear to
reflect the exegetical traditions of the Amoraim, and
that they were written at a stage at which Targumim were
a matter of literary production as much as of teaching in
synagogues.[5] In order to clearly represent that
consensus, it has been proposed to rename the corpus: we
are dealing with a rich inheritance of Tiberian Targumim,
not with a unitary, ancient "Palestinian Targum."[6] Those

Isaiah Targum: Journal for the Study of the Old Testament
Supplements 23 (Sheffield: JSOT, 1982) 7-11, and
bibliography is given on pp. 118, 119. Pivotal articles
in the discussion are presented in J. A. Fitzmyer, *Essays
on the Semitic Background of the New Testament*: Sources
for Biblical Study 5 (Missoula: Scholars Press, 1974); *A
Wandering Aramean. Collected Aramaic Essays*: Society of
Biblical Literature Monograph Series 25 (Missoula:
Scholars Press, 1979).

[5]Just those points are recognized by Le Déaut, *Targum du
Pentateuque* I, p. 40, who nonetheless goes on vaguely to
assert that "*il* (sc. Neophyti I) *représente l'une des
mise par écrit d'une tradition orale bien plus ancienne.*"
He acknowledges that the "antiquity" -- by which he means
relevance to the study of the New Testament -- of "the
Palestinian Targum" cannot be presumed (p. 65), and yet
he asserts it at every available opportunity, even when
the evidence he cites makes the assertion problematic.

[6]The proposal is made in an article forthcoming in
Aufstieg und Niedergang der römische Welt, entitled
"Targumische Traditionen innherhalb des Neuen
Testaments."

documents therefore have a place in our consideration, but that place is not at -- or even near -- the beginning.

The period of scholarly discussion which has seen the falsification of the hypothesis of a "Palestinian Targum" has seen another revolution of equally dynamic proportions. The Prophets' Targum, both to the Former and the Latter Prophets, has received renewed attention as the best source for the explication of scripture in synagogues during periods of early Judaism and rabbinic Judaism. The current phase of discussion is predicated upon the fundamental work of Pinkhos Churgin, who located Targum Jonathan in the intersection between worship in synagogues and rabbinic discussion.[7] Today, it may seem obvious that the principal Targumim are the result of the dynamics between synagogues and schools,[8] but there have been times when an almost entirely folk origin has been

---

[7]Cf. *Targum Jonathan to the Prophets:* Yale Oriental Series -- Researches XIV (New Haven: Yale University Press, 1927).

[8]Cf. A. D. York, "The Dating of Targumic Literature," *Journal for the Study of Judaism* 5 (1974) 49-62; "The Targum in the Synagogue and the School," *Journal for the Study of Judaism* 10 (1979) 74-86; Chilton, *The Isaiah Targum:* The Aramaic Bible 11 (Wilmington: Glazier and Edinburgh: Clark, 1987) xxv-xxviii.

proposed.[9] Churgin held that Targum Jonathan emerged during the formative period of rabbinic influence, between the second century B. C. and the seventh century A. D. Linguistic discussion, primarily the work of A. Tal, E. Y. Kutscher, and M. Goshen-Gottstein,[10] focused attention particularly on the second century A. D., that is, just subsequent to the Aramaic of Qumran, and transitional to the language of the Amoraim, as the

---

[9]Cf. R. Le Déaut, *Introduction à la littérature targumique* (Rome: Pontifical Biblical Institute, 1966); J. Bowker, *The Targums and Rabbinic Literature. An Introduction to Jewish Interpretation of Scripture* (Cambridge: Cambridge University Press, 1969); McNamara, *Targum and Testament.*

[10]Cf. Tal, *The Language of the Targum of the Former Prophets and its Position within the Aramaic Dialects* (Tel Aviv: 1975 [Hebrew]); Kutscher, "Das zur Zeit Jesu gesprochene Aramäische," *Zeitschrift für die neutestamentliche Wissenschaft* 51 (1960) 46-54; (tr. M. Sokoloff), *Studies in Galilean Aramaic*: Bar Ilan Studies in Near Eastern Language and Culture (Ramat Gan: Bar Ilan University Press, 1976); Goshen-Gottstein, "The Language of Targum Onqelos and the Model of Literary Diglossia in Aramaic," *Journal of Near Eastern Studies* 37 (1978) 169-179. Although the discussion cannot now detain us, mention should also be made here of Fitzmyer's contributions, already cited, and to two articles which appeared in 1973, M. Delcor, "Le Targum de Job et l'araméen du temps de Jésus," *Exégèse biblique et judaisme* (ed. J.-E. Ménard; Strasbourg: Faculté de théologie catholique, 1973) 78-107; S. Kaufman, "The Job Targum from Qumran," *Journal of the American Oriental Society* 93 (1973) 317-327.

likely period of formation. But one of the features noted has been the stable, one might say standard, quality of the Aramaic employed in Targum Jonathan, which makes an assessment of date predicated upon linguistic considerations alone appear inadequate.[11]

A decade ago, the present writer took up a method of comparative analysis which was designed to substantiate or to qualify the work of linguists.[12] The exegeses incorporated in the Targum of Isaiah were compared systematically with departures from the Hebrew text evidenced in the Septuagint, the Apocrypha and Pseudepigrapha, the scrolls of Qumran, the New Testament, the Mishnah, the two Mikiltas, *Sifra*, *Sifre*, the two Talmuds, Midrash Rabba, the two Pesiktas, the *Pirqe de R. Eliezer*, and the *Yalkut Shimoni*. The conclusion was that targumic traditions were incorporated within an exegetical framework, a version -- perhaps incomplete -- of Isaiah in Aramaic composed by a meturgeman who flourished between A. D. 70 and 135.[13] That work was

---

[11]Cf. *The Glory of Israel*, pp. xi. Since the time I wrote those pages, however, discussion of the development of the Aramaic language has tended to offer further support of the position which I developed upon an exegetical basis, as remarks below will indicate; cf. *The Isaiah Targum*, p. xxi.

[12]Cf. Chilton, *The Glory of Israel*.

[13]Within that early framework, materials were incorporated

completed by another meturgeman, associated with Rabbi Joseph bar Ḥiyya of Pumbeditha, who died in 333.[14] Throughout the process, however, the communal nature of the interpretative work of the meturgeman was acknowledged; insofar as individuals were involved, they spoke as the voice of synagogues and of schools.

The theme of a characteristically prophetic message of repentance is represented in both frameworks, and there is tragic recognition that the departure of the Shekinah spells the end of prophecy (cf. 5:5, 6; 8:16, 17).[15]

---

which appear to reflect the interpretations of earlier periods, including the period of Jesus, cf. Chilton, *A Galilean Rabbi and his Bible. Jesus' Use of the Interpreted Scripture of His Time*: Good News Studies 8 (Wilmington: Glazier, 1986; also published with the subtitle, *Jesus' own interpretation of Isaiah*; London: SPCK, 1984).

[14]*The Glory of Israel*, pp. 2, 3; *The Isaiah Targum*, p. xxi. For the sections of the Targum most representative of each meturgeman; cf. *The Isaiah Targum*, p. xxiv.

[15]Cf. *The Glory of Israel*, pp. 98, 54–5. For the latter theologoumenon, cf. (for Is. 5:5, 6) Ecclesiastes Rabba 11.3, and (for 8:16, 17) Genesis Rabba 43.3.2. The first statement is attributed to Aquila, and second is anonymous. Cf. Peter Schäfer, *Die Vorstellung vom heiligen Geist in der rabbinischer Literatur*: Studien zum Alten und Neuen Testament 28 (München: Kösel, 1972) 75, 135, 136, 139, 140, 143; *The Glory of Israel*, 48–52; L. Smolar and M. Aberbach, *Studies in Targum Jonathan to the Prophets* (New York: Ktav, 1983) 11; K. J. Cathcart and R.

Within both frameworks, the *incipit,* "The prophet
said...," is frequently added. It has been rather lamely
suggested[16] that the innovation is merely a liturgical
help, much as "Jesus" replaces "he" in many modern
lectionaries. What the suggestion utterly ignores is the
most obvious and crucial factor: within both exegetical
frameworks, meturgemanin preface some of their most
innovative renderings with the introduction.[17] In
aggregate, the Aramaic interpreters implicitly claim to
speak with quasi-prophetic authority, in the wake of the
departed Shekinah. Two such cases permit us to see the
work of the meturgemanin of the two frameworks, virtually
side by side, in chapters 21 and 22.

Chapter 21 is redolent of the military power of the
Sassanids and the nascent threat of Arabians,[18] and

P. Gordon, *The Targum of the Minor Prophets*: The Aramaic
Bible 14 (Wilmington: Glazier and Edinburgh: Clark, 1989)
199 n. 5, with its citation of Babba Bathra 12a.

[16] By Cathcart and Gordon, *op. cit.,* 150.

[17] *The Glory of Israel,* pp. 52–53, 55; *The Isaiah Targum,*
pp. xiii, xiv. The observation is confirmed in respect of
Targum Jonathan more generally in R. Hayward, *The Targum
of Jeremiah*: The Aramaic Bible 12 (Wilmington: Glazier
and Edinburgh: Clark, 1987) 32. Cathcart and Gordon, *op.
cit.,* themselves translate an instance in which the
Targumic *incipit* prefaces an expansive rendering at
Habakkuk 2:1f.

[18] *The Isaiah Targum,* pp. 40–43.

indulges in proleptic glee at "Babylon's" demise. The Amoraic setting of the meturgeman is also betrayed in the particular statement (21:12);

> The prophet said, "There is reward for the righteous and retribution for the wicked. If you are penitent, repent while you are able to repent."[19]

The meturgeman addresses those who are prepared to listen (cf. 33:13; 57:19), while the usual assumption of the Targum is that Israel is obdurate.[20] Repentance is here associated more with the eschatological judgment of individuals than with the restoration of the Temple and the people, Israel's intended *telos* in the earlier framework. The usage of the *incipit* here is Amoraic, as it is at 21:8, 9, where reference is innovatively made to the imminent fall of Babylon. Perhaps the closest approximation to the reading is to be found in Numbers Rabba 16.23, which cites Is. 21:12 and observes, "when the time of the world to come arrives...we shall know in whom he delights."[21]

---

[19]As in *The Isaiah Targum*, italics indicate innovative material in the Targum, as compared to the Hebrew of the Masoretic Text.

[20]*The Glory of Israel*, pp. 37–46.

[21]The passage also connects Malachi 3:18 with Is. 21:12, which is reminiscent of the Isaian passage in Targum Jonathan. For a further discussion, including references to other analogies, cf. *The Glory of Israel*, pp. 43, 44.

The emphasis is quite different in the following chapter, which focuses on the depredations of Jerusalem, the victories of the Romans, and the fate of the sanctuary,[22] characteristic interests of the Tannaitic meturgeman. A particular threat is directed against those who feast in a time when the prophet calls for fasting (22:12, 13), and the threat, articulated at 22:14, is couched in language also found in the Revelation of John:

> The prophet said, With my ears *I was hearing when this was decreed before* the LORD God of hosts: "Surely this *sin* will not be forgiven until you die *the second death,"* says the LORD God of hosts."

The fact that the same theologoumenon appears in Revelation 2:11; 20:6, 14; 21:8 does not alone settle the questions of the chronology and meaning of the phrase. Charles Perrot and Pierre-Maurice Bogaert cite the usage in various Targumim and in *the Pirqe de R. Eliezer* (34).[23]

---

[22]Cf. *The Isaiah Targum*, pp. 42–45 and Chilton, "Shebna, Eliakim, and the Promise to Peter," *The Social World of Formative Christianity and Judaism* (eds J. Neusner, P. Borgen, E. S. Frerichs, R. Horsley; Philadelphia: Fortress, 1989) 311–326, also available in *Targumic Approaches to the Gospels. Essays in the Mutual Definition of Judaism and Christianity*: Studies in Judaism (Lanham and London: University Press of America, 1986) 63–80.

[23]*Les Antiquités bibliques* II: Sources Chrétiennes 230 (Paris: Les éditions du Cerf, 1976) 56 n. 3.

But at Is. 22:14, the rabbis from the second century regularly refer to death in the straightforward sense (cf. Mekilta Bahodesh 7.24; cf. Yoma 86a),[24] so that the communal eschatology of the Tannaitic meturgeman appears to be reflected here.

The idea of a phasal development within Targum Jonathan, resulting in two exegetical frameworks, the one developed prior to A. D. 135, and the other of Aramaic provenience, has been generalized from the Isaiah Targum to other documents within Jonathan in a way which could only be intimated a decade ago.[25] In his commentary, Robert Hayward observes that the "translation of 'prophet' in certain cases as 'scribe' produces the association of

---

[24] Cf. *The Glory of Israel*, p. 56.

[25] *The Glory of Israel*, p. 117. The same paradigm is applied in D. J. Harrington and A. J. Saldarini, *Targum Jonathan of the Former Prophets*: The Aramaic Bible 10 (Wilmington: Glazier and Edinburgh: Clark, 1987) 3; Hayward, *op. cit.*, p. 38; S. H. Levey, *The Targum of Ezekiel*: The Aramaic Bible 13 (Wilmington: Glazier and Edinburgh: Clark, 1987) 3, 4; Cathcart and Gordon, *op. cit.*, pp. 12–14. Levey's acceptance of the paradigm is especially noteworthy, in that he had earlier argued that Targum Jonathan (especially Isaiah) should be placed within the period of the ascendancy of Islam, cf. "The Date of Targum Jonathan to the Prophets," *Vetus Testamentum* 21 (1971) 186–196. Although the model has been applied, the editions cited do not, in fact, test it critically, which is the method recommended in *The Glory of Israel*.

priests with scribes" in the Jeremiah Targum, an
association also made in Josephus and the New Testament.[26]
Scribes, then, are "a *powerful and influential group*"
during the time of the Targum's composition.[27] Care should
be taken, however, not to apply Hayward's suggestion
globally. There are instances in which the association is
not operative in the Jeremiah Targum,[28] and the "prophets"
of the Masoretic Text often become "prophets of
falsehood" as well as "scribes" in the Targum.[29]
Meturgemanin of Jeremiah, as those of Isaiah,[30] evidently
wished to insulate the unqualified usage of "prophet"
from any charge of deception. That results in referring
to prophets who lie,[31] and in the grouping of other

---

[26]Hayward, *op. cit.*, pp. 36, 37. He cites Tg. Jer. 8:10;
14:18; 23:11, 33, 34; 26:7, 8, 11, 16; 29:11 and
Antiquities 12.3.3 @ 142; Mark 11:27; Matthew 2:4; 16:21:
20:18; Acts 4:5, 6.

[27]Hayward, *op. cit.*, p. 33. His argument was earlier
developed in "Some Notes on Scribes and Priests in the
Targum of the Prophets," *Journal of Jewish Studies* 36
(1985) 210-221.

[28]Cf. 6:13; 18:18, from Hayward's own lists (pp. 32, 36,
37).

[29]Hayward, *op. cit.*, p. 32; as he notes, and as is the
case elsewhere in the Targum Jonathan, "teacher" is a
possible surrogate for "prophet" in the Masoretic Text.

[30]Cf. *The Glory of Israel*, p. 54, citing 9:14; 28:7.

[31]Hayward, *op. cit.*, p. 33 corrects the surmise of Churgin
that idolatrous prophets are particularly in view when
the phrase "prophets of falsehood" appears.

classes of leaders in criticisms from which prophets are protected. That is quite a different matter from the presentation of the Gospels, in which priestly and scribal leaders are particularly in view as a result of their alleged responsibility in the execution of Jesus.[32]

Hayward's comparison of the Jeremiah Targum with the Gospels illustrates a difficulty in the assessment of the Targumim in respect of more ancient documents. Words and phrases are more easily shared than are meanings, especially among speakers who commonly -- and independently -- refer to an authoritative collection of scriptures. The meturgemanin of Jeremiah sometimes referred to "scribes" in order to protect "prophets" from criticism; the Gospels' framers attack "scribes" in order to discredit an alternative system of religion. Unless the sense of references is evaluated, observations of brute similarities of usage are pointless, and may prove misleading.[33]

Hayward also notes a tendency to introduce the term "prophet" in the Targum Jeremiah, as at 35:4 (in

---

[32]Cf. Michael J. Cook, *Mark's Treatment of the Jewish Leaders*: Supplements to Novum Testamentum (Brill: Leiden, 1978).

[33]Cf. the method of exegetical comparison recommended in *Targumic Approaches to the Gospels*, cited above.

reference to Hanan, the son of Yigdaliah). He does not observe, however, that the usage cited is part of a pattern within Jonathan generally, in which prophecy is associated with the cult (cf. also the Isaiah Targum 8:2, in respect of Uriah the priest); that positive assessment of a priestly charism emerges only sporadically, and likely rests upon an ancient claim, much in the manner of Josephus.[34] Generally speaking, the whole of Jonathan represents a tendency to portray "prophecy as a unified phenomenon which is understood as true contact with God involving revelatory significance," and to introduce characterizations designed to protect the perceived integrity of prophecy.[35] That is the conclusion of Harrington and Saldarini in respect of the Targum of the Former Prophets, and it is sufficiently unexceptionable to be applied to the corpus as a whole.

From the second century, the rabbis taught that prophecy was a phenomenon proper to the land promised by God to his people (cf. Mekilta Pisha 1.42f.). Such an understanding was at apparent odds with the experience of

---

[34]Cf. J. Blenkinsopp, "Prophecy and Priesthood in Josephus," *Journal of Jewish Studies* 25 (1974).

[35]Harrington and Saldarini, *op. cit.*, pp. 11, 12. Cf. also Saldarini, "'Is Saul Also Among the Scribes?' Scribes and Prophets in Targum Jonathan," *Essays on Aggadah and Judaica for Rabbi William G. Braude* (New York: Ktav, 1986).

Ezekiel, and was a problem which needed to be confronted in the Aramaic rendering of the book. As Samson H. Levey points out, the meturgemanin resolved the difficulty by having Ezekiel's revelation in 1:3 begin in Jerusalem.[36] Cathcart and Gordon similarly associate the presentation of the prophets within the Targum of the Minor Prophets with the theology of the Amoraim. Unlike Hayward, they locate the usage of "scribe" in that latter phase of the Targum's development, on the grounds that the rabbis held that prophecy had passed from the prophets to the sages.[37] Obviously, that analysis fails to take account of the negative sense which sometimes accompanies use of the term "scribe" in Jonathan; if they are more correct than Hayward in their chronology, they are equally deficient in their exegesis. Moreover, they do not call attention to the connection of priesthood and prophecy at Hosea 4:4,[38] nor to the repeated theme of Israel's rejection of the prophetic message (cf. Hosea 6:5; 9:7; Zephaniah

---

[36]Levey, op. cit., p. 13.

[37]Cathcart and Gordon, op. cit., pp. 3, 199 n. 5, citing Babba Bathra 12a. Cf. also Gordon, "Targum as Midrash: Contemporizing in the Targum to the Prophets," Proceedings of the Ninth World Congress of Jewish Studies (ed. M. Goshen–Gottstein; Jerusalem, 1988) 61–73.

[38]A reference to priesthood there in the Masoretic Text occasions the statement, "For they say, 'The scribe shall not teach, and the prophet shall not admonish.' So your people argue with their teachers."

3:2); both of those features are important links to the Tannaitic phase of Targum Jonathan. Finally, they do not observe the vital link between their Targum and the rest of Jonathan in its received form: the tendency to present the message of all the prophets as consonant. That is particularly accomplished by identifying the biblical prophets as such, despite the impression of redundancy which sometimes results (cf. Nahum 1:1; Habakkuk 1:1; Zephaniah 1:1; Haggai 2:1; Zechariah 1:1; 7:4; 11:4, 15).[39]

The model of the phasal development of two exegetical frameworks which was developed in respect of the Isaiah Targum, and then generalized for Jonathan, has recently been deployed in order to understand Targum Onqelos.[40] Grossfeld has subjected Onqelos to the same sort of comparative analysis with rabbinic sources which was conducted in the case of Isaiah, so that his findings may be cited with greater confidence than is the case with the less comprehensive treatments of the Targums of the Former Prophets, Jeremiah, Ezekiel, and the Latter

---

[39]Their distinction from the false prophets, cf. Micah 3:5; Zephaniah 3:4; Zechariah 13:2, 4 is another link to the normal pattern of Jonathan.

[40]Cf. Bernard Grossfeld, *The Targum Onqelos to Genesis*: The Aramaic Bible 6 (Wilmington: Glazier and Edinburgh: Clark, 1988) 11, 16, 18, 32, 33, 34, 35.

Prophets. Much as the Isaiah Targum has been linked with Rabbi Joseph bar Ḥiyya, Grossfeld connects Targum Onqelos with Rab, the Amora of the third century, while a Tannaitic phase, characterized by similarities to the so-called Halakhic Midrashim (*Mekilta*, *Sifra*, *Sifre*) is also posited.[41] Together with Moses Aberbach, Grossfeld observes that, when Rebecca claims prophetic knowledge that no curse would come upon Jacob for deceiving his father (27:13), that accords with the understanding of Midrash Rabba.[42] The cognate theme of patriarchal inspiration also emerges at 41:38 and at 49:24, of Joseph.[43] Indeed, such is the intensity of the conviction that a single "spirit of prophecy" is responsibility for the disclosure of truth, it is said to have resided even in Balaam (Numbers 24:2).

---

[41]Grossfeld is rather ambivalent in regard to the date of the "final redaction:" is that event to be placed in the fourth century (p. 16), the fifth century (p. 18), or the third century (p. 32)?

[42]At Genesis 67.9. Cf. the discussion in Aberbach and Grossfeld, *Targum Onqelos to Genesis* (New York: Ktav, 1982) 101.

[43]Cf. Aberbach and Grossfeld, *op. cit.*, pp. 138, 171, and the reference to Genesis Rabba 89.3 on the latter page. The appearance of the phrase "spirit *of prophecy*" at Numbers 11:25, 26, 29 might be mentioned, but it is scarcely remarkable, in view of the meaning of the passage in Hebrew. Cf. Grossfeld, *The Targum Onqelos to Leviticus and The Targum Onqelos to Numbers*: The Aramaic Bible 8 (Wilmington: Glazier, 1988) 101 n. 15.

It is not surprising that the Targum called Neophyti I should largely agree with the thematic emphasis already described in the case of Onqelos, in that its textual basis was also laid during the Amoraic period.[44] As is consistently the case in the Tiberian Targums, readings are frequently more expansive and innovative, at times overtly haggadic. Prophecy is closely associated with Abraham (Genesis 15:4; 18:1), but also with Bezalel (Exodus 31:3), in view of his connection with the cult.[45] A notable reading at Exodus 32:5 associates the prophet Hur with Aaron in his apostacy, much as in Amoraic literature.[46] There was evidently a tendency during that period to loosen the strictures in regard to what might be associated with prophecy, although Neophyti also relates it emphatically to the people of Israel and to Moses in particular.[47] Moses and Miriam benefit from the association in Numbers (11:26;[48] 12:16), and Moses' role

---

[44]Cf. Le Déaut, *Targum du Pentateque* I (1978) 40. The fifth volume is an *Index Analytique* (1981), which was of great utility in the preparation of the present paper.

[45]Cf. 35:30f.

[46]Cf. Leviticus Rabba 10.5 and Sanhedrin 7a.

[47]Cf. Exodus 1:21; 2:12, in both instances, marginal readings; Leviticus 27:33 presents a alignment of Moses and the prophets in the margin.

[48]As in the cognate case in Onqelos, the reference to Eldad and Medad in prophetic terms is not remarkable, in

as a prophet is reinforced again in Deuteronomy (30:12; 32:1, 12, 13). The specificity of that role becomes startling at 32:1, in that Isaiah is also named as such. The case of the *mesith* in chapter 13, by contrast, is specified as false prophecy (vv. 2, 4, 6).

The Targum conventionally known as Pseudo–Jonathan, which was produced during the seventh century, simply extends the pattern established in Neophyti I.[49] Now Joseph (Genesis 41:3), Jacob (45:27; 46:2), and Sarah (21:12)[50], and the prophetic endowment of Israel as a whole, may also be taken as characteristic of the emphasis of Pseudo–Jonathan (cf. also 35:11). That theme is repeated in Exodus, 33:16; 36:21, although the old idea of Bezalel's status is also found here (35:31; 37:8). Likewise, the continuity between the seventy and Moses is stressed (Numbers 11:17, cf. 25ff.), and the prophetic designation of Miriam is quite emphatic (Numbers 33:17).[51]

---

view of the Masoretic Text.

[49]The question of dating is adddressed by Le Déaut, *Targum du Pentateuque* I, pp. 29–37. Owing the their fragmentary character, the manuscripts of the Cairo Geniza and the Fragments Targum have not been included within the present survey.

[50]Cf. Exodus Rabba 1.1.

[51]The idea in itself, of course, is unexceptionable, cf. Exodus 15:20 in the Masoretic Text. Cf. Le Déaut, *Targum du Pentateque* II, p. 129.

Pseudo-Jonathan shares the vision of Neophyti in regard to any *mesith* (Deuteronomy 13:2, 4, 6) and the identity of Moses (32:1, 12, 13). But instead of the comparison with Isaiah in particular, there is rather an insistence upon the continuity of prophecy as God's own gift (Deuteronomy 18:14,[52] 19; 32:1, 7).

The Targum of Ruth extends the sphere of prophetic revelation to include Boaz (2:11; 3:16) and Ruth (3:15), just as surely as it incorporates the rabbinic idea of the withholding of prophecy as a punishment (1:1). Etan Levine has argued that the Targum derives "from an early, Palestinian sect."[53] But his argument is based entirely on the notion "that whatever is anti-mishnaic is pre-mishnaic." Pseudo-Jonathan is manifestly post-Mishnaic, in its reference to Adisha and Fatima, the wife and daughter of Mohammed (Genesis 21:21), and just as manifestly "anti"-Mishnaic, in that Mishnah Megillah 4:9 insists that Leviticus 18:21 ("You must not give of your seed, to deliver it to Moloch") should *not* be interpreted in respect of sexual intercourse with

---

[52]Notably, a comparison is here made between priestly consultation of Urim and Thumim and the role of the prophets. Whenever the wording was formulated, Pseudo-Jonathan here articulates an ancient idea.

[53]*The Aramaic Version of Ruth*: Analecta Biblica 58 (Rome: Biblical Institute Press, 1973) 7.

Gentiles, which is just the interpretation the Targum indulges. By the time of the Tiberian Targums, sufficient distance from the origins of the form in the worship of synagogues had been achieved to allow of what amounts to academic play: marginal variants of the sort of Neophyti's, and countervailing interpretations as in Pseudo-Jonathan and Ruth. But typical themes such as that of prophecy permit us to place such Targumim within a plausible scheme of development.

The Targum of Chronicles provides a suitable *terminus ad quem* for the present exercise, in that it is widely agreed to have been composed at the turn of the eighth and ninth centuries.[54] Here, too, there is an extension of the sphere of prophecy. It may generally include the prophets and scribes who succeeded Joshua (1 Chron. 4:22), but also the daughter of Pharaoh who named Moses (and later converted and married Caleb; 4:18),[55] the father of Hosea (5:6),[56] members of David's entourage

---

[54]Cf. R. Le Déaut and J. Robert, *Targum des Chroniques*: Analecta Biblica 51 (Rome: Biblical Institute Press, 1971) 27. As in the case of other Targumim, Le Déaut posits an earlier form (p. 25), in the present case reaching back to the fourth century.

[55]Cf. Megillah 13a and Le Déaut, Robert, *op. cit.*, p. 49.

[56]Cf. Hosea 1:1 and Le Déaut, Robert, *op cit.*, p. 52.

(11:11; 17:3; 21:9; 25:5), David himself (22:8; 23:27;[57] 2
Chron. 8:14), and those who confronted later kings (2
Chron. 11:2; 12:7; 15:1; 18:18, 27, 33; 25:9; 33:10).[58]

The fundamental concerns of the Targumim in regard to
prophecy, then, are characteristic of their identified
strata. The Tannaim were consumed with the failure of
Israel as a whole to attend to the prophetic message, and
with the resulting punishment. The Amoraim were more
optimistic, but also conceived of the rewards of
attending to prophecy in more individually eschatological
terms. Targum Jonathan represents those strata quite
clearly. The thought that Israel might indeed attend to
God's message through his prophets later resulted in a
certain playfulness in respect of identifying prophets
from the past. There was a precedent for that exercise in
the association between priesthood and prophecy within
early Judaism, which Targum Jonathan already attests. But
by the time of Neophyti I and Pseudo-Jonathan (that is,
near the middle and towards the end of the Amoraic
period), there is a positive and inventive enjoyment in
"identifying" the prophetic bearers of the past, an
enjoyment which the emergence of Targum as a literary

---

[57]Moses, by contrast, is by now "the great scribe," 24:6.

[58]Cf. the reference to prophets who lie, 2 Chron. 18:9,
21.

form only encouraged. What might or might not be countenanced in the school could be indulged in Targumim, particularly as their applicability to worship in synagogues (with the currency of Arabic) became problematic.

The treatment of Balaam in the Tiberian Targums may serve to illustrate the point. For Philo, he is a problematic figure. He is not properly a prophet, but renowned for μαντaία (*De Vita Mosis* I @ 264), and covetous of prophetic fame (I @ 266).[59] Left to his own devices, he would be a failure, but he is grasped by a prophetic spirit (προφητικοῦ πνεύματος ἐπιφοιτήσαντος; I @ 277 cf. I @ 283). In fact, before Balaam can give his most famous oracle from scripture, Philo has him giving his own, personal advice to Balak: introduce prostitutes into Israel, so as to weaken them (I @ 294f., an interpretation inspired by Numbers 25 and 31:16). The heroic intervention of Phineas purifies the camp, and defeats Balaam's advice. Philo's view of Balaam is not unique, although his account of prophecy is characteristic: Josephus has Balaam giving similar advice (cf. *Antiquities* 4.6.6 @ 129, 130).[60] By contrast, the

---

[59]Cf. Roger Arnaldez, Claude Mondésert, Jean Pouilloux, Pierre Savinel, *De Vita Mosis I-II*: Les Oeuvres de Philon D'Alexandrie (Paris: Les édition du Cerf, 1967) 153.

[60]*Op. cit.*, p. 168. It may be of interest that Balaam's

Tiberian Targums repeatedly refer to Balaam in unashamedly prophetic terms,[61] and present the gist of his message (Numbers 24:23) as comparable to Isaiah's (21:12).[62] The figure whom for Philo and Josephus is

---

prophecy was involved with a priestly act, and that Phineas' counteraction is both prophetic and priestly in Numbers. The treatment of Balaam in Onqelos and the *Liber Antiquitatum Biblicarum* 18 is conservative, as is generally the case in the Tiberian Targumim, although the ancient idea of his malicious advice is incorporated; cf. Grossfeld, *op. cit.*, 138 and Perrot and Bogaert, *op. cit.*, p. 128 n. 13. It appears that the oracle of Balaam had assumed such importance during the movement of Simon bar Kosiba, with its classic expectation of a star from Jacob in 24:17, that Balaam himself was protected somewhat from the earlier haggadah which Philo and Josephus report by a more direct reference to the biblical text.

[61]Cf. Neophyti Numbers 23:7, 10, 19, 23; 24 :3, 10, 23; 24:3, 4, 15, 16, 20, 21, 23; Pseudo-Jonathan Numbers 23:7; 24:3; 24:4, 15, 16, 20, 21, 23; E. E. Urbach, "Homilies of the Rabbis on the Prophets of the Nations and the Balaam Stories," *Tarbiz* 25 (1956) 272-289. The importance of the oracle in Numbers 24:17 to the movement of Simeon bar Kosiba (cf. the interpretation in Onqelos) might explain the greater deference accorded Balaam from the second century; cf. *Damascus Document* 7.19, 20, however, for the early origin of the interpretation itself; Samuel Abramsky, "Bar Kokhba," *Encyclopedia Judaica* 4 (New York: Macmillan, 1971) 228-239.

[62]Both Neophyti and Pseudo-Jonathan frame 24:23 in terms of rewards for the righteous and vengeance enacted from the impious, and the former theme is especially emphasized in Neophyti 23:23. In each Targum, however, the eschatological judgment of individuals is at issue contextually.

exceptional and troubling becomes, by the Amoraic period, a cipher for the prophetic message generally. And in the generality of their message, if not in all of the exegeses they convey,[63] the Targumim convey the Amoraic

---

[63]It is notable, for example, that Pseudo-Jonathan portrays Balaam as both as benighted by the abundance of his knowledge (cf. Acts 26:24 and Le Déaut, *Targum du Pentateuque* III, p. 208) and as impious (cf. 23:9, 10, 21 and Philo's use of related terms in *De Migratione Abraham* 112, 113; *De Confusione Linguarum* 159; *De Cherubim* 32; *Quod Deterius Poterio Insidiari Soleat* 71, and Aboth 5.19). Pseudo-Jonathan also brings to especial emphasis the theme that Balaam benefited from the revelation of what had been concealed from all the prophets (24:3, 4 [with Neophyti], 15, 16; cf. Matthew 13:17/Luke 10:24 and McNamara, *Targum and Testament,* pp. 139-141). But the observation of Amoraic elements of interpretation requires some emphasis in the light of a contribution from Geza Vermes, "The Story of Balaam -- The Scriptural origin of Haggadah," *Scripture and Tradition in Judaism*: Studia Post-Biblica 4 (Leiden: Brill, 1961) 127-177. Vermes concludes that "Since targumic and midrashic literature embodies ancient exegetical tradition, it provides a reliable basis for research into the mind of the last redactors of the Bible" (p. 177). Quite evidently, his homogenizing approach violates a critical understanding of chronology and the development of meaning; he even associates Philo and Josephus with a *later* embellishment of the "ancient exegetical tradition" (1. 162). He does not reflect, for example, on Pseudo-Jonathan's development of the theme of Balaam's advice to refer to building taverns to seduce the Israelites with food and drink (24:14, cf. 25:1), an obvious incorporation of the later haggadah reflected in Yerushalmi Sanhedrin 28 and Numbers Rabba 20.23.

inheritance.

RECENT AND PROSPECTIVE DISCUSSION OF מימרא

In his recent book, *Divine Revelation and Divine Titles in the Pentateuchal Targumim,*[1] Andrew Chester sides with George Foot Moore, in seeing מימרא as a phenomenon of translation, rather than of theology.[2] Where Moore was resisting the tendency to see in מימרא a precursor of λόγος in Christian theology, Chester sets himself against the more sophisticated schemes of Domingo Muñoz Leon and Robert Hayward. Chester's resistance to a theological understanding of מימרא is especially striking, in that it appears in a work in which exegetical and theological aspects are elsewhere, in respect of other terms, held to be complementary. Observing, for example, that the verb אתגלי is used as a verbal replacement in theophanic contexts, Chester speaks of the usage quite categorically:

> It is not, then, merely a negative device, but is used with positive exegetical and theological purpose, to indicate one way in which God can be spoken of as active and present in the world.[3]

---

[1] Number 14 in the series, Texte und Studien zum Antiken Judentum (Tübingen: Mohr, 1986).

[2] Chester, *Divine Revelation*, 308-9.

[3] P. 243, cf. 152, 245, 261, 262. It may be noted that I had earlier made a similar argument for the usage of the same verb in Targum Zechariah 14.9, in "Regnum Dei Deus

Given that Chester is fully capable of a nuanced co-ordination of the exegetical and theological strands of a usage, we may ask, Why does he bifurcate them in the case of מימרא, and then unequivocally give preference to the exegetical strand?

Chester proceeds in his work by means of a careful evaluation of the history of discussion in regard to the various sorts of revelational language in which he is interested. Indeed, the care of his historical description is such that sometimes the value of his book transcends the merits of the particular case which he argues. In the instance of מימרא, Chester's lucid resumé is capped by the observation that recent discussion has polarized:

> Thus from the recent work of Muñoz Leon and Hayward on the one hand (even allowing for the important differences between them) and Aufrecht on the other, we appear to be presented with two diametrically opposed interpretations of Memra and its significance. The one holds that Memra is an

---

Est," *Scottish Journal of Theology* 31 (1978) 261–270, (now reprinted in *Targumic Approaches to the Gospels. Essays in the Mutual Definition of Judaism and Christianity*: Studies in Judaism [Lanham: University Press of America, 1986] 99–107, 101). As a note there observes, Dalman and Moore had already traced the cognate usage within Rabbinica.

important creative theological concept, above all in N[eophyti], the other that it is simply a limited type of translation, basically a metonym, with no theological significance whatever.[4]
Faced with a choice between the poles of a dichotomy, Chester prefers the exegetical alternative to the theological one.[5]

Chester is brought to his choice by means of an analysis of the arguments of Muñoz Leon and Hayward, both of which he finds seriously wanting. Muñoz Leon, in Chester's estimation, imposes a scheme upon Neophyti I which is, at the end of the day, apologetic:

> That is, he imposes a theological system on N and its usage of Memra, and reads theological significance into this usage both in detail and in general, without taking proper account of the

---

[4]P. 305. The references are to: Domingo Muñoz Leon, *Dios-Palabra. Memra en los Targumim del Pentateuco:* Institución San Jerónimo 4 (Granada: Santa Rita--Monachil, 1974); C.T.R. Hayward, *The Use and Religious Significance of the Term Memra in Targum Neofiti I in the Light of the Other Targumim* (Oxford: D.Phil., 1975), a revised form of which was published as *Divine Name and Presence: The Memra:* Oxford Centre for Postgraduate Hebrew Studies (Totowa: Allanheld, Osmun and Co., 1981); W. E. Aufrecht, *Surrogates for the Divine Name in the Palestinian Targums to Exodus* (Toronto: Ph.D., 1979).

[5]Cf. pp. 308-9, 313.

inconsistencies that do not fit this theory. Further, the theological categories he uses appear preconceived; thus, his characterization of Memra as "the creative, revealing and saving Word" fits his understanding of the Johannine Logos but not at all obviously the evidence of the Targumim themselves.[6]

It should be noted, before Chester's evaluation is accepted at face value, that the suspicion of an incipiently Christological understanding of מימרא in the work of Muñoz Leon is not consistently supportable, in that he adamantly corrects against the tendency of earlier discussion to conceive of מימרא as independent of God.[7] Nonetheless, there is a persistent recourse in his work to the language of substitution, and even of hypostasis,[8] which must seem odd in the wake of Moore's definitive assertion that "nowhere in the Targums is *memra* a 'being' of any kind or in any sense, much less a

---

[6]P. 306.

[7]We might give the example of the category, "Sustitución Memrá en lugares que expressan reacciones divinas," pp. 57f. Essentially, the emphasis upon God's unity is manifest here, cf. B. D. Chilton, *The Glory of Israel. The Theology and Provenience of the Isaiah Targum:* Journal for the Study of the Old Testament Supplements Series 23 (Sheffield: JSOT, 1982), 56–69 and 140–146, and Hayward, *Divine Name,* 6.

[8]Cf. Hayward, *Divine Name,* 6, 7.

personal being."[9] Chester rightly discerns the weakness in the analysis of Muñoz Leon, which finally fails to engage Moore's classic assertion that "*memra* is purely a phenomenon of translation, not a figment of speculation."[10] The unavoidable result of Moore's study is that מימרא should not, without argument, be taken as the object of systematic reflection among meturgemanin.

Just the last criterion of recent discussion is ignored, even more comprehensively than by Muñoz Leon, by Robert Hayward. His study is the most daring attempt ever to fasten a univocal meaning upon מימרא. He was inspired by the work of Pamela Vermes on Martin Buber, in which a link between מימרא and the divine name as disclosed in Exodus 3 is explored. Indeed, Chester's basic problem with Hayward's argument is its aetiology; he complains that Hayward "takes over uncritically the argument of P. Vermes connecting Memra with the divine name, and builds his whole thesis on hers."[11] In justice, it must be

---

[9]G. F. Moore, *Judaism in the First Centuries of the Christian Era. The Age of the Tannaim* I (Cambridge: Harvard University Press, 1927) 419 and "Intermediaries in Jewish Theology," *Harvard Theological Review* 15 (1922) 41-85, 53, 54.

[10]*Judaism*, 419; "Intermediaries," 54.

[11]*Divine Revelation*, 307. Hayward has taken issue with Chester in a review, claiming that he worked independently of Mrs Vermes (*Journal of Jewish Studies* 38

observed that Hayward does attempt to honor Moore's position:

> ...the <u>Memra</u> is neither an hypostasis, nor a pious periphrasis for the Name of YHWH, but...an exegetical term which stands for the Name revealed by God to Moses at the burning bush, the Name 'HYH I AM/I WILL BE THERE."[12]

What Hayward appears not to have recognized, however, is that such a specific locus of meaning, generated within a profoundly resonant passage and distributed generally through the Targumim, makes מימרא no longer an "exegetical term," but the engine of a systematic idea.

What is at issue at this point in Hayward's thesis might more accurately be called an exegetical theology, and the more generally it is imputed to the Targumim as a whole, the less plausible it appears. Hayward's own characterization of the meaning of מימרא in Neophyti makes it evident that his understanding is far from Moore's:

> N's point is therefore clear: the covenant with Jacob at Bethel is God's assurance that He, in His

---

[1987] 261-266, 265). That clarification would appear to contradict the "Preface" of *Divine Name* (p. ix).

[12]Hayward, "The Holy Name of the God of Moses and the Prologue of St John's Gospel," *New Testament Studies* 25 (1978-9) 16-32, 17.

Memra, will be with Jacob and the Jerusalem Temple is the outward and visible proof of the fulfilment of that oath, since it is the point of contact between earth and heaven, the place where God's presence in His Memra is most keenly apprehended.[13] Hayward so restricts the meaning of מימרא, that in order to explain its actual appearances elsewhere in the Targumim, he must rely on the expedient of supposing that its original meaning had been forgotten.[14] Essentially, Hayward appears unaware of the conceptual difficulties of his own thesis.[15]

Confronted, then, with two unsuccessful attempts at a systematic understanding of מימרא in the Targumim, Chester's preference for a genuinely exegetical approach is understandable:

> It is in fact more plausible to see Memra (in form a substantival infinitive) as basically a translational and exegetical term, drawing on the various senses of the underlying verb אמר and its

---

[13]*The Use*, 113.

[14]For these and other criticisms, cf. *The Glory of Israel*, 67, 68 and 143-4 n. 31; 144-5 n. 38; 145-6 nn. 39-46.

[15]There is, it must be said, a certain naïveté in his bland assertion of his own, unproven case, cf. "Memra and Shekhina: A Short Note," *Journal of Jewish Studies* 31 (1980) 210-13.

related noun forms, with connotations such as "utterance, speech, word, promise, command."[16] Chester is at pains to stress that מימרא is not a "theologically sophisticated" usage; and he argues that "it simply portrays one main mode of God's activity, intelligible at a popular level and intended primarily as an interpretation of the biblical text."[17]

Chester's last statement is offered by way of conclusion; conceptually, it serves only to highlight the paradox of his position. On the one hand, מימרא is held not to be a usage of a theological nature, while on the other it is described as portraying a "main mode of God's activity." If the term in fact conveys a reference to divine action, then it is not simply exegetical or -- in Moore's language -- translational. Of course, Chester's pre-emptive defence against such an objection is to insist that, even if technically theological, the usage is not sophisticated: the activity of God simply falls within an ordinary range of the associations of אמר.

---

[16]*Divine Revelation*, 308-9, citing V. Hamp, *Der Begriff "Wort" in den aramäischen Bibelübersetzungen. Ein exegetischer Beitrag zur Hypostasen-Frage und zur Geschichte der Logos Spekulation* (München: Filser, 1938) 79-102. Cf. also *The Glory of Israel*, 144 (the continuation of n. 31).

[17]*Divine Revelation*, 313.

Just at this point, however, a fundamental objection to the procedure used by Chester, along with Hayward and Muñoz Leon, may be registered. We have long since passed the point when all Targums may be supposed to adhere to a single sense of מימרא, be it unsophisticated or otherwise. Some such basic meaning as "speech" or "utterance" is -- of course -- assumed, and has been recognized by scholars otherwise as much at variance as Moore and Hayward.[18] But the effort has persistently been made to typify that meaning further, and so to arrive at the underlying sense of מימרא. Hayward represents the most extreme case of attempts to typify the whole from a particular part: Neophyti Genesis 3:14; 4:12 are for him paradigmatic. Because מימרא is associated with אהיה there, it is everywhere. Moore represents a far more adequate procedure of typing, from general usage to overall sense. He observes the usage in Onqelos and Jonathan especially, in the interests of "brevity and simplicity."[19] He concludes that the types of use include command,[20] the obedience of command,[21] the acceptance of a

---

[18]Cf. Moore, "Intermediaries," 47; Hayward, *Divine Name*, 1.

[19]"Intermediaries," p. 60 n. 7. In fact, the usages cited below, from Moore's study, are all taken from Onqelos, with occasional reference to Pseudo-Jonathan.

[20]P. 47.

[21]Pp. 47-8.

command,[22] divine speaking,[23] divine meeting with others,[24] oracles,[25] swearing by God,[26] his fighting for Israel,[27] his protection,[28] his establishing covenant.[29] Whatever may be said of Moore's contribution conceptually, he represents a procedural advance in permitting the Targums to typify their own sense of מימרא. That is precisely what Chester, Hayward, and Muñoz Leon do not do.

Chester offers the possibility of an important distinction of usage between Onqelos and the so-called Palestinian Targumim, but he does not himself explore that possibility. In a work published in 1982, the present writer offered a typology of מימרא in the Isaiah Targum, based upon Moore's approach, but applying it to new material (cf. n. 19).[30] In that study, however, the refinement was introduced, that the order of categories

---

[22]P. 48.

[23]Pp. 48-9.

[24]P. 49.

[25]Pp. 49, 50.

[26]P. 50.

[27]Pp. 50-1.

[28]P. 51.

[29]P. 51. In all of these classifications, I have categorized on the basis of Moore's own, characteristically discursive, descriptions.

[30]*The Glory of Israel*, 56-69.

was determined by the order of appearance of the first instance of each category. The types present מימרא as an occasion for rebellion,[31] an agent of punishment,[32] a demand for obedience,[33] an edict,[34] a voice,[35] divine protection,[36] an eternal witness,[37] an intermediary of prayer.[38] The overlap with Moore's categories is evident, but not complete. His typology, on the basis of Onqelos, included categories and a precedence of categories not found in Jonathan's Isaiah, and vice versa. The possibility emerges that Targum Isaiah is distinctive in its usage of מימרא, precisely by virtue of its focus upon Israel's disobedience, and God's demand for a reversal on the basis of his election of his people. In other words, literary variation might appropriately be built into our characterization of מימרא, rather than explained away or ignored.

---

[31]Pp. 57-8.

[32]Pp. 58-60.

[33]P. 60.

[34]P. 61.

[35]Pp. 61-2.

[36]Pp. 62-3.

[37]P. 63.

[38]Pp. 63-4. It should be clearly understood that I immediately cited Hamp's observation, that an intermediary need not imply a hypostasis, cf. p. 143 n. 31.

The testing of any such hypothesis is obviously impossible, if it must rely solely upon the comparison of, say, Moore's analysis of the Pentateuch in Onqelos, and my analysis of Isaiah in Jonathan. What is required is a comparison of cognate documents, preferably from demonstrably related strams of tradition. The so-called Palestinian Targumim, of course, make just that comparison practicable.[39] By comparing Neophyti I and Pseudo-Jonathan from Targum to Targum, and also from document to document within each Targum, we will be in a position to say whether there is in fact a significant variation in the types of usage of מימרא.

The more technical requirements of the comparison include access to critical editions of the two Targums which are cognate in their policies of textual criticism, and which are indexed even-handedly. For that reason, the five volumes of Roger LeDéaut have been been used as the basis of the collation.[40]

---

[39]Moore, needless to say, did not have access to Neophyti I, and he simply evinced no strong interest in Pseudo-Jonathan.

[40]*Targum du Pentateuque. Traduction des deux recensions palestiniennes complètes avec introduction, parallèles, notes et index* 1-5: Sources Chrétiennes 245, 256, 261, 271, 282 (Paris: Les editions du Cerf, 1978, 1979, 1979, 1980, 1981). By their very nature, the Fragments Targum

Because, in the nature of the case, we must move from book to book within Torah, it is impracticable to employ my earlier method, of ordering the categories according to the precedence of appearance within the text. At the same time, it is necessary within the logic of a typological analysis that the text (rather than the interpreter) in some way establish precedence. For that reason, the lead will be taken from the *frequency* of types within each book of each Targum.[41] As a rule of

---

and the materials from the Cairo Genizah are not sufficiently comprehensive for such a comparison as is proposed here.

[41]In this connection, it might be noted that, had the same procedure been followed in the instance of the Isaiah Targum, the result would actually have been to heighten thematically central usages, and to reduce the attention given to less prominent concerns:

demand for obedience	22
divine protection	22
edict	19
rebellion against	12
witness	12
agent of punishment	10
voice	7
intermediary	2.

The usages have been tabulated on the basis of my previous survey, as presented in *The Glory of Israel*, pp. 56–69. The last two usages are in fact of little conceptual importance within the Isaiah Targum. The arrangement by frequency, rather than precedence, gives greater emphasis to the imperative ("demand for obedience") and positive ("divine protection," "edict") aspects of מימרא, rather than the negative aspects of rebellion and punishment. Such an emphasis probably does

thumb, only types consisting of 10% of the total usages of מימרא within the document will be considered to characterize the usage of the document in question.[42] That additional constraint will help us considerably to resolve a portrait of מימרא document by document, because there are not eight, but fifteen types in play throughout Neophyti and Pseudo-Jonathan.[43]

---

greater justice to the theology of the document (cf. *The Glory of Israel,* 97-111).

[42]Were that rule applied to the Isaiah Targum, with its 106 usages, the types of voice and intermediary would be omitted, which are precisely the types of least conceptual import (cf. the previous note). During the development of the present exercise, usages representing only slightly less than 10% of the total were also considered.

[43]The types present מימרא as speaking, blessing, creating, a voice, giving law, involved in worship, deliberating, acting, influencing, aiding, being with others, involved in covenant, swearing, demanding obedience, occasioning revolt. The arrangement and designation of the categories is heuristic. Their meaning is largely self-explanatory, although reference might be made to the distinction operative between "acting" and "influencing." The former includes transitive acts of direct impact, such as striking, throwing, taking, closing, protecting, etc., while the latter is concerned when the action involved indirectly makes itself felt, as when the מימרא manifests itself, appears, converses, realizes, causes descent, gratifies, gives sons, tempts, etc. Obviously, no hard and fast division between these two categores has been possible to draw. Indeed, all of the categories need to be applied elastically, once usage establishes them, if a typological approach is to be developed at all. Moreover,

In   Neophyti's   Genesis,   מימרא   is   characteristically
portrayed as:

speaking	13 of 62 occurrences
involved in worship	10 of 62 occurrences
influencing	9 of 62 occurrences
involved in covenant	8 of 62 occurrences
creating	8 of 62 occurrences.

Lest it be thought Genesis simply demands such usages by
virtue of its subject matter, it must be borne in mind
that   Pseudo-Jonathan's   Genesis   delivers   a   different
impression of מימרא:

aiding	13 of 50 occurrences
deliberating	7 of 50 occurrences
involved in covenant	7 of 50 occurrences
influencing	7 of 50 occurrences

Only the types involving covenant and influence present
points of obvious overlap, and only the first of the two
may be regarded as generated by the content of Genesis,
in   that   the   second   proves   to   be   distributed   generally

---

a single use may sometimes be said to invoke more than
one   category,   although   in   the   present   paper   double
counting is avoided, provided one category is used with
emphasis. A tabular list of all the usages surveyed is
included as an appendix. It must be stressed that the
typologies   here   explored   are   provisional,   and   were
evolved by assessing the sense of each passage in its
context,   not   by   means   of   a   dictional   or   semantic
analysis.

within the Pentateuch. Neophyti's Genesis, alone of all the Targums we shall consider, gives priority to the מימרא as speaking,[44] but then also imagines it as acted upon in worship,[45] as involved in covenant,[46] as well as influencing (the typically Targumic portrayal) and creating.[47] The conception in Pseudo-Jonathan is more unequivocally active,[48] although a certain reflexivity, manifest in deliberation,[49] is also apparent.

Both Targums alter their usage in Exodus. Neophyti I gives us a largely new list:

being with others   13 out of 43 occurrences

---

[44]1:3, 5, 6, 8, 9, 10, 11, 20, 24, 28; 17:3; 18:17; 20:6. Such usages would be vastly augmented, were marginal variants taken into account. It is striking that the מימרא's speaking is made made prominent in Neophyti by virtue of its importance in chapter one (cf. the type, "creating").

[45]4:26; 8:20; 12:7, 8; 13:4; 15:6; 16:13; 21:33; 22:14; 26:25.

[46]9:12, 13, 15, 16, 17; 17:7, 8, 11. Other covenantal moments might obviously have occasioned the usage: the covenants involving Noah and Abraham are of especial concern to the meturgemanin. The distribution in Pseudo-Jonathan is virtually the same.

[47]1:9, 11, 16, 25, 27; 2:2; 14:19, 22.

[48]Cf. the portrayl of the מימרא as "aiding," 21:20, 22; 26:28; 28:15, 20; 31:3, 5; 35:3; 39:2, 3, 23; 48:21; 49:25.

[49]6:6, 7; 8:1, 21; 29:31; 41:1; 50:20.

influencing	9 out of 43 occurrences
deliberating	5 out of 43 occurrences
involved in worship	5 out of 43 occurrences
demanding obedience	4 out of 43 occurrences.

The first, fourth and last of these may be regarded as required by the content of Exodus,[50] since they also show up among the prominent types of usage in Pseudo-Jonathan, and are not featured in Genesis:[51]

acting	10 out of 51 occurrences
demanding obedience	7 out of 51 occurrences
being with others	7 out of 51 occurrences
involved in worship	7 out of 51 occurrences
influencing	6 out of 51 occurrences.

"Influencing" is so far common to all four lists, and may be held to be endemic within the ethos of Neophyti I and Pseudo-Jonathan. That leaves very little that is distinctive within Exodus. Deliberating appears to be the emphasis of Neophyti I at this point,[52] while acting is

---

[50] As a matter of fact, the correspondence between Neophyti and Pseudo-Jonathan within these categories is fairly high (cf. the appendix).

[51] Only the type of involvement in worship shows up there, and even then in Neophyti alone.

[52] 3:17; 15:2; 17:1, 16; 18:11. Of these usages, 17:1 hardly represents deliberation in any substantial sense, but formal emphasis is perhaps for that reason all the more apparent.

stressed most emphatically in Pseudo-Jonathan.[53] It is not obvious why deliberating should be stressed in Neophyti, especially when it appeared only once in Genesis (against seven usages in Pseudo-Jonathan): evidently, the emphasis is not a matter of mere convention, but reflects how the meturgemanin understood divine activity in Exodus in particular. Pseudo-Jonathan, however, seems consistent, so far, in a portrayal of מימרא as comparatively active.

Leviticus occasions the fewest number of references to מימרא in both of the Palestinian Targums.[54] In both cases, the by now conventional portrait of the מימרא as influencing is obvious. On the other hand, Neoophyti I manifests its greater concern for the involvement of מימרא in worship,[55] while Pseudo-Jonathan breaks new ground in its focus on the מימרא as giving law[56] and as demanding obedience:[57]

---

[53]2:5; 7:25; 12:23, 29; 13:8, 17; 14:25; 15:1, 8; 33:22.

[54]That Hayward does not explain this distributional factor, in making his case of a cultic association of מימרא, is unfortunate.

[55]16:8. 9. The numbers are far too small to bear much weight in isolation, but the coherence with the usage in Neophyti's Genesis (and, to a lesser extent, Exodus) supports the generalization.

[56]9:23; 24:12; 26:46. The ground broken, however, is not broad (cf. the last note).

[57]8:35; 18:30; 22:9; cf. the previous note.

Neophyti

influencing	8 out of 14 occurrences
involved in worship	2 out of 14 occurrences

Pseudo-Jonathan

influencing	4 out of 13 occurrences
giving law	3 out of 13 occurrences
demanding obedience	3 out of 13 occurrences

It appears clear that the meturgemanin of Pseudo-Jonathan are here concerned for a reading of מימרא within Leviticus in particular which is more prescriptive, as compared both to other books in Pseudo-Jonathan and to Neophyti at this point.

The deliberation involved in מימרא,[58] and its demand for obedience,[59] which surfaced in Neophyti in Exodus, also characterizes Neophyti in Numbers:

deliberating	12 out of 55 occurrences
demanding obedience	12 out of 55 occurrences
influencing	10 out of 55 occurrences
being with others	6 out of 55 occurrences
occasioning revolt	5 out of 55 occurrences.

The aspect of influencing is, again, consistently a feature of Neophyti's portrayal of the מימרא, but the

---

[58] 9:18, 20; 10:13; 11:20; 14:41; 20:24; 22:18; 24:13; 27:14; 33:2, 38; 36:5.

[59] 3:16, 39, 51; 4:37, 41, 45, 49; 14:24; 20:12, 21; 32:12, 15.

appearance of the type of מימרא as occasioning revolt may be determined by the content of Numbers, as it also appears in Pseudo-Jonathan:[60]

demanding obedience	17 out of 50 occurrences
influencing	10 out of 50 occurrences
occasioning revolt	6 out of 50 occurrences
deliberating	5 out of 50 occurrences.

Of course, the types of deliberating and demanding obedience also appear in Pseudo-Jonathan, but those types are established as typical of Neophyti before Numbers. What is striking in Pseudo-Jonathan is the more deliberative, deuteronomistic aspect of the מימרא in Numbers,[61] as compared to the more dynamic portrayal earlier.

Both Targums evince a fresh, distinctive and vigorous view of מימרא in Deuteronomy. Although Neophyti's usual emphasis upon the מימרא as influencing is present, for the first time its function as a voice is significantly present, and in fact predominates:[62]

---

[60]As the appendix indicates, the overlap between the two Targums is impressive, although not complete.

[61]Just this aspect is reminiscent of the Isaiah Targum (cf. n. 41).

[62]4:12, 30, 33, 36; 5:23, 24, 25, 26; 8:20; 9:23; 13:5, 19; 15:5; 18:16; 26:14; 27:10; 28:1, 2, 15, 45, 62; 30:2, 8, 10, 20; 34:10.

voice	26 out of 117 occurrences
influencing	21 out of 117 occurrences
acting	11 out of 117 occurrences
demanding obedience	10 out of 117 occurrences

The dynamic quality of מימרא is here also suggested by the presence of acting as a type of usage, for the first time in Neophyti.[63] On the other hand, by this stage the type of demanding obedience appears simply to be characteristic of both Targums after Genesis. Pseudo-Jonathan also averts to the vocal sense of מימרא in Deuteronomy,[64] and presents it as even more active than Neophyti does:[65]

acting	21 out of 75 occurrences
demanding obedience	17 out of 75 occurrences
occasioning revolt	9 out of 75 occurrences
voice	8 out of 75 occurrences.

Clearly, the vocal associations may be triggered by the content of Deuteronomy, although the reference of Pseudo-Jonathan to revolt[66] may be considered a

---

[63]3:21; 4:3; 5:24; 9:4, 19, 20; 11:23; 29:22, 23; 32:39; 33:27.

[64]4:33, 36; 5:5, 24, 25, 26; 26:14; 34:10. (All usages but 5:5 are included within Neophyti.)

[65]1:30; 2:21; 3:22; 4:3, 24; 5:24; 11:23; 18:19; 19:15; 24:18; 26:5; 28:20, 22, 27, 28, 35; 29:22; 32:39, 43; 33:27; 34:6.

[66]1:26, 32, 43; 8:20; 9:23; 21:20; 25:18; 32:18, 51.

characteristic convention.

As the types of usage are viewed within Neophyti and Pseudo-Jonathan, and compared to one another, so that distinctive elements are identified, a profile of each Targum emerges:

Neophyti:
> Genesis: speaking, involved in worship, creating
> Exodus: deliberating
> Leviticus: involved in worship
> Numbers: deliberating
> Deuteronomy: voice

Pseudo-Jonathan:
> Genesis: aiding, deliberating
> Exodus: acting
> Leviticus: giving law, demanding obedience
> Numbers: demanding obedience
> Deuteronomy: occasioning revolt.

Neophyti, at the beginning and end of the Pentateuch, presents מימרא in its vocal association, but also portrays it as creating (Genesis), involved in worship (Genesis, Leviticus), and deliberating (Exodus, Numbers). Pseudo-Jonathan proceeds in a more sequential manner, from the activity of מימרא in aiding, deliberating, and acting (Genesis, Exodus) to its demanding obedience to the law (Leviticus, Numbers), and thence to the inevitable revolt (Deuteronomy). That מימרא is to be related to the verb אמר, and assumes a divine subject, is indeed a necessary occasion of such usages, but the patterns of types manifest within Neophyti and Pseudo-Jonathan suggest that the association is not the sufficient condition of the usages. Rather, the immediate inference from the patterns of distribution observed is that God is portrayed as speaking in different ways and at different points within Neophyti and Pseudo-Jonathan. In other words, מימרא is not simply a metonym for God, or even for God understood as speaking, but is the term which conveys the sense of God's distinctively vocal, deliberative, creative, and worshipped aspects in Neophyti, and his distinctively active, demanding, and resisted aspects in Pseudo-Jonathan.

In the most general of terms, one may therefore infer that מימרא is the Targumic category of God's activity of commanding. Within that activity, a meturgeman might think of commanding as what is ordered, as the response to the order, or as what is behind the order. There are a range of emphases, both interior to the act of commanding, informing the decision of command, and exterior to the act, devolving from it, which מימרא might theoretically convey.[67] At just this point, however, it is crucial not to mistake the categories with which we are dealing. Although מימרא is used variously, there is no warrant for saying that there is such a thing as a *concept* of God's מימרא which can take distinctive forms. Following the lead of Moore, we may say that מימרא is not a personal being, a being, a figment of speculation (so far Moore), or even (we now conclude) a systematic idea, consistent from Targum to Targum. What links the Targumim, in their usage of מימרא, is not a theological thought, but a theological *manner* of speaking of God.

But having spoken in largely negative terms, we must also

---

[67]Precisely because the usage of מימרא is flexible, and has to do with effective command, it seems unwise to discount the possibility of a relationship with Philo's use of λόγος, which refers to the more interior, or intentional, aspects of command, cf. Chilton, *Glory*, 145, 146 (n. 46), and "Commenting on the Old Testament (with particular reference to the pesharim, Philo, and the Mekilta)" *It is Written: Scripture Citing Scripture. Essays in Honour of Barnabas Lindars, SSF* (eds D. A. Carson and H. G. M. Williamson; Cambridge: Cambridge University Press, 1988) 122-140, 129, 130, 131-3. Indeed, the procedure defended here, of reading מימרא inductively, and inferring a sense therefrom, is analogous to H. A. Wolfson's in respect of the Philonic λόγος, cf. *Philo: The Foundations of Religious Philosophy in Judaism, Christianity, and Islam* I, II (Cambridge: Harvard University Press, 1947, 1948) I.229f., 235f., 240, 244f., 253f., 291, 331; II.32 and Muñoz Leon, 34, 49.

guard against the recent tendency, so to discount the coherent reference of מימרא, as to deny the sensibility of its usage. It has now become evident that מימרא in Neophyti and Pseudo-Jonathan (as in the Isaiah Targum) evinces patterns of usage. Obviously, those patterns do not amount to a systematic theology. But it is equally obvious that מימרא within a given Targum is not invoked haphazardly when some verb of speaking happens to be used of God in the Hebrew text which is rendered. The Targums to hand suggest an alternative hypothesis for the understanding of מימרא: *the usage of the term reflects the manner in which given meturgemanin conceive of God's activity of commanding, whether from the point of view of God's intention in the command, or the human response to what is effected (or affected) by the command.* Within the history of each Targum's development, the typologies of usage vary, and the principal variables at issue are (1) the notion of how God commands (and what response his command elicits), and (2) the complex of ideas triggered by a given book. מימרא might therefore be understood as covering the conceptual field[68] of divine speaking, inclusive of the deliberation behind, and the results of, that speaking. The term performs taxonomically, invoking

---

[68]Cf. Georges Mounin, *Les problèmes théoretiques de la traduction* (Paris: Gallimard, 1963) 71-112. A personal conversation with Koenraad Kuiper suggested the description of the use of מימרא in terms of taxonomy.

the possibility that a range of terms within the appropriate lexical field might be employed. In the Masoretic Text, the same *sorts* of action or event may be described, but the taxonomic system is not as well regulated.[69]

APPENDIX
Typologies of Usage, by Book and Targum

Genesis: Neophyti 62; Pseudo-Jonathan 50

speaking-- Neophyti 14 (1:3, 5, 6, 8, 9, 10, 11, 20, 24, 28; 17:3; 18:17; 20:6)

Pseudo-Jonathan 1 (20:6)

blessing-- Neophyti 3 (1:22; 24:1; 26:3)

Pseudo-Jonathan 2 (24:1; 26:3)

creating-- Neophyti 8 (1:9, 11, 16, 25, 27; 2:2; 14:19, 22)

Pseudo-Jonathan 0

voice-- Neophyti 2 (3:8, 10)

Pseudo-Jonathan 2 (3:8, 10)

---

[69]By contrast, דבור in Neophyti and Pseudo-Jonathan is a later development, retricted to particular disclosures of God, usually involving Moses (cf. Exodus 29:3; Leviticus 1:1; Numbers 7:89 in Neophyti, and Exodus 33:11; Leviticus 1:1; Numbers 7:89; Deuteronomy 4:12; 5:22, 23; 18:16 in Pseudo-Jonathan. Both Targums associate the usage with Jacob at Genesis 28:10.

giving law-- Neophyti 0

    Pseudo-Jonathan 1 (3:24)

involved in worship-- Neophyti 10 (4:26; 8:20; 12:7, 8; 13:4; 15:6; 16:13; 21:33; 22:14; 26:25)

    Pseudo-Jonathan 4 (4:26; 15:6; 18:5; 21:33)

deliberating-- Neophyti 1 (29:31)

    Pseudo-Jonathan 7 (6:6, 7; 8:1, 21; 29:31; 41:1; 50:20)

acting-- Neophyti 1 (20:13)

    Pseudo-Jonathan 4 (7:16; 12:17; 16:1; 20:18)

influencing-- Neophyti 9 (12:7; 15:1; 16:3; 17:1; 18:1, 19; 19:24; 20:3; 46:4)

    Pseudo-Jonathan 7 (11:8; 15:1; 16:13; 19:24; 22:1; 27:28; 48:9)

aiding-- Neophyti 2 (31:5; 49:25)

    Pseudo-Jonathan 13 (21:20, 22; 26:28; 28:15, 20; 31:3, 5; 35:3; 39:2, 3, 23; 48:21; 49:25)

being with others-- Neophyti 2 (28:15; 31:3)

    Pseudo-Jonathan 1 (46:4)

involved in covenant-- Neophyti 8 (9:12, 13, 15, 16, 17; 17:7, 8, 11)

    Pseudo-Jonathan 7 (9:12, 13, 15, 16, 17; 17:2, 7)

swearing-- Neophyti 0

    Pseudo-Jonathan 2 (21:23; 31:50)

demanding obedience-- Neophyti 3 (22:18; 24:3; 26:5)

    Pseudo-Jonathan 3 (22:18; 24:3; 26:5)

occasioning revolt-- Neophyti 0

Pseudo-Jonathan 0

Exodus: Neophyti 43; Pseudo-Jonathan 51

speaking-- Neophyti 0

Pseudo-Jonathan 2 (10:29; 33:12)

blessing-- Neophyti 0

Pseudo-Jonathan 0

creating-- Neophyti 1 (12:42)

Pseudo-Jonathan 0

voice-- Neophyti 2 (19:5; 23:22)

Pseudo-Jonathan 0

giving law-- Neophyti 1 (15:25)

Pseudo-Jonathan 2 (13:17; 15:25)

involved in worship-- Neophyti 5 (4:31; 5:23; 14:31; 17:15; 34:5)

Pseudo-Jonathan 7 (14:31; 17:15; 20:7; 26:28; 33:19; 34:5; 36:33)

deliberating-- Neophyti 5 (3:17; 15:2; 17:1, 16; 18:11)

Pseudo-Jonathan 3 (2:23; 3:17; 15:2)

acting-- Neophyti 3 (12:23; 15:1, 8)

Pseudo-Jonathan 10 (2:5; 7:25; 12:23, 29; 13:8, 17; 14:25; 15:1, 8; 33:22)

influencing-- Neophyti 9 (3:8, 12, 14; 6:3; 11:4; 19:9, 20; 20:4; 31:17)

Pseudo-Jonathan 6 (1:21; 3:8; 12:27; 13:15; 31:17; 33:9)

aiding-- Neophyti 1 (18:4)

Pseudo-Jonathan 3 (3:12; 10:10; 18:19)

being with others-- Neophyti 13 (3:12; 4:12, 15; 8:18; 10:10; 12:12; 13:21; 25:22; 29:43, 45; 30:6, 36; 31:17)

Pseudo-Jonathan-- 7 (4:12, 15; 25:22; 29:43; 30:6, 39; 31:17)

involved in covenant-- Neophyti 0

Pseudo-Jonathan 0

swearing-- Neophyti 0

Pseudo-Jonathan 1 (6:8; 13:5; 17:16)

demanding obedience-- Neophyti 4 (15:26; 17:1; 19:5; 23:22)

Pseudo-Jonathan 7 (5:2; 14:7; 15:26; 17:1, 13; 19:5; 23:22)

occasioning revolt-- Neophyti 0

Pseudo-Jonathan 1 (16:8)

Leviticus: Neophyti 14; Pseudo-Jonathan 13

speaking-- Neophyti 0

Pseudo-Jonathan 1 (1:1)

blessing-- Neophyti 0

Pseudo-Jonathan 0

creating-- Neophyti 0

Pseudo-Jonathan 0

voice-- Neophyti 0

Pseudo-Jonathan 0

giving law-- Neophyti 1 (26:46)

Pseudo-Jonathan 3 (9:23; 24:12; 26:46)

involved in worship-- Neophyti 2 (16:8, 9)

    Pseudo-Jonathan 0

deliberating-- Neophyti 1 (26:42)

    Pseudo-Jonathan 0

acting-- Neophyti 0

    Pseudo-Jonathan 1 (9:23)

influencing-- Neophyti 8 (9:4; 16:2; 19:2; 20:23; 25:38; 26:9, 12, 45)

    Pseudo-Jonathan 4 (20:23; 26:11, 12, 30)

aiding-- Neophyti 0

    Pseudo-Jonathan 0

being with others-- Neophyti 0

    Pseudo-Jonathan 0

involved in covenant-- Neophyti 1 (26:46)

    Pseudo-Jonathan 1 (26:46)

swearing-- Neophyti 0

    Pseudo-Jonathan 0

demanding obedience-- Neophyti 0

    Pseudo-Jonathan 3 (8:35; 18:30; 22:9)

occasioning revolt-- Neophyti 1 (26:23)

    Pseudo-Jonathan 0

Numbers: Neophyti 55; Pseudo-Jonathan 50

speaking-- Neophyti 2 (1:1; 22:12)

    Pseudo-Jonathan 0

blessing-- Neophyti 4 (6:27; 10:29; 23:8; 24:5)

    Pseudo-Jonathan 3 (6:27; 23:8, 20)

creating-- Neophyti 0

    Pseudo-Jonathan 0

voice-- Neophyti 0

    Pseudo-Jonathan 0

giving law-- Neophyti 1 (13:3)

    Pseudo-Jonathan 1 (14:35)

involved in worship-- Neophyti 1 (18:9)

    Pseudo-Jonathan 0

deliberating-- Neophyti 12 (9:18, 20; 10:13; 11:20; 14:41; 20:24; 22:18; 24:13; 27:14; 33:2, 38; 36:5)

    Pseudo-Jonathan 5 (9:18, 23; 14:41; 22:18; 24:13)

acting-- Neophyti 1 (23:5)

    Pseudo-Jonathan 2 (21:6; 22:28)

influencing-- Neophyti 10 (11:17; 14:14; 17:19; 18:20; 22:9, 20; 23:3, 4, 12, 16)

    Pseudo-Jonathan 10 (12:6; 17:19; 21:35; 22:9, 20; 23:3, 4, 16; 24:23; 27:16)

aiding-- Neophyti 0

    Pseudo-Jonathan 4 (14:9, 43; 23:21; 31:8)

being with others-- Neophyti 6 (6:27; 14:9, 21, 28; 23:19, 21)

    Pseudo-Jonathan 2 (25:4; 23:19)

involved in covenant-- Neophyti 0

    Pseudo-Jonathan 0

swearing-- Neophyti 1 (11:21)

    Pseudo-Jonathan 0

demanding obedience-- Neophyti 12 (3:16, 39, 51; 4:37,

41, 45, 49; 14:24; 20:12, 21; 32:12, 15)

Pseudo-Jonathan 17 (3:16, 39, 51; 4:37, 41, 45, 49; 9:20, 23; 10:13; 13:3; 20:12; 21:8, 9; 33:2, 38; 36:5)

occasioning revolt— Neophyti 5 (11:20; 14:11, 43; 21:5, 7)

Pseudo-Jonathan 6 (11:20; 14:11; 16:11; 20:24; 21:5; 27:14)

Deuteronomy: Neophyti 117; Pseudo-Jonathan 75

speaking— Neophyti 9 (5:5, 28; 9:10; 10:4; 17:16; 31:2; 32:12; 33:2; 34:4)

Pseudo-Jonathan 2 (31:2; 32:49)

blessing— Neophyti 5 (5:28; 8:10; 15:4; 21:5; 33:7)

Pseudo-Jonathan 1 (24:19)

creating— Neophyti 1 (32:15)

Pseudo-Jonathan (8:3)

voice— Neophyti 26 (4:12, 30, 33, 36; 5:23, 24, 25, 26; 8:20; 9:23; 13:5, 19; 15:5; 18:16; 26:14; 27:10; 28:1, 2, 15, 45, 62; 30:2, 8, 10, 20; 34:10)

Pseudo-Jonathan 8 (4:33, 36; 5:5, 24, 25, 26; 26:14; 34:10)

giving law— Neophyti 4 (1:1; 4:23; 8:3; 34:9)

Pseudo-Jonathan 0

involved in worship— Neophyti 6 (4:7; 18:5, 7, 19, 20, 22)

Pseudo-Jonathan 2 (4:7; 18:7)

deliberating-- Neophyti 7 (1:1; 12:14; 17:10; 32:23, 26; 33:27; 34:5)

Pseudo-Jonathan 6 (12:5, 11; 26:18; 32:23, 26; 33:27)

acting-- Neophyti 11 (3:21; 4:3; 5:24; 9:4, 19, 20; 11:23; 29:22, 23; 32:39; 33:27)

Pseudo-Jonathan 21 (1:30; 2:21; 3:22; 4:3, 24; 5:24; 11:23; 18:19; 19:15; 24:18; 26:5; 28:20, 22, 27, 28, 35; 29:22; 32:39, 43; 33:27; 34:6)

influencing-- Neophyti 21 (1:27; 4:20, 27; 5:24; 8:18, 19, 20; 9:4, 23; 10:5, 15; 11:17, 21; 13:18; 26:17, 18; 30:3; 31:4; 32:30; 34:1, 11)

Pseudo-Jonathan 34 (1:10; 4:20; 5:24; 11:12; 28:7, 9, 11, 13, 21, 25, 48, 49, 61, 63, 65, 68; 29:1, 3; 30:3, 4, 5, 7, 9; 31:5, 15; 32:12, 36, 39, 50; 33:29; 34:1, 5, 6, 11)

aiding-- Neophyti 3 (31:8, 23; 32:9)

Pseudo-Jonathan 4 (2:7; 20:1; 31:8, 23)

being with others-- Neophyti 2 (32:39, 40)

Pseudo-Jonathan 0

involved in covenant-- Neophyti 1 (4:23)

Pseudo-Jonathan 0

swearing-- Neophyti 0

Pseudo-Jonathan 2 (5:11; 31:7)

demanding obedience-- Neophyti 10 (1:36; 2:1; 6:2; 7:4; 10:8; 13:5, 11; 25:18; 29:17; 31:27)

Pseudo-Jonathan 17 (4:30; 11:1; 13:5, 19; 15:5;

26:17; 27:10; 28:1, 2, 15, 45, 62; 30:3, 8, 10, 20; 31:12)

occasioning revolt-- Neophyti 7 (1:26, 32, 43; 9:7, 23; 32:18, 51)

Pseudo-Jonathan 9 (1:26, 32, 43; 8:20; 9:23; 21:20; 25:18; 32:18, 51)

Eight Theses on the Use of Targums in Interpreting the New Testament

The work of an international project, aimed at translating all extant Targumim into English, is nearly complete.[1] The Former and the major Latter Prophets are now available to scholars in a way which makes the use of these sources of early and rabbinic Judaism far more likely. For some thirty years, since the late Alejandro Díez Macho identified a previously unappreciated Targum of the Pentateuch,[2] Aramaists and a small group of Neutestamentler have been grappling afresh with Targumic study, but now the documents will be available more generally, for good or ill. The questions emerge: what might be done with them, and what must not be done with them? The history of interpretation is littered with instances of citing Targumim, as if they were uniformly pre-Christian, and ignoring them, as if they were utterly unreflective of that Judaism which is the milieu of the

---

[1]Publication is in a series entitled "The Aramaic Bible," which was first produced by Michael Glazier, Inc., under the general editorship of Martin McNamara. The Liturgical Press later acquired Glazier's imprint

[2]Cf. his own description of the discovery in *Neophyti 1. Targum Palestinense Ms de la Biblioteca Vaticana*I (1968) 19, 20. Among the first of a new generation of scholars which was influenced by the discovery was Martin McNamara, who has produced a lucid and compact history of research in *The New Testament and the Palestinian Targum to the Pentateuch:* Analecta Biblica (1966).

New Testament in its earliest phase.[3]

The only and obvious way to avoid those pitfalls, and others, is to become familiar with the documents themselves, and their use among critical exegetes. As an aid and incentive within that process, the following theses are offered.

(1) The Targums generally were composed after, and

---

[3]Examples of the former tendency are evident in the work of B. F. Westcott, cf. his *Introduction to the Study of the Gospels* (1896) 134–139. It must, however, be stressed that Westcott responded critically to the subject, within the bibliographical terms of reference then available. The latter tendency is implicit in the jejune dismissal of the Targumic understanding of *memra* as a possible antecedent of *logos* in the fourth Gospel by C.K. Barrett in *The Gospel according to St John* (1978) 153. Barrett cites only a straightforward usage of *memra* as a possible antecedent of *logos* in John, in coming to the global judgment that "*Memra* is a blind alley in the study of the biblical background of John's logos doctrine." His index of rabbinic literature (pp. 619–621) refers to works later than the Targumim, but not to any Targumic work. That the literature is programmatically ignored is a conclusion that it is difficult to resist. An arguably more egregious failure is that scholars of the Hebrew Bible who have elaborated theories of its textual history on the strength of the relationship between the MT and the LXX do so without reference to Targumic evidence, cf. D. J. A. Clines, *The Esther Scroll. The Story of the Story*: JSOTS (1984) in comparison to the valuable material available in Grossfeld's study of the Targum (cited in n. 11).

without reference to the paramount concerns of, the New Testament. Because the Targums are, among things, renderings of the Hebrew Bible, their distinctive concern is to convey and illuminate scripture among those for whom Torah was the sole guarantor of the integrity of Israel. The destruction of the Temple (definitvely, in A.D. 135/136) and the consequent crisis of eschatological hope in the restoration of Israel, caused the Aramaic interpreters, as representaives of rabbinic Judaism, to confront afresh what the choice of Israel, the Davidic promise, the Temple itself, the coming of the messiah, the predictions of the prophets, and the commands of Torah might mean.[4] Some of the Targumim partially

---

[4]The exegetical vocabulary of the Targumim, particularly the more expansive instances of the genre, is geared to precisely such issues, as has been shown in *The Glory of Israel. The Theology and Provenience of the Isaiah Targum* (1982). The cessation of cultic sacrifice was a particularly painful reality for the meturgemanin, as is shown by the following passage from the Isaiah Targum (53:10):

> Yet before the LORD it was a pleasure to refine and to cleanse the remnant of his people, in order to purify their soul from sins; they shall see the kingdom of their Messiah, they shall increase sons and daughters, they shall prolong days; those who perform the law of the LORD shall prosper in his pleasure; from the slavery of the Gentiles he shall deliver their soul, they shall see the retribution of their adversaries. They shall be satisfied with the plunder of their kings: by his wisdom shall he make innocents to be accounted innocent, to subject

represent the concerns of early Judaism, as preceding and contemporary with Jesus and his first followers, but on the whole they address the distinctive agena of a later period.[5]

(2) The Targumic agenda is essentially rabbinic. Rabbis were concerned with how scripture was rendered in synagogues, and they were in the end responsible for the Targums as they can be read today.[6]

---

many to the law; and he shall beseech concerning their sins. Then I will divide him the plunder of many peoples, and he shall divide the spoil, the possessions of strong fortresses; because he handed over his soul to the death, and subjected the rebels to the law; yet he will beseech concerning the sins of many, and to the rebels it shall be forgiven for him.

[5]Cf. McNamara's later book, *Targum and Testament. Aramaic Paraphrases of the Hebrew Bible: A New Light on the New Testament* (1972).

[6]Cf. B. Grossfeld, "Bible. Translations. Ancient Versions. Aramaic: the Targumim," *Encylcopedia Judaica* 4 (1971) 841–851, 841, 842. The presentation of Genesis 22 in the Palestinian Targumim provides an instance of exegesis comparable to the rabbinic understanding of the passage, cf. S. Spiegel (tr. J. Goldin), *The Last Trial. On the legends and lore of the command to Abraham to offer Isaac as a sacrifice: the Akedah* (1967) and B.D. Chilton, "Recent Discussion of the Aqedah," *Targumic Approaches to the Gospels. Essays in the Mutual Definition of Judaism and Christianity: Studies in Judaism* (1986) 39. To give but one example, Genesis Rabbah 55:4 and Pseudo-Jonathan 22:1 agree that, in a

Sometimes, Targumic renderings are at variance with an expressed rabbinic preference,[7] and such tensions may be taken to evidence the folk provenience of Targumic traditions, but allowance must be made for the influence, and even the direct composition, of the rabbis within the extant witnesses.[8]

(3) Within early and Rabbinic Judaism, the provenience and programme of the Targumim are variegated. There are Targumim such as Onqelos, which correspond formally to their Hebrew *Vorlagen,* once allowance is made for their reverential periphrases in speaking of God, and of his

---

dispute over priority between Ishmael and Isaac, the latter volunteered to yield all his members to God.

[7]A notorious instance is the contradiction between Megillah 4:10, prohibiting the rendering of Genesis 35:22 (which speaks of Reuben's taking his father's concubine), and all the extant Targumim of the verse, which render it. The truncated version of the Hebrew presented in Neophyti 1 may represented an attempted accommodation with the Mishnaic prescription.

[8]Codex Reuchlianus particularly must be watched for this tendency. At Isaiah 33:7, for example, a version of the Aqedah is appended (cf. Chilton, "Recent Discussion of the Aqedah," *Targumic Approaches* (1986) 39–49. The connection between that verse and Genesis 22 might seem inexplicable, until it is borne in mind that the lectionary by the medieval period association the two passages (cf. Spiegel, *op. cit.,* 149 n. 68 and Genesis Rabbah 56:5).

revelation to his people.[9] Others, such as Neophyti I,[10] are more globally paraphrastic and expansionistic. Still others, such as the Targum to Esther, present a markedly mixed character.[11] There is no general tendency over time towards either correspondence or expansion: both Onqelos and Neophyti are commonly dated within the third century, and the later Targumim, such as those to Esther, represent both tendencies. Although the Targums in their initial purpose are directed to liturgical, popular usage, in the end they were preserved after Aramaic was no longer the Jewish *lingua franca*. In the case of marginalia in the Codex Reuchlianus (cf. n. 8), we find rabbis of the medieval period engaged in a exercise of esoteric play.[12] The myth of the Targums as the Bible of the people has been exploded.

---

[9]For ease of a comparison between Onqelos, Pseudo-Jonathan, and the Fragmentary Targum, recourse might still be made to J.W. Etheridge, *The Targums of Onqelos and Jonathan ben Uzziel on the Pentateuch with the Fragments of the Jerusalem Targum* (1968).

[10]Cf. Díez Macho, *op. cit.*

[11]B. Grossfeld characterizes *The First Targum to Esther* (1983, p. iv) as alternatively correspondent and expansive. Cf. his comments in respect of the Targum Sheni and the text of the Antwerp Polyglot on pp. iv-vi.

[12]Cf. also B.D. Chilton, "Sennacherib: a Synoptic Problem in Targumim of Isaiah," *Targumic Approaches* (1986) 163-177.

(4) There is no "Palestinian," "pre-Christian" Targum. Elements within the Targumim may arguable antedate, or be contemporaneous with, documents of the New Testament, but such a case remains always to be made, and may not be assumed. Discoveries at Qumran, Naḥal Ḥever, and Murraba'at make it quite clear that the Aramaic of the Targumin is not that of the first century.[13] Each Targum remains to be dated relative to rabbinic, early Judaic, and Christian sources, and characterized by its style of interpretation, so that elements which might illuminate that New Testament can be shown to be plausibly related to it. Apart from such analysis, serious, comparative work is not possible, and any other comparison is uncritical.

(5) A Targumic approach to the New Testament is to be distinguished from an Aramaic approach. In view of their history, the Targums are of less moment for reconstructing the dialect of Jesus than are the finds mentioned under the fourth thesis.[14] What distinguishes

---

[13]Cf. J.A. Fitzmyer, "The Phases of the Aramaic Language," *A Wandering Aramean. Collected Aramaic Essays:* SBLMS 25 (1979) 57-84.

[14]Precisely this fact to some degree vitiates M. Black's *An Aramaic Approach to the Gospels and Acts* (1967). With Paul Kahle, Black takes "the Palestinian Targum" as representative of Aramaic as spoken in the time of Jesus, and therefore as the most appropriate instrument for

the Targumim from such finds is that they offer understandings of the Hebrew Bible which may (or may not) shed light on the Judaism of the first century.

(6) A Targum of a date later than the New Testament might, on occasion, represent a tradition which was current in the period of the New Testament, albeit not in a Targumic context. The Pentateuchal Targum called Pseudo-Jonathan, which is no earlier than the seventh century, provides a near analogy to Luke 6:36 at Leviticus 22:18.[15] But the injunction to be merciful, as our heavenly father is merciful, has no necessary

---

reconstructing the words of Jesus. Subsequent research has not validated the linguistic thesis implicit under such a usage of the sources. A critique of Black's method precisely on those grounds is offered in J.A. Fitzmyer's review in *CBQ* 30 (1968) 417-428. Moreover, the operative assumption in respect of the message of Jesus under Black's approach is that individual words of Jesus were handed on verbatim at the stage of transmission in Aramaic, and that substantive development of an interpretative nature awaited translation into Greek. If the Gospels developed at all analogously to rabbinic sources, however, we should expect to encounter interpretative activity from the very beginning. Moreover, if Luke is to be taken at the word of the Gospel's opening, *some* historical interest apparently grew as the traditions concerning Jesus developed.

[15]Cf. McNamara, *The New Testament* (1966) 133-138. The *terminus post quem* of the document as a whole is given by its reading at Genesis 21:21, where the wife and daughter of Muhammed are mentioned.

connection with the passage in Leviticus, and the understanding that such a connection was traditional at the time Luke 6:36 was created does nothing whatever to illuminate its meaning. (On the other hand, the Lukan passage does not explain the Targumic passage: the logical possibility of Targumic dependence on the Gospel does not appear to be plausible in this case.) In such instances, the Targums are merely accessible sources of certain materials of early Judaism; they are useful heuristically, and instances of this kind prove nothing in respect of the dating of Targumim.

(7) On more rare occasions, a Targum might provide us with a tradition which was—at the time of the New Testament—already of an exegetical nature. The most obvious instance of this kind is provided by the Targum of Isaiah 6:9, 10, in relation to Mark 4:12. The apparent peculiarity of the Markan citation of Isaiah, in reference to people being forgiven, rather than healed (as in the Masoretic Text and the Septuagint) is explained by the Targumic rendering.[16] Apparently, the

---

[16]Cf. Chilton, *A Galilean Rabbi and His Bible. Jesus' own interpretation of Isaiah* (1984) 90-98. A recent review of the work by Morna Hooker provides a classic instance of the attempt to trivialize the import of Targumic analogies within the Gospels (cf. *New Blackfriars 66* [1985] 550-552). She complains that such analogies are "only to be expected," although she herself made no

Targum shows us that, in this respect, the understanding of scripture attributed to Jesus was conventional. Generalization is only possible, however, to the extent of agreement with the New Testament in both wording and scriptural contextualization.

(8) The Targums instance, not only traditions which may be reflected in the New Testament, but a process of conveying those traditions which might be illuminating. Once the history of Targumic development is reckoned with, it becomes obvious that their greatest use for the student of the New Testament lies in their provision, not of antecedents, but analogies. It has long been recognized that there is something of a synoptic relationship among the Pentateuchal Targumim styled as Palestinian,[17] and that may be a clue that the Gospels and

---

reference to the Targumim in investigating the phrase "the son of man," as attributed to Jesus (cf. *The Son of Man in Mark* [1967]). Having made her dismissive comment, she then complains at the observation that Jesus appears to have departed as far from the Targum of Isaiah as he did from any other extant version. But if his usage of Targumic traditions is "only to be expected," how is any evidence of his non-usage of such traditions anything other than notable? It is evident that there is a tendency within the discipline to bridle at recourse to early Judaism, even if the evasion requires self-contradictory logic.

[17]Cf. Chilton, *Targumic Approaches* (1986) 113–135; 137–149; 163–177.

the Targumim are mutually illuminating textual phenomena.
Only comparative study can determine the extent to which
this comparability is a function of their mutual matrix
in early Judaism, along with other texts of that
provenience.[18]

But while that determination is being made, we will
become more familiar with specific examples from
antiquity of how sacred texts and revered traditions
together intersected, in the instance of Targumim, to
provide a continuing construal of the meaning of
scripture. It may be that the properly religious function
of scripture within, and after, the period of the New
Testament will become plainer and more explicable in the
light of the Targumim.

---

[18]Cf. B. Gerhardsson (tr. E.J. Sharpe), *Memory and Manuscript. Oral Tradition and Written Transmission in Rabbinic Judaism and Early Christianity* (1961); (tr. E.J. Sharpe), *Tradition and Transmission in Early Christianity* (1964); (J. Toy), *The Testing of God's Son (Matt 4:1-11 & Par)* (1966); *The Origins of the Gospel Traditions* (1979).

MODERN AUTHOR INDEX

Hamp, V., 180

Harrington, D. J., 255

Hayward, Robert, 255-8, 272, 275-7, 279-80, 288

Herrenbrück, Fritz, 10

Hill, David, 16

Hooker, Morna, 311-12, 313-14

Jeremias, Joachim, 41-2, 43, 44, 71-2, 160-1

Kahle, Paul, 245, 311

Kittel, G., 186

Koester, Helmut, 134-6

Kutscher, E. Y., 249

Lach, Samuel Tobias, 112, 118

Lagrange, M. J., 166, 169

Le Déaut, Roger, 47-8, 245-6, 247, 263, 265, 282

Leon, Harry B., 234, 240

Levey, Samson H., 255, 259

Levine, Etan, 264

Lifshitz, Baruch, 242

Lindars, Barnabas, 76, 83

Lund, Shirley, 52

Luz, Ulrich, 140

McNamara, Martin, 305, 308, 312

Moore, G. F., 177-80, 271, 274-5, 246, 279, 282

South Florida Studies in the History of Judaism

South Florida Academic Commentary Series

The Talmud of Babylonia, An Academic Commentary

South Florida-Rochester-Saint Louis
Studies on Religion and the Social Order

South Florida International Studies in
Formative Christianity and Judaism